MW00484323

Financial Accounting
in an Economic Context

4th Edition

Jamie Pratt

Professor of Accounting

Indiana University, Bloomington

Prepared by

Joseph H. Anthony

Michigan State University

Robin P. Clement

Louisiana State University

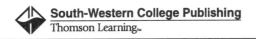

South-Western College Publishing
Thomson Learning™

Australia • Canada • Denmark • Japan • Mexico • New Zealand • Philippines
Puerto Rico • Singapore • South Africa • Spain • United Kingdom • United States

Study Guide to *Financial Accounting in an Economic Context*, 4th edition
Prepared by Joseph H. Anthony and Robin P. Clement

Accounting Team Director: Richard Lindgren
Acquisitions Editor: Rochelle Kronzek
Senior Developmental Editor: Ken Martin
Marketing Manager: Dan Silverburg
Manufacturing Coordinator: Doug Wilke
Printer: Globus Printing, Inc.

Printed in the United States of America
1 2 3 4 5 02 01 00 99

For more information contact South-Western College Publishing, 5101 Madison Road, Cincinnati, Ohio, 45227 or find us on the Internet at http://www.swcollege.com

For permission to use material from this text or product, contact us by
• **telephone: 1-800-730-2214**
• **fax: 1-800-730-2215**
• **web: http://www.thomsonrights.com**

ISBN: 0-324-01524-0

This book is printed on acid-free paper.

TABLE OF CONTENTS

PREFACE

This study guide was prepared to accompany the fourth edition of Pratt's **FINANCIAL ACCOUNTING**. The study guide is intended to both supplement and complement the text. Each chapter contains a *Review of Key Concepts*. The review expands the discussion of important concepts from the text, offering additional examples to aid student comprehension. Where appropriate, we provide alternative approaches to understanding the concepts presented in the text.

Each chapter also includes a set of multiple choice questions and several short exercises for student review. Answers are provided for the multiple choice questions as well as detailed solutions to the exercises.

INSTRUCTIONS TO THE STUDENT

The instructions which follow are intended to allow you to get the most value for your investment in this *STUDY GUIDE*. If used properly, the *STUDY GUIDE* should be of great assistance in learning the materials of introductory financial accounting. Take a few minutes to carefully review the instructions which follow.

1. We recommend reviewing chapters in this *STUDY GUIDE* <u>only after</u> you have read the assigned materials in your text. The *STUDY GUIDE* provides a review of key concepts. In many instances these will be presented in an alternative way from that used in the text. In other cases we follow the text presentation but provide you with alternative examples.

2. We <u>**DO NOT**</u> recommend using the *STUDY GUIDE* instead of the text. Our Review of Key Concepts is not comprehensive. Rather, we have selected for inclusion <u>only</u> those topics, which in our experience, are most troublesome for students. Less difficult topics are excluded.

3. The questions and exercises should provide you with a means of self-testing and practice for examinations in the course. We typically include twenty multiple choice questions and five short exercises/problems per chapter. The following approach is suggested.

   a. Complete all odd-numbered multiple choice questions before reading the Review of Key Concepts. CIRCLE YOUR RESPONSES. Check your responses against the solutions provided.

   b. Identify your mistakes and the areas which are giving you difficulty. Carefully read the Review of Key Concepts sections where you need additional work.

   c. Complete the short exercises/problems for those topics which you found difficult. You may also want to use these to supplement assignments from the text given by your instructor. We have provided sufficient space for you to work the exercises and problems directly in the *STUDY GUIDE*. All short exercises/problems have detailed solutions provided. You may find it convenient to tear out the completed problems to allow easier comparison to the solutions.

   d. Use the even-numbered multiple questions to create your own examinations. Complete these questions prior to your in-class examinations. Time yourself. Allow approximately the same time as is available on the scheduled examinations. Multiple choice questions are widely used in introductory accounting classes due to the large number of students enrolled. This self-testing provides an excellent preparation for actual examinations. Once again, it may be useful to tear out the pages to construct your self-examination.

   Timing yourself carefully and evaluating your performance on these self-tests should help to eliminate pre-examination jitters.

ACKNOWLEDGEMENTS

We wish to acknowledge the efforts of the Accounting and Taxation Team of ITP/South-Western College Publishing in completing the manuscript. We also wish to thank all users of the prior edition who offered comments, corrections, and suggestions.

CHAPTER 1

Financial Accounting and Its Economic Context

REVIEW OF KEY CONCEPTS

Our coverage of Chapter 1 deviates somewhat from the presentation in your text. The text provides important introductory information on the role of financial accounting. You should carefully read this material. This chapter defines accounting and introduces the basic accounting system, often referred to as the accounting information system or the **accounting model**. The simple model presented herein provides the conceptual basis for virtually all the material to be covered in an introductory financial accounting course. This coverage will give you a head start on the material which will appear in the next four chapters of the text.

Accounting Defined

Accounting is the process of identifying, measuring, recording, and communicating information about the production, development, and management of wealth involving an individual, a business, or a country.

The objective of financial accounting, the focus of this text, is to provide the suppliers of wealth (creditors and owners) with information regarding where management has invested that wealth. Accounting also provides a summary of changes in that wealth due to the operations of the business. Investors and creditors can use such information to assess the performance of management over time and to compare investment opportunities across companies.

The purpose of a business is generally assumed to be to increase the wealth of its owners. The accounting model is a collection of rules and definitions which are designed to measure the total wealth invested in the business at a point in time as well as changes in wealth over time. A **model** is a description of a process that attempts to capture important or critical dimensions of an object or social structure. The accounting model's rules attempt to measure in a concise and understandable way the events affecting wealth during a time period. The model is a representation of economic events a business engages in, using assumptions, estimates, and other devices to approximate wealth and changes in wealth over time.

The Accounting Model

The foundation of the accounting model is the following equation:

$$\text{Assets} = \text{Liabilities} + \text{Owners' Equity}$$

Assets are the specific economic resources that the invested wealth of creditors and owners is allocated among. When investments are made by owners or loans are received from creditors, managers choose the specific assets in which to invest the money. As the firm operates its business, economic resources are acquired through selling a product or service. Economic resources are consumed in providing that service or product.

The accounting rules define an asset as a resource:
(1) having an anticipated future economic benefit, and
(2) being the result of a past transaction.

The first criterion requires that the item contributes to the process of generating future wealth in some way. For example, if a building is purchased to be used in future business operations, it qualifies as an asset. But, if the building is found to be contaminated with a substance to the point it cannot be repaired, the building's status as an asset becomes questionable. Even though the business legally owns the building, the building is not necessarily an asset since its ability to contribute to future wealth is impaired.

The second criterion requires that an asset be the result of a past transaction. A **transaction** is the result of performing or doing something. Usually, an exchange of some sort is required before the item is recorded as an asset. The act of entering into a contract to perform a service or provide goods in the future does not result in an asset. As the service is performed or the product delivered, assets are being acquired.

Liabilities are probable claims to economic resources or services to be fulfilled at some time in the future. Like an asset, a liability must be the result of a past transaction or event.

Owners' equity is the amount of wealth (measured by the accounting model) invested by owners at a point in time. It is the amount of assets remaining after satisfying the claims of creditors. Owners' equity is sometimes referred to as the residual claim on assets since it is the difference between assets and the claims of creditors. Rearranging the accounting equation:

$$\text{Assets - Liabilities = Owners' Equity}$$

The focus to this point has been describing economic resources and claims to those resources at a point in time. The **balance sheet** or **statement of financial position** lists the assets and claims to assets (liabilities and owners' equity) at a point in time. It is included in the financial information provided to investors and creditors.

Accounting for Changes in Financial Position

Investors are also interested in detail regarding how wealth changes over time. Specifically, they are interested in changes in the owners' equity account from one point in time to another, such as from one year-end to the next. An owner's investment in the business can change due to three activities: additional investment, withdrawal of investment, and the operations of the business. The **statement of owners' equity** provides information regarding these three activities.

Since the primary motivation for investing in a company is to increase wealth from the business's operation, a summary of operating transactions, called the **income statement**, provides more detail to investors about changes in their invested wealth due to the operating activities of the business. The change in invested wealth due to operations is separated into transactions which increase wealth, called **revenues and gains**, and those decreasing wealth, called **expenses and losses**.

Revenues arise when, in exchange for the business's services or products, the company receives either an asset (usually cash or a promise to pay cash, which is called a receivable) or the discharge of a liability. As an example of the latter, assume a customer pays in advance for a service. Cash is increased, and a liability is incurred. Owners' wealth is unaffected because the cash received has not yet been earned. When the service is provided, the liability is discharged and the owner has earned the cash previously received. Thus, revenues are increases in owners' wealth due to providing services or goods.

Expenses reduce owners' equity. Expenses represent the costs of providing services or goods to customers. Either an asset is consumed or a liability arises when performing the service or selling the product. For example, when a department store sells a shirt, its inventory is reduced. The inventory is an asset. The store also employs sales people to help customers. Their salaries may be paid immediately (reducing assets) or may be paid in the future (increasing liabilities). The net affect is a reduction in owners' wealth.

For a business to successfully operate, in the long-run, revenues or increases in owners' wealth due to operations must exceed expenses or decreases in owners' wealth. The difference between revenues and expenses is called **net income** or profit.

Investors find the listing of types of revenues and expenses on the income statement useful in assessing the management of resources across time and in comparing companies' abilities to increase owners' wealth.

A Comprehensive Example

Some of the more important basic concepts underlying the use of the accounting model to develop financial statements for a business are illustrated below.

The following information involves **Jewelbox**, a small jewelry store owned by Jane Blalock, during June, 1999, its first month of business. For each item presented, the effect on the accounting model is discussed. Following the final transaction, the financial statements are prepared.

Transactions and Analysis (in chronological order)

1. The business opens a checking account from which its bills will be paid by depositing the $50,000 original investment of Ms. Blalock. The business's resources are increased, and the claimant to those resources is Ms. Blalock.

Model Component	Specific Account Affected
Assets	**Cash** increases by $50,000
Liabilities	No account affected
Owner's Equity	**J. Blalock, Capital** increases by $50,000

2. The business purchases land for $5,000 and a building for $25,000. These are **assets** because the business will be conducted from this site now and in the future. Current and future years' operations are likely to be enhanced from such a purchase.

    The business purchased these resources by exchanging other resources (Cash, $10,000) and entering into a loan contract with the bank. Thus, total resources or assets are increased by $20,000 ($5,000 + $25,000 - $10,000), and the claims on the total resources of the business are increased by $20,000. The claimant is not the owner, but the bank who provided the loan of $20,000.

Model Component	Specific Account Affected
Assets	**Cash** decreases by $10,000 **Land** increases by $ 5,000 **Building** increases by $25,000 Net change: Assets increase by $20,000
Liabilities	**Notes Payable** increases by $20,000
Owner's Equity	No account affected

3. The business purchases a display case for $2,000 cash. The display case presumably will be used by the business for several years. The purchase represents the exchange of one economic resource, Cash, for another, Equipment.

Model Component	Specific Account Affected
Assets	**Cash** decreases by $2,000 **Equipment** increases by $2,000 Net change is zero
Liabilities	No account affected
Owner's Equity	No account affected

4. Mary Johnson is hired as a sales clerk. A contract exists between Ms. Johnson and Jewelbox. However, this type of event is usually not recorded in the accounting records because the accounting model's components are unaffected. Since Ms. Johnson has not yet performed services, she does not have a claim on the business's resources. When Ms. Johnson actually begins to work, the company will record as revenues the sales price received for merchandise sold to customers. The company will record as expenses the cost of purchasing merchandise sold and the cost of Ms. Johnson's salary. The change in owner's wealth for the period is the difference between revenues and expenses (**net income**).

5. The business purchases $5,000 of merchandise from GEM, Inc. The purchase is on account. The merchandise purchased is intended for resale to Jewelbox's customers. Merchandise intended for resale (retailers) or raw materials to be used to produce products for sale (manufacturers) are included in **Inventory** accounts.

    When purchases or sales are **on account,** a contract is created promising to pay the amount owed in the future. Businesses usually have a group of suppliers they purchase inventory from on a regular basis. Amounts owed such suppliers are recorded in **Accounts Payable**.

Model Component	Specific Account Affected
Assets	**Inventory** increases by $5,000
Liabilities	**Accounts Payable** increases by $5,000
Owner's Equity	No account affected

6. The business sells jewelry for $2,000 cash. The jewelry cost Jewelbox $1,500. This transaction involves an outflow of an economic resource, the jewelry that cost Jewelbox $1,500. The $2,000 cash received from the customer represents an inflow of resources. Assets have increased by $500 (Cash increased by $2,000 and Inventory decreased by $1,500). The owner is the claimant to the increase in resources. The change in owner's equity is recorded in two accounts, Jewelry Revenue is increased by $2,000 and Cost of Goods Sold is increased by $1,500, representing the inflow and outflow of resources resulting from the transaction.

Model Component	Specific Account Affected
Assets	**Cash** increases by $2,000 **Inventory** decreases by $1,500 Net change: Assets increase by $500
Liabilities	No account affected
Owner's Equity	**Revenues** increase by $2,000 **Expenses** increase by $1,500 Net change: Owner's Equity increases by $500

7. The business sells jewelry for $3,000 that cost Jewelbox $2,000. The sale was on account. As mentioned in (5), sales of merchandise to customers or purchases of merchandise from suppliers can be **on account**. The customer is contracting with Jewelbox to pay the $3,000 in the future. Obviously, Jewelbox enters into such contracts only if the customer has a good credit history. The promise to pay for the jewelry in the future is an asset since cash is expected to be received in the future.

    Like transaction (6), assets are increased by the difference between the assets received and assets given up, or $1,000 ($3,000 - $2,000). Owner's equity is also increased by $1,000. The change in owner's equity is recorded as an increase in Jewelry Revenue of $3,000 and an increase in Cost of Goods Sold of $2,000.

Model Component	Specific Account Affected
Assets	**Accounts Receivable** increases by $3,000 **Inventory** decreases by $2,000 Net change: Assets increase by $1,000
Liabilities	No account affected
Owner's Equity	**Revenues** increase by $3,000 **Expenses** increase by $2,000 Net change: Owner's Equity increases by $1,000

8. The business pays GEM, Inc., for item purchased in (5). The creditor's (GEM, Inc.) claim is settled by the $5,000 payment. Both assets and liabilities are decreased. Owner's equity is unaffected.

Model Component	Specific Account Affected
Assets	**Cash** decreases by $5,000
Liabilities	**Accounts Payable** decreases by $5,000
Owner's Equity	No account affected

9. The business pays Mary Johnson's salary of $500. Cash decreases by $500 and the owner is charged for Ms. Johnson's work for the month.

Model Component	Specific Account Affected
Assets	**Cash** decreases by $500
Liabilities	No account affected
Owner's Equity	**Salary Expense** increases by $500 Net change: Owner's Equity decreases by $500

From the above analysis, the resources and claims to resources of Jewelbox can be determined at the end of the month.

Resources: Assets

Cash is affected by transactions 1, 2, 3, 6, 8, and 9.
    $50,000 (1) - $10,000 (2) - $2,000 (3) + $2,000 (6) - $5,000 (8) - $500 (9)
    = $34,500.
Jewelbox's accounting records indicate it has a cash balance of $34,500 at the end of the month.

Accounts Receivable is affected by transaction 7 only and shows a $3,000 balance at the end of the month.

Inventory is affected by transactions 5,6, and 7 and has an end-of-month balance of $1,500.
   $5,000 (5) - $1,500 (6) - $2,000 (7) = $1,500.

Land's balance is $5,000 (2).

Building's balance is $25,000 (2).

Equipment's balance is $2,000 (3).

Assets total **$71,000** ($34,500 + $3,000 + $1,500 + $5,000 + $25,000 + $2,000).

Claims to Resources: Liabilities + Owner's Equity

Liabilities: Notes Payable balance is $20,000 (2).

Owners Equity: J. Blalock, Capital balance is affected by transactions 1,6,7, and 9.
   $50,000 (1) + $2,000 (6) - $1,500 (6) + $3,000 (7) - $2,000 (7) - $500 (9) = $51,000.

Claims to Resources total **$71,000** (Liabilities, $20,000 + Owner's Equity, $51,000).

Financial Statements: The formal financial statements are presented below in an order that highlights how the statements interrelate.

Jewelbox
Income Statement
For the Month Ended June 30, 1999

Revenues			$ 5,000
Expenses:	Cost of goods sold	$ 3,500	
	Salaries	500	4,000
Net income			$ 1,000

Jewelbox
Statement of Owner's Equity
For the Month Ended June 30, 1999

J. Blalock, capital June 1, 1999		$ 0
Add: Contribution by owner	$ 50,000	
Net income for June	1,000	51,000
J. Blalock, capital June 30, 1999		$ 51,000

Jewelbox
Balance Sheet
June 30, 1999

Assets:		Liabilities:	
Cash	$ 34,500	Notes payable	$ 20,000
Accounts receivable	3,000		
Inventory	1,500		
Land	5,000	Owner's Equity:	
Building	25,000	J. Blalock, capital	51,000
Equipment	2,000		
		Total liabilities	
Total assets	$ 71,000	and owner's equity	$ 71,000

QUESTIONS FOR YOUR REVIEW

1. Which financial statement shows the assets and claims to those assets at a point in time?
   a. income statement
   b. balance sheet
   c. statement of retained earnings
   d. statement of cash flows

2. Suzie's Nuts paid $15,000 cash for a new refrigerated display case. What effect did this transaction have on assets, liabilities, and owner's equity?

	Assets	Liabilities	Owner's Equity
a.	none	none	none
b.	lower	lower	none
c.	lower	lower	lower
d.	lower	none	lower

3. A balance sheet:
   a. presents assets and claims to those assets during a period of time.
   b. shows the changes in owner's equity during a period of time.
   c. shows revenues earned and the expenses used to earn them over a period of time.
   d. presents assets and claims to those assets at a point in time.

4. A transaction which decreases both total assets and total owner's equity is:
   a. payment of salaries earned by employees during the month.
   b. payment of a bank loan.
   c. the purchase of inventory on account.
   d. collection of an account receivable.

5. Barkely Stores purchased a new cash register for $2,500 and promised to pay the seller in 90 days. This transaction:
   a. increases total assets and decreases total liabilities.
   b. increases total assets and increases total liabilities.
   c. is a "wash." Total assets are unaffected.
   d. is not recorded since no cash is involved.

6. A user of accounting information with a direct financial interest in the business is a(n):
   a. owner.
   b. taxing authority.
   c. regulatory agency.
   d. labor union.

7. Most business enterprises in the United States are:
   a. sole proprietorships.
   b. partnerships.
   c. corporations.
   d. governmental units.

Questions 8 through 12 are independent and refer to the following information.

Gill Decorating Company had the following balance sheet accounts and balances:

Accounts Payable	$16,000	Equipment	$14,000
Accounts Receivable	2,000	S. Gill, Capital	?
Building	?	Land	14,000
Cash	6,000		

8. If the balance in the capital account is $44,000, the building account's balance is:
   a. $4,000
   b. $14,000
   c. $24,000
   d. $48,000

9. If the building account's balance is $30,000, the total of liabilities and owner's equity is:
   a. $30,000
   b. $50,000
   c. $60,000
   d. $66,000

10. If the building account's balance is $40,000 and the equipment is sold for $14,000, the balance in owner's equity is:
    a. $40,000
    b. $42,000
    c. $60,000
    d. $76,000

11. If the building account's balance is $20,000 and $6,000 of accounts payable is paid using cash, the balance in owner's equity is:
    a. $34,000
    b. $40,000
    c. $56,000
    d. $60,000

12. If equipment is sold for $14,000, the owner's equity balance is:
    a. increased by $14,000.
    b. decreased by $14,000.
    c. increased by $28,000.
    d. unchanged.

Questions 13 through 16 are independent and refer to the following information.
The total assets and liabilities at the beginning and end of the year for Tulane Corporation are as follows:

	Assets	Liabilities
Beginning of the year	$ 7,000	$3,000
End of the year	10,000	5,000

13. Assuming Tulane received no investments in the business and no owner withdrawals occurred, net income for the year is:
    a. $5,000
    b. $1,000
    c. $9,000
    d. $3,000

14. Assuming Tulane received no investments in the business and the owner withdrew $4,400, net income for the year is:
    a. $7,200
    b. $2,800
    c. $3,200
    d. $800

15. Assuming Tulane received an investment of $1,000 in the business and no owner withdrawals occurred, net income for the year is:
    a. $2,000
    b. $4,000
    c. $10,000
    d. $0

Chapter 1

16. Assuming Tulane received an investment of $1,000 in the business and the owner withdrew $2,200, net income for the year is:
    a. $2,200
    b. $6,200
    c. $3,800
    d. ($200)

17. The beginning of the year account balances for Fred's Bookstore are:

Total assets	$40,000
Total owner's equity	20,000

    During the year, total assets increased by $18,000 and total liabilities increased by $12,000. The owner withdrew $4,000 from the business. Net income for the year is:
    a. $14,000
    b. $10,000
    c. $30,000
    d. not determinable using the available information.

18. A revenue:
    a. increases assets and liabilities.
    b. increases assets and owner's equity.
    c. increases assets and decreases owner's equity.
    d. affects only the income statement.

19. Animal Kingdom Company purchased twenty black cats for $500 cash. This transaction:
    a. does not affect total assets.
    b. increases total assets by $500.
    c. decreases total assets by $500.
    d. increases total assets by $1,000.

20. Spartan Manufacturing reported the following amounts:

	June 1	June 30
Total assets	$750,000	$930,000
Total liabilities	600,000	640,000

    During the month, the owners withdrew $50,000 in cash from the business. There were no additional investments by the owners. What is Spartan's net income for the month?
    a. $140,000
    b. $240,000
    c. $190,000
    d. It cannot be determined without additional information.

21. Identify each of the following transactions as either an owner's investment, withdrawal, revenue, or expense. Briefly explain your response.

   (a)   Received cash for providing a service.

   (b)   Owner transferred assets to the business.

   (c)   Paid service station for gasoline.

   (d)   Paid cash to employee for services performed.

Chapter 1

Questions 22 through 25 refer to the following information. Show all required calculations to support your answers.

On September 30, 1999, Tony's Hot Dog Company had the following account balances:

Cash	$ 6,900
Accounts payable	2,900
Accounts receivable	11,340
Tony, capital (Sept. 1, 1999)	23,040
Sales revenue	4,400
Wage expense	1,500
Hot dog inventory	3,400
Restaurant equipment	6,800
Rent expense	400

22. What are the total assets for Tony's Hot Dog Company?

23. What are the total liabilities for Tony's Hot Dog Company?

24. What is the net income for Tony's Hot Dog Company?

25. What is the total owner's equity at September 30, 1999?

CHAPTER 1 SOLUTIONS

1.	b	6.	a	11.	b	16.	a
2.	a	7.	a	12.	d	17.	b
3.	d	8.	c	13.	b	18.	b
4.	a	9.	d	14.	c	19.	a
5.	b	10.	c	15.	d	20.	c

21. a. **Revenue**. Owners' claims on the business's resources are increased by the sale of products. The increase is recorded in revenue accounts.

b. **Investment**. Owners' claims on the business's resources are increased by the additional investment amount.

c. **Expense**. Gasoline is used to deliver goods which are sold to customers. This cost is one among many costs incurred to earn revenue. Owners are charged for the use of this resource.

d. **Expense**. Employees are typically necessary to conduct business, including the production of revenue. Their wages are a cost incurred to earn revenue. Owners are charged for the use of this resource.

22. The assets are:

Cash	$ 6,900
Accounts receivable	11,340
Hot dog inventory	3,400
Restaurant equipment	6,800
Total	$28,440

23. Liabilities consist of Accounts Payable only. Therefore, total liabilities are $2,900.

24. Net income is $2,500. Net income is the change in owners' wealth during a time period due to business operations. Revenues represent increases in owners' wealth and expenses represent decreases in owners' wealth. Net income is calculated as follows:

Sales revenues		$4,400
Expenses:		
Wage expense	$1,500	
Rent expense	400	1,900
Net income		$2,500

25. The balance is $25,540. Tony's capital at September 30, 1999, is computed as follows:

Tony, capital (September 1, 1999) $23,040
Add net income   2,500
Tony, capital (September 30, 1999) $25,540

CHAPTER 2

The Financial Statements

REVIEW OF KEY CONCEPTS

This chapter provides more detail regarding the basic financial statements. These statements are provided to owners and creditors to help them judge the performance of the business and to use as a basis for comparing its performance to other businesses' performance. After completing this chapter, you should be able to describe each of the four basic financial statements. Your description should include a discussion of the type of information each furnishes and the names and definitions of each statement's basic elements.

The Financial Statements

The information contained in the annual report includes the following financial statements:
(a) balance sheet
(b) income statement
(c) statement of cash flows
(d) statement of retained earnings

These four statements are accompanied by footnotes that provide information considered important in fully understanding the financial statements. Footnotes usually contain more detail about economic events summarized in the body of the financial statements.

The notes always contain a **summary of significant accounting procedures**. This footnote summarizes the rules and assumptions used in the preparation of the financial statements. Since companies can select from a variety of different assumptions, rules, and procedures within Generally Accepted Accounting Principles (GAAP) (the rules required to be followed to prepare audited financial statements), the investor comparing companies' financial performance must factor in differences in accounting choices in their computations of ratios. Only then can financial statements be compared accurately. The notes aid in this task.

In preparing financial statements, economic events are analyzed using the set of assumptions, rules, and procedures selected by the business from GAAP. The result of this analysis is formally recorded using the mechanical process to be discussed in Chapter 5. The financial statements are prepared from the data set which results from this analysis and recording process.

As discussed in Chapter 1, the model which serves as the foundation for GAAP is:

Assets = Liabilities + Owners' Equity

Economic Resources = Claims to Resources

The financial statements are used to evaluate investment opportunities. A business's primary objective is to create wealth for its owners. Financial statements are used to determine how well businesses manage the invested wealth. The criteria used by investors and potential investors to judge the health of the business include:

1. The ability to pay off business obligations as they come due, which is called **solvency**.

2. The ability to use business resources in such a way that the inflows from their use (**revenues**) are greater than the outflows of resources used to earn those revenues (**expenses**). A company is **profitable** if inflows exceed outflows. Investors are also interested in how skillfully the business's managers use the resources with which they are entrusted as compared to their competitors. This is called **operational efficiency**.

3. The ability to take advantage of government regulations and financial opportunities so that the maximum can be earned on each dollar invested by the owners (**profitability** of the business).

The financial statements are a raw material to be used in the production of conclusions about a business's health. Analysts and investors add labor, tools (such as computers and related software), and information from the financial press to come to conclusions about a business's current and future performance. These conclusions help investors to decide in which businesses to invest and how much of their money to invest in each business.

Financial statement analysis includes comparing total dollar and percentage changes in reported financial statement numbers across time. For example, the percentage increase in sales from one year to the next might be computed or the dollar increase in sales from year to the next might be used. **Ratio analysis** is widely used in financial statement analysis as well. Ratios are mathematical combinations of numbers reported in one or more of the financial statements. The number combinations are based upon economic theory and the ratios are used to determine how solvent, operationally efficient, and profitable the business is over time and compared to other businesses. Specific ratios, their computation, and their interpretation are discussed in a later chapter.

The Financial Statements

The financial statements are arranged to assist investors and creditors in **financial statement analysis**. The organization of each financial statement and its association with ratio analysis is discussed below.

Classified Balance Sheet

The **balance sheet** lists the assets (resources), liabilities (debts), and owners' equity (owners' investment) of the firm at a point in time. Typically, the balances of these accounts are listed for the current year and one or two prior years. The reader can compute percentage changes across time using this format. The order in which accounts are listed is usually comparable across companies since most companies are required to present **classified** balance sheets.

The accounting principle which defines the dollar amount at which assets are initially recorded is the **historical cost principle**. **Historical cost** is the cash equivalent price at which economic resources are acquired and readied for their intended use within the business. Cash equivalent price means that interest is usually excluded from the cost of an asset. For example, if a delivery truck is purchased for $20,000 using a bank loan to be repaid over 3 years at 10 percent interest, $20,000 is the historical cost of the asset. The interest paid over the three years to finance the truck is charged to owners' equity using the interest expense account as the interest accumulates.

The second aspect of the historical cost principle is that all additional costs incurred to prepare the asset for its intended use are included in the cost of the asset. For example, if the delivery truck's operation required special training, the cost of training the initial driver to operate the truck is also included in the truck's cost. Typical additional costs which may be included in an asset's historical cost are brokerage fees paid when purchasing investments and delivery costs for purchased inventory and factory assets.

Assets

The balance sheet asset classifications are **current assets**; **long-term investments**; **plant, property, and equipment**; and **intangibles**. A **current asset** is an asset expected to be converted into cash or consumed within one year or the **operating cycle**, whichever is longer.

The **operating cycle** is the amount of time required to invest cash in the product that the corporation is in business to sell, to sell the product, and to turn the asset back into cash. For a manufacturing firm, the steps of the **operating cycle** can be represented as:

1. Invest cash.
2. Buy raw materials.
3. Convert raw materials to the finished good to be offered to customers for sale by adding labor and machine effort.
4. Market the product.
5. Deliver the product to a customer and receive in return either cash or a promise to pay cash in the future.
6. Collect cash.

The operating cycle for most businesses is less than one year. For some businesses, such as whiskey distillers, the operating cycle can be several years. The asset accounts which may exist at a point in time related to the operating cycle are Cash, Accounts Receivable, Raw Materials Inventory, Work-in-Process Inventory, and Finished Goods Inventory.

A well-managed company will attempt to shorten the various steps in the operating cycle without sacrificing quality or the ability to meet customer demand. A shorter operating cycle means that customers can be serviced with a smaller average investment in economic resources. This means more money is available for other investments, meeting debt obligations, and paying dividends. The ratios constructed from financial statement elements related to various aspects of the operating cycle can be used to assess changes in this aspect of management performance over time.

The current asset section also includes assets that are not directly related to the operations, but which are either expected to be converted into cash or used up within one year or the operating cycle, whichever is longer. Other types of current asset accounts include Temporary Investments and Prepaid Expenses. The former are investments of cash that is not needed immediately to pay bills, but will be needed in the future. Instead of earning no interest or a lower interest rate from a checking account, excess cash is invested in low-risk (but higher yielding) securities such as U.S. Treasury Bills or the common stock of other businesses. Prepaid Expenses are assets purchased with benefits to be received in the future. Prepaid expenses are considered assets because they represent future benefits, such as prepayment of insurance or rent. For example, an insurance company typically requires that policy premiums be paid one year in advance, or a landlord may require rent prepayment for three months when leasing an office.

The current asset section lists assets in order of decreasing liquidity (the ability to be quickly converted into cash) or closeness to cash or time to be converted into cash. Cash is listed first, then Temporary Investments, Accounts Receivable, Inventory (Raw Material, Work-in-Process, and Finished Goods) and Prepaid Expenses.

On the balance sheet, current assets are followed by **long-term investments**. Long-term investments are investments of economic resources that do not directly relate to the operations of the business. For example, idle plant or land held for future use are typically listed here. They do not contribute to the main production or operating activities of the business. Other examples include long-term investments in another company's stock.

Plant, property, and equipment represent the assets which house the production and are actually used to manufacture and sell the product. These are **long-lived assets** because the business typically uses them in operations for a number of years.

Intangibles are assets without a physical existence. They generally represent **purchased** rights or value of some type. **Goodwill** is the difference between the price paid for another company and the market value of identifiable assets at the purchase date. Thus, to be recorded on the financial statements, goodwill must be purchased. Other examples of intangibles include the price paid to people outside the business for costs related to patent development.

Liabilities

Like assets, liabilities are classified as **current** and **long-term**. Current liabilities are obligations to be paid with current assets or services to be rendered, or to be replaced with other current liabilities within one year or the operating cycle, whichever is longer. Current liabilities include **Accounts Payable**, which is the amount due to suppliers on purchases of material that become a part of Inventory.

Long-term liabilities are due in more than one year or the operating cycle, whichever is longer. Mortgage Payable, Bonds Payable, and Lease Obligations are examples of long-term liabilities. The mortgage loan is used to purchase long-lived assets such as buildings. The loan is guaranteed by the asset that is being purchased with its proceeds. If a company fails to meet its mortgage payments, the creditor can take possession of the asset being purchased by the loan. This process is called foreclosure. Mortgage payments due within one year are reclassified as a current liability-the current portion of long-term debt.

A bond payable is actually several individual loans made by creditors. Unlike most loans, bonds are traded in a market similar to stock. Each bond of a particular issue is identical regarding the cash flow payments to repay the loan and regarding the due date. Companies issue bonds when they need large amounts of money to finance projects. Since each bond is identical and the market mechanism reduces the search cost and negotiation cost of each loan, large amounts of money can be raised less expensively.

A lease obligation is a contract to use a particular long-lived asset in operations in exchange for rental payments. Accounting rules distinguish between leases which are effectively purchases of long-lived assets and those which are not. If leases are deemed, in effect, purchases of long-lived assets with long-term debt, the lease obligation and the leased asset are included in the balance sheet as liabilities and assets, respectively. If a lease term is of a relatively short duration, the lease is not considered a purchase and the asset and liability are not recorded; the lease payments are simply charged against income when they are paid.

Stockholders' Equity

The stockholders' equity section typically reflects the legal organization of ownership. If a business is formed as a sole proprietorship or partnership, the owners' wealth (as measured by the accounting system) is recorded in **capital** accounts.

If the business is formed as a corporation, the amount originally invested by owners when the stock was initially sold is recorded in the **contributed capital** section. If the stock sold has a **par value** associated with the stock, then the contributed capital has two parts: par value and paid-in-capital in excess of par. Par value represents the minimum amount for which stock can sell in order for owners to enjoy limited liability, an appealing feature of the corporation. If stock sells initially at less than par, owners can be liable for the difference between par value and the amount paid if the firm goes bankrupt. State laws governing incorporation establish par value requirements. If stock is sold above par value, the stockholder is not liable to pay anything more.

The second section of a corporation's stockholders' equity is **retained earnings**. The balance in Retained Earnings represents the total earnings less payments to owners from the beginning of the corporation's existence to the present time period. As the name implies, the balance represents the amount of owners' wealth from operating the corporation that is reinvested or retained in the business.

Owners of a corporation are the owners of its common stock. Since the owners are stockholders, this section of the corporate balance sheet is also known as the **stockholders' equity**.

Income Statement

The income statement provides detail regarding the change in owners' equity due to business operations during a time period. As mentioned in Chapter 1, revenues represent increases in the owners' share of the total economic resources of the business resulting from inflows of resources from business operations. Expenses are decreases in the owners' share of total economic resources of the business resulting from outflows of resources due to business operations.

In addition to revenues and expenses, the income statement includes changes in owners' wealth from activities outside the normal operations of the business. For example, if the business sells land for more than its historical cost, total economic resources have increased by the difference. This difference belongs to the owners. The difference is called a **gain on disposal of assets**. If total economic resources decline (the land is sold for less than its cost), the owners' wealth is reduced by a **loss on the disposal of assets**.

The **revenue recognition** and **matching** principles determine when and at what amount revenues and expenses are recorded in the accounting database. The **revenue recognition criteria** are:

1. the earnings process must be substantially complete, and
2. the net amount to be ultimately received must be estimable.

The first criterion relates to when the owners of the business have provided sufficient services or products to be able to claim an increase in wealth. Revenue is not recorded upon signing a contract to provide services in the future since no service or product has been provided. Revenue is recorded when the services are actually provided.

The second criterion requires that the net increase in owners' wealth must be estimable. If uncertainties exist regarding the collectibility of the contracted amount or future services to be rendered by the business to fulfill the contract, then the act of recording revenue must be delayed. For example, if a warranty is included in the contract and the potential liability under the warranty is not estimable, the act of recording revenue must be delayed until this uncertainty is reduced to a tolerable level.

The **matching principle** determines when expenses are recorded. The net increase or decrease in owners' wealth due to the goods or services provided by the business is relevant for decision making. Accordingly, if possible, expenses are recorded in the same period in which related revenue is recorded.

Costs directly traceable to the good or service provided to customers are termed **product costs**. When the good or service is provided, the product cost is included in the income statement as **Cost of Goods Sold** or **Cost of Sales**.

Unfortunately, matching cannot be applied to all expenses. Some expenses are not directly traceable to the individual good or service being provided. Office staff salaries and advertising are examples of costs necessary to conduct business which are incurred to create a climate conducive to business. They are not a direct cost of the good or service being provided.

Like the balance sheet, the income statement's elements are organized to aid investors' analysis. A **multi-step** income statement groups together elements that result from operations, and then the other elements are listed. Within the operating section, Sales Revenues (from the sale of products) or Service Revenues (from rendering of services) are listed first, net of any returns or discounts. **Cost of Goods Sold**, the cost directly traceable to such sales, is listed after Sales Revenue. Cost of Goods Sold is deducted from Sales Revenue to arrive at the **Gross Profit** subtotal. Cost of Goods Sold represents the cost per unit of the items sold times the quantity sold. Thus, gross profit represents the amount available to cover all the other costs necessary to produce and sell the good and generate a profit.

Operating expenses are deducted from gross profit to arrive at income from operations. The other **operating expenses** or period costs include the cost of marketing the good and administrative costs. Commissions and advertising are included as marketing costs. Administrative costs include the accounting department, purchasing department, and other support functions within the business.

After income from operations, the other items that are not directly related to operations but which affect owners' wealth are listed. Interest Expense, Interest Revenue and Gains and Losses on Disposal of Assets are examples of these nonoperating items.

Finally, Income Tax Expense is deducted to arrive at the net income or net loss for the period. Net income is included in the **statement of stockholders' equity** representing the portion of the change in owners' equity over the period related to business operations. Other components of the Statement of Stockholders' Equity include additional contributions by owners and withdrawals by owners. The withdrawals by the stockholders (the owners of the corporation) are known as **Dividends**.

The Statement of Cash Flows

The statement of cash flows provides a detailed summary of the transactions affecting the asset account, which has the most transactions affecting it during the year. Cash can be viewed as the life's blood of the business since ultimately all transactions have cash consequences. If a company is unable to maintain sufficient cash balances to meet obligations as they come due, the business will fail.

The statement of cash flows divides the transactions affecting cash into three categories. **Cash from operations** is the amount that cash increased or decreased during the period as a result of the business's on-going operations. Examples of sources of cash from operations are cash collections on sales and accounts receivable. Examples of uses or outlays of cash from operations include paying for inventory or paying salaries and utilities.

Cash from investing activities is the amount that cash increased or decreased due to the acquisition or disposal of noncurrent assets. Examples include the purchase of buildings or sale of equipment.

Cash from financing activities is the amount that cash increased due to the issuance of stocks or bonds and additional contributions of owners or decreased due to the repayment of debt or withdrawals by owners.

The Statement of Retained Earnings

A summary of the current period transactions affecting the earnings reinvested in the company is provided in the statement of retained earnings. Retained earnings is increased by net income and is reduced by net losses and dividends.

Summary

Historical cost, revenue recognition, and the matching principle are the accounting concepts followed to determine when and at what amount assets, revenues, and expenses are initially recorded. The format of the balance sheet, income statement, and statement of cash flows was also explained.

QUESTIONS FOR YOUR REVIEW

The following information relates to questions 1 and 2.

Lambert, Inc., began business in January 1999. The following transactions occurred during January. Common stock was issued for $30,000. A bank loan for $10,000 was received (the loan will be paid in two years). Inventory was purchased for $20,000 (the bill will be paid next month). Inventory that cost $15,000 was sold for $25,000. The customer paid $22,000 in cash immediately and will pay $3,000 next month. Lambert bought a parcel of land for $10,000. Lambert paid a $10,000 dividend.

1. The total current assets at January 31, 1999 is:
    a. $60,000
    b. $53,000
    c. $52,000
    d. $50,000

2. What is net income (loss)?
    a. $12,000
    b. $10,000
    c. $0
    d. ($10,000)

3. Expense is:
    a. another word for a liability.
    b. a cash payment for costs incurred to earn revenues.
    c. a cost (whether paid or not) incurred to produce revenues.
    d. a decrease in assets.

4. Profitable operations are evident when:
    a. assets increase.
    b. the difference between assets and liabilities increases.
    c. common stock increases.
    d. retained earnings increases.

5. An important benefit of a corporation compared to a partnership or proprietorship is:
    a. the owners are directly involved in the day-to-day operations of the company.
    b. dividend income is taxable.
    c. the stockholder is generally only liable for his initial investment.
    d. only the corporation allows distributions of earnings to its owners.

6. The amount of cash received from the sale of plant and equipment is located on the:
    a. income statement.
    b. balance sheet.
    c. statement of cash flows.
    d. statement of retained earnings.

7. The net book value of a company is:
    a. total assets less any depreciation and amortization.
    b. the retained earnings balance.
    c. the common stock balance.
    d. the total common stock and retained earnings balances.

The following information is used for questions 8 through 11.

The Turner Company engaged in the following transactions during 1999:

(1) Sales totaled $50,000. All but $5,000 has been collected during the year. The goods sold cost $35,000. All the goods sold were bought and paid for during 1999.
(2) 10,000 shares of common stock were sold for $250,000.
(3) A bank loan of $20,000 was received.
(4) Land was sold for $60,000; the land originally cost the company $61,000.
(5) A truck was purchased for $50,000 cash.
(6) Dividends of $6,000 were paid.
(7) Employees were paid $3,000.

8. What is net income (loss)?
    a. $15,000
    b. $12,000
    c. $11,000
    d. $6,000

9. What is net cash from (used in) operations?
    a. $15,000
    b. $12,000
    c. $7,000
    d. $1,000

10. Net cash from (used in) investing activities is:
    a. $60,000
    b. $10,000
    c. ($10,000)
    d. ($50,000)

11. Net cash from (used in) financing activities is:
    a. $270,000
    b. $264,000
    c. $244,000
    d. $20,000

Questions 12 and 13 are based on the following information.

The Magenta Company began business in 1997. The following is Magenta's revenues, expenses, and dividends from 1997 to 1999.

	Revenues	Expenses	Dividends
1997	$100,000	$120,000	$ 0
1998	200,000	150,000	10,000
1999	250,000	180,000	30,000

12.   Compute Magenta's net income for 1997, 1998, and 1999.

    1997

    1998

    1999

13. Compute Magenta's Retained Earnings balance for 1997, 1998, and 1999.

1997

1998

1999

CHAPTER 2-SOLUTIONS

1.	d	5.	c	9.	c
2.	b	6.	c	10.	b
3.	c	7.	d	11.	b
4.	d	8.	c		

12. Net income for Magenta:

	1997	1998	1999
Revenues	$100,000	$200,000	$250,000
- Expenses	(120,000)	(150,000)	(180,000)
Net income	$ (20,000)	$ 50,000	$ 70,000

13. Retained Earnings balance for Magenta:

		1997	1998	1999
	Beginning retained earnings	$ 0	$(20,000)	$ 20,000
+	Net income (loss)	(20,000)	50,000	70,000
-	Dividends	0	(10,000)	(30,000)
	Ending retained earnings	$(20,000)	$ 20,000	$ 60,000

CHAPTER 3

Using Financial Statement Information

REVIEW OF KEY CONCEPTS

This chapter discusses how financial accounting numbers can be used in business decision making. The chapter also reviews technical procedures involved in the analysis of financial statements and focuses on how to use the output of these analyses.

Control and Prediction

The two major uses of financial accounting information are **control** and **prediction**. Investors and creditors are interested in assessing the future cash flows to be provided by a business. It is the future cash flows which give value to the investment. Historical data provided in the financial statements is useful in predicting the business's future cash flows. The financial data is also useful in monitoring or controlling the performance of company management.

The financial statements report historical accounting data concerning past operating performance. The financial statements do not attempt to directly measure future cash flows. However, research results indicate that historical data is useful in predicting future performance. Specifically, financial accounting numbers are useful in assessing the **solvency** and **profitability** of a company.

Solvency is the company's ability to pay liabilities as they come due. Profitability is the company's ability to generate future cash flows and increases in wealth through business operations. Profitability measures the company's ability to generate the cash flows needed to meet obligations (earning power). Solvency and profitability are closely related. Operating activities are a primary source of the cash used to meet obligations and liabilities as they come due. An insolvent company cannot survive. An insolvent company cannot maintain earning power or profitability.

Also closely related to profitability is the concept of **earnings persistence**. Earnings persistence is a measure of the likelihood that reported income numbers will persist, or continue in future periods. For example, a large gain from the sale of a portion of the business's assets has low earnings persistence. The assets have already been sold. This gain will not appear again in future years. On the other hand, income earned from long-term service contracts will continue for at least the term of the existing contracts. Such income has a higher earnings persistence.

Financial accounting numbers are also used to monitor and control the decisions of company management. Stockholders might directly use the numbers, assess past performance, and simply vote to change management when that past performance does not meet their expectations. While this has occurred in the past, control is usually accomplished in another way. Financial accounting measures and numbers are included as **contracting** variables.

For example, **creditors** will include financial ratios and other accounting numbers as covenants in debt contracts. Such covenants serve to limit the flexibility of management and provide additional protection for the financial interests of the creditors. Typical debt covenants are restrictions on the payment of dividends to shareholders, requiring a company to maintain a minimum level of the current ratio, or a maximum level for the debt/equity ratio.

Stockholders wish to have management act in their own best interests as a means of maximizing their wealth. One means of accomplishing this is to contract with management by basing management compensation, at least in part, on the operating performance of the company. It is very common to observe compensation contracts that base a significant portion of management's total compensation on the reported net income of the company.

Assessing Profitability and Solvency

There are four primary tools used to assess the profitability and solvency of a company. Investors and creditors should include a careful review of (1) the **audit report**, (2) **significant transactions**, (3) the company's **credit rating**, and (4) **financial statement analysis**.

The audit report is prepared by the certified public accountant hired as the company's external auditor. Financial statements are prepared by the company's management. The independent external auditor is hired to review the company's financial records and provide additional assurance to the users of the financial statements. The auditor will normally indicate that the financial statements **fairly present** the **operations** and **financial position** of the company. The audit report will also indicate that all necessary tests and audit procedures were conducted and that the financial statements have been prepared in accordance with generally accepted accounting principles. When all the above conditions have been met, the audit report is referred to as a **standard audit report**.

When some conditions are not met, the auditor will issue a departure from the standard report. The following are reasons for issuing a non-standard report.

- One or more standard and necessary audit tests could not be completed. This is known as a scope limitation.
- The auditor has relied on another auditor to perform a portion of the work.
- The financial statements do not fully conform to generally accepted accounting principles.
- Major accounting principles or methods have been changed during the period since the last financial statements.
- The future outcome of uncertainties affecting the financial statements cannot be reasonably estimated.
- There is extreme uncertainty. The company's ability to continue as a going concern is in question.

Significant transactions are also important in assessing the profitability and solvency of a company. It is important for investors and creditors to recognize that single, large transactions may often distort the numbers presented in the financial statements. Normally, such single significant transactions will be discussed in the footnotes that accompany the financial statements.

Professional credit rating agencies provide additional reports which can be useful to both investors and creditors. Such reports are based in part on financial statement analysis. The credit rating agencies provide formal ratings or rankings on the riskiness of a company's outstanding debt issues.

The final important step is to conduct financial statement analysis. Financial statement analysis normally includes vertical analysis, horizontal analysis, and ratio analysis. **Vertical analyses**, techniques which convert the financial statements to percentages, are also known as **common-size financial statements**. This is especially useful to compare a company's operating performance to other companies in the same industry. It is highly unlikely that two companies will have exactly the same numbers appearing in their financial statements. However, companies in the same industry should have similar technologies and face similar costs in material and labor input markets. Therefore, companies within an industry should have similar operating performances.

Horizontal analysis techniques are used to compare a company's performance over time. **Ratio analysis** focuses on key relationships of items presented in the financial statements. The three types of analysis are normally combined in the overall financial statement analysis for a company. Details of technical procedures to complete the analyses are reviewed in the next section.

Assessing Solvency

In order to survive, a company must remain solvent. **Insolvency**, or **bankruptcy**, imposes significant costs on investors, creditors, and the economy as a whole. As previously noted, the goal of solvency assessment is to determine whether the company can generate sufficient future cash flows to meet liabilities and obligations as they come due. Evaluation of future cash flows is based on consideration of **operating performance**, **financial flexibility**, and **liquidity**.

Operating performance is a measure of the company's ability to increase net assets from normal operating activities. Companies provide goods and/or services to customers. A company can only increase net assets if such operating activities are profitable. Profitable operating activities are the primary source of a company's cash inflows and outflows.

Financial flexibility is a measure of the company's ability to generate cash flows from sources other than operating activities. Other sources are an important secondary source of cash flows to the company. Debt and equity markets are the most important other source for cash flows. A company will have less financial flexibility if it has exhausted its ability to borrow, or if recent stock market prices for its shares are depressed.

Liquidity is a measure of how quickly a company can convert its existing assets into cash. Current assets are more liquid than operating assets such as property and equipment. For example, by definition, there is a ready market for a company's investments in marketable securities. These can normally be converted into cash as the need arises by a simple call to the company's broker. On the other hand, it may be difficult to find a buyer for certain types of specialized production machinery and equipment. While the productive assets may be sold, considerable time may elapse before these can be converted to cash. Higher liquidity indicates a lower risk of insolvency.

Financial Statement Analysis Techniques

Financial statement analysis is an important skill for managers, investors, creditors, and others interested in assessing the financial performance of a company. Financial statement analysis is based on three primary tools: horizontal, vertical, and ratio analyses.

Horizontal analysis is an analysis technique which compares a company's financial statement data across two or more time periods. Vertical analysis (also known as common-size financial statements) converts raw dollar amounts in the financial statements to percentages to facilitate comparisons. For example, all balance sheet amounts are divided by total assets. Vertical analysis emphasizes the interrelation of the various financial statement numbers. **Ratio analysis** places an even greater emphasis on financial statement interrelations. Ratios are fractions using one (or more) account balance in the numerator and another (or more) account balance in the denominator.

Analysts frequently combine the above horizontal and vertical analyses. As an example, it is common to first prepare common-size financial statements and then to analyze the percentage-changes in the common-size amounts from year to year. It is also common to see analyses in which ratios are computed and then compared for percentage-changes over time.

It is worth your time to reinforce the concepts presented in Chapter 3 by some additional practice. You will have an opportunity to do some combined analyses of your own in completing the comprehensive review problem at the end of this chapter. Once you have completed the problem, you should be comfortable with the various calculations and you will have gained a greater appreciation of the techniques employed in financial statement analysis.

Before turning to the review problem, take a few minutes to read the paragraphs below which should refresh your memory on completing the various financial statement analysis procedures. You should also carefully read those sections in your text which deal with interpreting the results of ratio analyses.

Preparing Common-Size Financial Statements

Common-size financial statements (vertical analysis) facilitate more direct comparisons from one period to another. Difficulties due to differences in reported financial statement balances because of inflation and overall growth in the company are mitigated when the comparisons are made in common-size amounts. Normally, an analyst will prepare both common-size income statements and balance sheets.

The preparation of common-size statements simply converts all dollar amounts into percentages. A common-size balance sheet uses total assets as the denominator in calculating the percentages. A common-size income statement uses net sales as the denominator in calculating the percentages.

Preparing Comparisons Across Time

Comparisons across time are another useful tool for financial statement analysis. Such intertemporal comparisons are also known as horizontal analysis or trend analysis. It is typical to see such analyses prepared on the basis of both changes in dollar amounts from one year to the next, and in percentage change format.

Ratio Analysis

Balance Sheet Ratios

Ratios computed using only balance sheet balances are discussed in this section. As discussed earlier, solvency is a criterion used by investors to assess the health of a business. Several ratios are used to assess the ability of the company to meet obligations as they come due.

The **quick** or **acid-test ratio** divides the combined total of cash, temporary securities, and accounts receivable by the total current liabilities. In other words, the ratio is the number of dollars of highly liquid assets per dollar of obligations due in the near future. The higher the quick ratio, the better the ability to meet obligations as they come due.

The **current** or **working capital ratio** divides current assets by current liabilities. Since the numerator includes more types of assets, the current ratio will be higher than the quick ratio. The additional assets included are inventory and prepaid expenses. According to the operating cycle, inventory is farther away from being converted into cash than accounts receivable. In economic downturns, companies may have more inventory on hand because they cannot sell it. An increase in the current ratio may not be a positive signal in such a situation. An investor must determine the reason for changes in inventory before interpreting this ratio.

The **debt/equity ratio** is the ratio of total liabilities to total stockholders' equity. This ratio provides the investor with a measure of the relative claims on economic resources by creditors and investors. Since the tax law allows deductibility of interest but not dividends, some degree of debt or leverage is advisable; however, too much debt may result in risk of bankruptcy.

Income Statement Ratios

Income statement and balance sheet items are combined to compute several ratios used to assess the solvency, operational efficiency, and profitability of the corporation over time and compared to other firms. Some of the more common ratios are discussed in this section.

Solvency

Net income + Interest expense + Income tax expense / Interest expense is called the **interest coverage ratio**. It measures the average number of times that interest is earned during the period. This ratio is used to assess the long-term ability of the business to meet its interest payments.

Accounts receivable turnover is net credit sales (if available) divided by average accounts receivable. Average accounts receivable is calculated by adding beginning and ending accounts receivable together and dividing by two. This ratio measures the average speed with which accounts receivable are collected. It is a measure of the efficiency of collection. For a company to remain solvent, the collection process must be efficient.

Inventory turnover is cost of goods sold divided by average inventory. Average inventory is calculated by adding together beginning and ending inventory and dividing by two. The inventory turnover measures the average liquidity in inventory.

The accounts receivable turnover ratio can be converted into the average number of days sales in the accounts receivable by dividing 365 days by the accounts receivable turnover ratio. The resulting number represents the average time period to collect accounts receivable after the sale. Average number of days sales in inventory is computed by dividing 365 days by the inventory turnover ratio. The resulting number represents the average time period until inventory is sold. The sum of the two days sales numbers is an estimate of the operating cycle. For example, if a company has an average of 20 days sales in inventory and another 30 days in accounts receivable, its operating cycle is approximately 50 days.

Profitability

Return on sales (profit margin) is net income plus interest expense divided by sales. It measures the residual amount of each sales dollar attributed to owners.

Return on assets is net income plus interest expense divided by average total assets. Average total assets is the beginning total assets plus ending total assets divided by two. Return on assets measures resources generated from using all the resources invested in the business.

Return on equity is net income divided by average stockholders' equity. Return on investment can be used by owners to compare alternative investments.

Market Ratios

Earnings per share is the ratio of net income available to common stockholders divided by the average number of shares outstanding. The individual shareholder can determine how much his personal wealth has increased according to the accounting model during the time period.

The **price/earnings ratio (P/E ratio)** expresses the market price as a multiple of the current year's earnings. Analysts calculate the ratio by dividing the market price per share by the earnings per share for the period. It is often compared to the P/E ratio of other firms in the industry as a rough gauge of whether the stock is over- or under-valued.

The **dividend yield ratio** is calculated by dividing dividends per share by the average market price per share. It is a measure of the cash return on the investment during the year, similar to the rate of interest earned on savings or other investment in interest bearing securities.

Annual return on investment is a market price-based version of return on equity. It is calculated by dividing the change in market price for the year plus dividends by the beginning of year market price.

Limitations of Financial Accounting Information

The primary limitation of financial accounting information is that it does not provide a direct measure of the variable of interest in investment and credit decision making. Investors and creditors are interested in the **future performance** of the company. The true value of a company is the present value of its future cash flows. The financial accounting numbers are the result of past transactions and events. As such, the financial statements provide book values, which are only imperfect measures of a company's true value.

Financial accounting information is prepared in accordance with generally accepted accounting principles, which are inherently limited because they do not include all relevant information about a company. It takes time to prepare and audit financial statements, rendering financial accounting information as deficient in not being available on a timely basis. Financial statements are prepared by management. As such, the application of generally accepted accounting principles is subject to the biases and judgment of management.

Financial statements include only the results of past transactions and events. Other relevant information for valuing a company is omitted, often because it cannot be quantified or objectively measured. Users must make subjective adjustments to the financial statements to consider such additional relevant information. For example, future changes in interest rates, inflation rates, and other economic trends may have a significant influence on the future performance of the company.

Current generally accepted accounting principles do not value a company's human resources. In a high technology industry, the skills of a company's employees (especially those involved in new product research and development) can be an extremely valuable, but omitted, asset. Human capital is omitted because its valuation is considered too subjective. A company's reputation in providing goods and services to customers is also an important asset. This reputation is an intangible asset known as goodwill. Current generally accepted accounting principles include only goodwill that has been purchased in a business combination. Once again, high subjectivity in assigning a value to internally generated goodwill precludes its inclusion on the balance sheet.

Financial accounting numbers are primarily based on historical costs. In periods of inflation, these numbers may be very different from current costs and current values. Current generally accepted accounting principles provide no adjustment for the impact of inflation.

QUESTIONS FOR YOUR REVIEW

1. Which of the following is *true* regarding the usefulness of financial accounting numbers?
    a. Financial accounting numbers can help to predict a company's future cash flows.
    b. Financial accounting numbers can provide an indication of a company's earning power and solvency position.
    c. Financial accounting numbers can help investors and creditors to influence and monitor the business decisions of a company's managers.
    d. Financial accounting numbers are useful in all the above situations.

2. Which of the following is *not* one of the FASB's financial reporting objectives?
    a. Providing investors and creditors with information to assess future cash flows.
    b. Providing useful information for making investment and credit decisions.
    c. Providing information to assist management decision making.
    d. Providing information about a business's resources and obligations.

3. Which of the following two characteristics of accounting information can be used to assess its usefulness?
    a. Verifiability and timeliness
    b. Relevance and reliability
    c. Comparability and neutrality
    d. Completeness and reliability

4. Which of the following is the *least* worrisome reason for a departure from an auditor's standard report?
    a. There is a question about whether the company can continue as a going concern in the future.
    b. Major accounting methods have been changed.
    c. The auditor's opinion is based in part on the work of another auditor.
    d. The scope of the auditor's examination is affected by conditions that preclude the application of one or more auditing procedures considered necessary.

5. Which of the following is the *most* worrisome reason for a departure from an auditor's standard report?
    a. There is a question about whether the company can continue as a going concern in the future.
    b. Major accounting methods have been changed.
    c. The auditor's opinion is based in part on the work of another auditor.
    d. The financial statements are affected by uncertainties concerning future events.

6. Which of the following is *not* a limitation of financial accounting information?
    a. Financial statements are significantly influenced by the subjective judgments and incentives of the managers who prepare them.
    b. Financial statements are not adjusted for inflation.
    c. Financial statements do not generally reflect market values.
    d. Financial accounting information suffers from all the above limitations.

7. Consistency refers to consistent use of alternative generally accepted accounting methods:
    a. by several different companies.
    b. by all firms within the same industry.
    c. by a single company across several accounting periods.
    d. by a single company throughout a single accounting period.

8. Where would you look for early signals of a change in a company's profitability?
    a. Interim financial statements
    b. Annual financial statements
    c. Annual reports to stockholders
    d. Annual reports to the SEC

9. Which of the following is *not* a useful employment of financial statement analysis?
    a. Evaluating a company's future performance
    b. Evaluating a company's current financial position
    c. Evaluating a company's past performance
    d. Evaluating a company's past risk

10. Financial accounting numbers that can be reproduced by another system and result in similar measures are called:
    a. relevant
    b. comparable
    c. verifiable
    d. consistent

11. A general rule in evaluating alternative investments is the greater the risk, the:
    a. lower the expected return required.
    b. greater the expected return required.
    c. lower the expected price of the investment.
    d. greater the expected price of the investment.

12. Which of the following are legally required to be audited by certified public accountants?
    a. All large, privately owned companies
    b. All companies whose stock is traded on public stock exchanges, regardless of size
    c. Only large, publicly traded companies
    d. All U.S.-based companies

13. Which of the following do *not* use credit ratings to evaluate the earning power and solvency of a company?
    a. Investors
    b. Creditors
    c. Auditors
    d. Managers

14. A company's ability to increase its net assets through operations is known as:
    a. financial flexibility.
    b. operating performance.
    c. solvency.
    d. earning power.

15. A company's ability to produce cash through means other than operations is known as:
    a. financial flexibility.
    b. operating performance.
    c. solvency.
    d. earning power.

16. Which of the following is an inherent limitation of generally accepted accounting principles?
    a. Firms may choose from among alternative acceptable accounting methods.
    b. Management may assist the board of directors in selecting an auditor.
    c. Financial statements are prepared by management, not by the auditors.
    d. Internally generated goodwill is not explicitly recognized on the financial statements.

17. One limitation of current generally accepted accounting principles is the lack of fair market value information. For which of the following accounts is this likely to present the most serious problem?
    a. Accounts Receivable
    b. Cash
    c. Property, Plant, and Equipment
    d. Accounts Payable

18. Where would an investor look to determine whether the financial statements have been prepared in accordance with generally accepted accounting principles?
    a. A credit rating agency, such as Moody's
    b. The auditor's report
    c. The Securities and Exchange Commission
    d. The Financial Accounting Standards Board

19. Which of the following should *not* be considered in assessing the earning power and solvency of a company?
    a. The audit report
    b. Significant transactions
    c. Financial statement analysis
    d. Letters of recommendation

20. The extent to which management has used its discretion in preparing the financial statement dollar amounts is known as:
    a. earning power.
    b. earnings persistence.
    c. earnings quality.
    d. all the above.

21. Which of the following is a profitability measure?
    a. Earnings per share
    b. Receivables turnover
    c. Current ratio
    d. Debt/equity ratio

22. Which of the following measures is most similar to return on assets?
    a. Asset turnover
    b. Debt/equity ratio
    c. Earnings per share
    d. Quick ratio

23. Which of the following should be used as a denominator in preparing a common-size income statement?
    a. Net income
    b. Cost of goods sold
    c. Gross profit
    d. Net sales

24. Why are common-size financial statements useful?
    a. Users can identify companies of the same size.
    b. Users can identify companies of the same fair market value.
    c. Users can assess the potential of two similar size companies in different industries.
    d. Users can compare two different size companies within the same industry.

25. Which of the following should be considered in conducting a horizontal analysis?
    a. Changes in financial statement format
    b. Changes in dollar amounts only
    c. Changes in percentages only
    d. Changes in both dollar amounts and percentages

26. What type of ratio is the current ratio?
    a. Profitability ratio
    b. Solvency ratio
    c. Activity ratio
    d. Market ratio

27. Which of the following transactions would increase a current ratio that is greater than 1.0?
    a. Company purchases merchandise on credit.
    b. Company converts a current liability to a long-term liability.
    c. Company borrows cash and issues a short-term note payable.
    d. Company pays a ten percent cash dividend on its common stock.

28. Which of the following formulas is used to calculate the inventory turnover ratio?
    a. Average inventory divided by net sales
    b. Average net sales divided by net income
    c. Cost of goods sold divided by average inventory
    d. Cost of goods sold divided by net income

29. Which of the following is an incorrect interpretation of a high inventory turnover ratio?
    a. A high turnover indicates that the inventory turns over frequently.
    b. A high turnover indicates that there is less invested for each dollar of sales.
    c. A high turnover indicates that the inventory is obsolete.
    d. A high turnover indicates that there is sufficient inventory to meet customer demand.

30. Spartan Corporation's current ratio increased during 1999, while the quick ratio decreased. Which of the following could explain this set of ratio changes?
    a. Spartan increased accounts payable.
    b. Spartan increased inventory levels.
    c. Spartan's accounts receivable decreased.
    d. Spartan sold marketable equity securities.

31. The current ratio is unaffected by:
    a. payment of a $3,000 accounts payable.
    b. purchasing inventory for $15,000.
    c. a customer's payment of an account receivable by giving land.
    d. payment of wage expense for the month.

32. The current ratio is unaffected by:
    a. sales of goods for cash.
    b. the purchase of inventory for cash.
    c. the purchase of inventory on account.
    d. the payment of wages accumulated during the month.

33. The Beasley Company's 2001 current ratio is 2:1 (current assets = $100,000). In 2000, the current ratio was 3:1 (current assets = $75,000). Current liabilities at the end of 2001 and 2000 are, respectively:
    a. $50,000 (2001) and $25,000 (2000).
    b. $33,333 (2001) and $18,750 (2000).
    c. $200,000 (2001) and $225,000 (2000).
    d. They cannot be determined from the given information.

34. Referring to question 33, which of the transactions could have resulted in the change in the current ratio from 2000 to 2001?
    a. $25,000 account receivable is collected.
    b. $25,000 account payable is paid.
    c. Inventory which cost $10,000 is sold for $35,000 cash.
    d. A truck which is recorded in the financial statements for $25,000 is surrendered to a creditor for full payment of a $25,000 account payable.

Questions 35 and 36 refer to the following information.

The following is an excerpt from Buckman Safari Country's 1999 annual report:

Selected information for 1997:

Accounts receivable, 12/31/97	$290,000
Inventory, 12/31/97	70,000
Total assets, 12/31/97	450,000
Stockholders' equity, 12/31/97	130,000

Buckman's balance sheet and income statement are provided below.

Buckman Safari Company
Balance Sheet
December 31, 1999 and 1998

Assets:	1999	1998
Cash	$ 70,000	$ 20,000
Accounts receivable	300,000	280,000
Inventory	100,000	60,000
Prepaid rent	10,000	5,000
Total current assets	$480,000	$365,000
Land held for future development	50,000	
Furniture and fixtures	30,000	35,000
Total assets	$560,000	$400,000
Liabilities and stockholders' equity:		
Accounts payable	$250,000	$225,000
Wages payable	50,000	60,000
Total current liabilities	$300,000	$285,000
Bonds payable	100,000	0
Total liabilities	$400,000	$285,000
Stockholders' equity:		
Common stock, $2 par value	$ 50,000	$ 50,000
Paid in capital in excess of par value	10,000	10,000
Total contributed capital	$ 60,000	$ 60,000
Retained earnings	100,000	55,000
Total stockholders' equity	$160,000	$115,000
Total liabilities and stockholders' equity	$560,000	$400,000

Buckman Safari Company
Income Statement
For the Years Ending December 31, 1999 and 1998

	1999	1998
Revenues	$600,000	$560,000
Cost of goods sold	445,000	409,400
Gross profit	$155,000	$150,600
Operating expenses:		
Wage expense	$100,000	$110,000
Rent expense	10,000	9,000
Depreciation expense	5,000	5,000
Total operating expenses	$115,000	$124,000
Operating income	$ 40,000	$ 26,600
Interest expense	10,000	0
Income before tax	$ 30,000	$ 26,600
Income tax	12,000	10,640
Net income	$ 18,000	$ 15,960

35. Complete the following table by computing the ratios for Buckman Safari Company.

Ratio	Formula	1999	1998
Quick ratio	(Cash + Accounts receivable + Marketable securities) / Current liabilities		
Current ratio	Current assets / Current liabilities		
Debt/Equity	Total liabilities / Total stockholders' equity		
Accounts Receivable Turnover	Revenues / Average accounts receivable		
Average days sales in Accounts Receivable	365 days / Accounts receivable turnover		
Inventory Turnover	Cost of goods sold / Average inventory		
Average Days Sales in Inventory	365 days / Inventory turnover		

Chapter 3

Interest Coverage Ratio	Net income before interest and taxes / Interest expense		
Return on Sales	Net income / Revenues		
Return on Assets	Net income + Interest expense/ Average total assets		
Return on Equity	Net income / Average stockholders' equity		
Common Stock Shares Outstanding	Common stock total par value/ Par value per share		
Earnings per Share	Net income / Average common stock shares outstanding		
Gross Profit	Gross profit / Revenues		

36. From your calculations in (35), answer the following. Show how you arrived at your answers.

    a. What is the approximate length of Buckman's operating cycle in 1999 and 1998, respectively?

    b. From your analysis, has the debt-paying ability of Buckman changed during 1999? Explain.

c. From your analysis, is Buckman more or less profitable to the stockholders in 1999 compared to 1998?

37. The balance sheet of the Hoosier Company appears as follows.

Assets:

Cash and marketable securities	$20,000
Other current assets	20,000
Property, plant, and equipment	30,000
Total assets	$70,000

Liabilities and stockholders' equity:

Accounts payable	$12,000
Long-term debt	38,000
Stockholders' equity	20,000
Total liabilities and stockholders' equity	$70,000

Hoosier entered into the following transactions during 1999:

1. Purchased $2,000 of inventory on account.
2. Sold inventory originally costing $5,000 to customers on account, at a profit of $500.
3. Recorded $3,000 of depreciation expense on the property, plant, and equipment.
4. Paid $1,800 in cash for three months rent in advance on December 1, 1999. The rent covers December, January, and February.
5. Purchased a piece of equipment for $8,000 in cash.

Required: Complete the following table, indicating the impact of each of the above independent transactions on the indicated ratios. Assume that the above balance sheet is correct prior to each transaction.

Transaction	Quick Ratio	Current Ratio	Debt/Equity Ratio
1			
2			
3			
4			
5			

INC = Increase
DEC = Decrease
NE = No effect

38. The December 31, 1998, balance sheet of Spartan Corporation is as follows.

Assets:
Current assets	$20,000
Long-lived assets	50,000
Total assets	$70,000

Liabilities and stockholders' equity:
Current liabilities	$15,000
Long-term liabilities	30,000
Stockholders' equity	25,000
Total liabilities and stockholders' equity	$70,000

On March 1, 1999, Spartan borrowed $30,000 from the bank on a long-term note payable. Spartan plans to use the cash to purchase various long-lived assets. The debt covenant specifies that Spartan must maintain a minimum current ratio of 2:1 over the term of the note.

Required:
a. How much of the $30,000 can Spartan invest in long-lived assets without violating the debt covenant?

b. Assume that Spartan invested the maximum amount in the long-lived assets. Also assume that Spartan has made no transactions other than the loan and the investment. What is the new current ratio? What is the new debt/equity ratio?

c. Assume that Spartan invested the maximum amount in the long-lived assets. Also assume that Spartan has made no transactions other than the loan and the investment and operating transactions, which earned a net income of $56,400 (all in cash). How large a dividend can Spartan declare and pay at December 31, 1998, without violating the debt covenant?

39. **Comprehensive Review Problem**

Presented on the following pages is a set of financial statements and additional information for the Hawkeye Corporation for the years ended December 31, 1998 to 2000. Use this information to complete the following exercises.

1. Prepare common-size balance sheets for 1998 and 1999. Also compute the percentage changes in the common-size numbers of each account from 1998 to 1999.

2. Prepare common size-income statements for 1998 and 1999. Also compute the percentage changes in the common-size numbers of each account from 1998 to 1999.

3. Compute the dollar change in each balance sheet account from 1998 to 1999. Also compute the percentage changes in each account from 1998 to 1999.

4. Compute the dollar change in each income statement account from 1998 to 1999. Also compute the percentage changes in each account from 1998 to 1999.

5. Complete the table of key ratios that follows. Make ratio calculations for the year ended December 31, 1999, unless otherwise indicated.

Hawkeye Corporation
Balance Sheets
December 31, 2000, 1999, and 1998

	2000	1999	1998
Assets:			
Current assets:			
Cash	$ 305	$ 159	$ 148
Marketable equity securities	12	8	17
Accounts receivable	615	632	585
Inventory	1,250	970	954
Other current assets	42	36	50
Total current assets	$2,224	$1,805	$1,754
Land	500	500	450
Plant and equipment (net)	1,268	981	950
Intangible assets	450	409	375
Total assets	$4,442	$3,695	$3,529
Liabilities and stockholders' equity			
Current liabilities:			
Accounts payable	$ 83	$ 28	$ 43
Notes payable	225	110	158
Other accrued liabilities	25	43	37
Total current liabilities	$ 333	$ 181	$ 238
Long-term debt	650	665	685
Deferred income taxes	253	242	215
Other long-term liabilities	180	216	161
Total liabilities	$1,416	$1,304	$1,299
Stockholders' equity:			
Common stock	$ 153	$ 98	$ 98
Retained earnings	2,873	2,293	2,132
Total stockholders' equity	$3,026	$2,391	$2,230
Total liabilities and stockholders' equity	$4,442	$3,695	$3,529

Hawkeye Corporation
Income Statements
For the Years Ended December 31, 2000, 1999, and 1998

	2000	1999	1998
Net sales	$11,586	$11,097	$10,613
Cost of sales	5,989	5,462	5,227
Selling expenses	2,704	2,809	2,735
Administrative expenses	2,387	2,328	2,194
Interest expense	113	71	68
Interest income	(34)	(19)	(17)
	$11,159	$10,651	$10,207
Income before taxes	$ 427	$ 446	$ 406
Income tax expense	178	134	125
Net income	$ 249	$ 312	$ 281

Other Information

1. All given financial statement amounts are in thousands of dollars.

2. Average common shares outstanding (thousands):
   2000: 112
   1999: 108
   1998: 105

3. Dividends per share:
   2000: $0.80
   1999: $0.75
   1998: $0.70

4. Market prices (per share):
   2000: High $40   Low $22   Close $38
   1999: High $38   Low $18   Close $35
   1998: High $35   Low $21   Close $30

YOU MAY WISH TO REMOVE THE INFORMATION PAGES TO FACILITATE
COMPLETION OF THE COMPREHENSIVE PROBLEM.

Common-Size Balance Sheets

	1999	1998	Percent Change
Assets:			
Cash			
Marketable equity securities			
Accounts receivable			
Inventory			
Other current assets			
Land			
Plant and equipment (net)			
Intangible assets			
Total assets			
Liabilities and stockholders' equity:			
Accounts payable			
Notes payable			
Other accrued liabilities			
Long-term debt			
Deferred income taxes			
Other long-term liabilities			
Common stock			
Retained earnings			
Total liabilities and stockholders' equity			

Common-Size Income Statements

	1999	1998	Percent Change
Net sales			
Cost of sales			
Selling expenses			
Administrative expenses			
Interest expense			
Interest income			
Income before taxes			
Income tax expense			
Net income			

Comparative Income Statements

	1999	1998	Dollar Change	Percent Change
Net sales				
Cost of sales				
Selling expenses				
Administrative expenses				
Interest expense				
Interest income				
Income before taxes				
Income tax expense				
Net income				

Comparative Balance Sheets

	1999	1998	Dollar Change	Percent Change
Assets:				
Cash				
Marketable equity securities				
Accounts receivable				
Inventory				
Other current assets				
Land				
Plant and equipment (net)				
Intangible assets				
Total assets				
Liabilities and stockholders' equity:				
Accounts payable				
Notes payable				
Other accrued liabilities				
Long-term debt				
Deferred income taxes				
Other long-term liabilities				
Common stock				
Retained earnings				
Total liabilities and stockholders' equity				

Ratio	Formula	Calculations	Answer
	Profitability Ratios		
Return on Equity			
Return on Assets			
Return on Sales			
Interest Coverage Ratio			
	Solvency Ratios		
Current Ratio			
Quick Ratio			
	Activity Ratios		
Receivables Turnover			
Inventory Turnover			
	Capitalization Ratios		
Financial Leverage			
Debt/Equity Ratio			
	Market Ratios		
Earnings per Share			
Price/Earnings Ratio			
Dividend Yield Ratio			
Return on Investment			

SOLUTIONS-CHAPTER 3

1.	d	10.	c	19.	d	28.	c
2.	c	11.	b	20.	c	29.	c
3.	b	12.	b	21.	a	30.	b
4.	c	13.	d	22.	c	31.	b
5.	a	14.	b	23.	d	32.	b
6.	d	15.	a	24.	d	33.	a
7.	c	16.	d	25.	d	34.	a
8.	a	17.	c	26.	b		
9.	a	18.	b	27.	b		

35.

Buckman Safari Company
Selected Ratios
1999 and 1998

Ratio	Formula	1999	1998
Quick Ratio	(Cash + Accounts receivable + Marketable securities) / Current liabilities	(70 + 300)/ 300 = 1.23	(20 + 280)/ 285 = 1.05
Current Ratio	Current assets/ Current liabilities	480/300 = 1.60	365/285 = 1.28
Debt/Equity Ratio	Total liabilities/ Total stockholders' equity	400/160 = 2.50	285/115 = 2.48
Accounts Receivable Turnover	Revenues/Average accounts receivable	600/ [(300 + 280)/2] = 2.07	560/ [(280 + 290)/2] = 1.96
Average Days Sales in Accounts Receivable	365 days/ Accounts receivable turnover	365/2.07 = 176.33 days	365/1.96 = 186.22 days
Inventory Turnover	Cost of goods sold / Average inventory	445/ [(100 + 60)/2]= 5.56	409.4/ [(60 + 70)/2] = 6.30
Average Days Sales in Inventory	365 Days / Inventory turnover	365/5.56 = 65.65 days	365/6.30 = 57.94 days

Interest Coverage Ratio	Net income before interest and taxes / Interest expense	40/10 = 4.0	N/A
Return on Sales	Net income / Revenues	18/600 = .0300	15.96/560 = .0285
Return on Assets	Net income + Interest expense / Average total assets	18 + 10 /[(560 + 400)/2] = .0580	15.96 + 0 /[(400+450)/2] = .0376
Return on Equity	Net income / Average stockholders' equity	18/ [(160 + 115)/2] = .1309	15.96/ [(115 + 130)/2] = .1303
Common Stock Shares Outstanding	Common stock total par value / Par value per share	$50,000 / $2 per share = 25,000	$50,000 / $2 per share = 25,000
Earnings per Share	Net income / Average common stock shares outstanding	18/[(25 + 25)/2] = .7200	15.96/[(25 + 25)/2] = .6384
Gross Profit	Gross profit / Revenues	155/600 = .2583	150.6/560 = .2689

36. a. Buckman's operating cycle length is estimated by adding together the days' sales in accounts receivable and days' sales in inventory. The operating cycle is 241.98 (176.33 + 65.65) days in 1999 and 244.16 (186.22 + 57.94) days in 1998.

During 1999, Buckman's customers typically pay in about six months (176.33/30 days per month), and it takes about two months (65.65/30 days per month) for Buckman to sell its inventory. Clearly, these are areas that are ripe for improvement. Buckman may adopt a policy of charging interest to customers who do not pay in full after a month or two to encourage payment. Buckman may need to study operations research to develop a system for inventory management to reduce the amount of inventory on hand and increase inventory turnover. Both of these strategies could reduce the operating cycle length so that more cash is available for additional investments in operating assets such as plant or equipment, or to pay liabilities and dividends.

b. Debt-paying ability can be assessed using the quick ratio, current ratio, accounts receivable turnover, and inventory turnover for debt due in a short time period. The debt to equity ratio and times interest earned can be used to assess the ability to meet long-term obligations.

As mentioned in part (a), Buckman's operating cycle length (using information derived from the accounts receivable turnover and inventory turnover ratios) is quite long, which could impede payment of debt. Even though Buckman has sufficient current assets to pay current liabilities, cash is required to pay those liabilities. If customers are not paying on a timely basis and if inventory is not selling on a timely basis, Buckman may not have enough cash to pay its bills as they come due.

More of Buckman's total resources are claimed by creditors according to the debt/ equity ratio, 250 percent. Buckman is leveraged. Buckman's income is four times as large as interest expense during 1999. Buckman's business is bringing in more resources than it costs to produce and sell those resources, which is a good sign. The net increase in resources is more than adequate to cover interest charges. Buckman must pay interest with cash. Thus, the low accounts receivable turnover ratio may be of concern since Buckman is not converting revenues into cash on a rapid basis.

c. Earnings per share increased by 12.5 percent [(0.72 - 0.64)/0.64] from 1998 to 1999. The profit margin increased by 5.26 percent. Buckman's return on investment increased by 0.5 percent. Buckman's stockholders' investment was slightly more profitable in 1999 compared to 1998.

Summary: Aside from cash-generating ability, Buckman seems to be in good shape.

37. If you have difficulty in determining the effects of transactions on ratios, you may wish to first record the journal entries (using only the available accounts). If you still have difficulty convincing yourself of the effects, then actually recompute the ratios after posting each of the transactions to the balance sheet. The journal entries are as follows.

1.	Other Current Assets (+A)	2,000	
	Accounts Payable (+L)		2,000
	Purchased inventory on credit.		
2.	Cash (+A)	5,500	
	Stockholders' Equity (R,+SE)		5,500
	Stockholders' Equity (E,-SE)	5,000	
	Other Current Assets (-A)		5,000
	Sold inventory on credit at a profit.		
3.	Stockholders' Equity (E,-SE)	3,000	
	Property, Plant, and Equipment (-A)		3,000
	Recognized depreciation.		
4.	Other Current Assets (+A)	1,800	
	Cash (-A)		1,800
	Paid three months rent in advance.		
5.	Property, Plant, and Equipment (+A)	8,000	
	Cash (-A)		8,000
	Purchased equipment.		

Transaction	Quick Ratio	Current Ratio	Debt/Equity Ratio
1	DEC	DEC	INC
2	INC	INC	DEC
3	NE	NE	INC
4	DEC	NE	NE
5	DEC	DEC	NE

38. A useful way to approach this problem is to prepare a balance sheet under each of the conditions. It is then relatively simple to make the ratio calculations and determine the required minimums to meet the debt covenant.

	12/31/98	After Borrowing	After Investing	After Net Income
Assets				
Current assets	20,000	50,000	30,000	86,400
Long-lived assets	50,000	50,000	70,000	70,000
Total assets	70,000	100,000	100,000	156,400
Liabilities and Equity				
Current liabilities	15,000	15,000	15,000	15,000
Long-term liabilities	30,000	60,000	60,000	60,000
Stockholders' equity	25,000	25,000	25,000	81,400
Total liabilities and equity	70,000	100,000	100,000	156,400

a. In order to maintain the 2:1 current ratio, look at the "After Borrowing" column. Spartan could invest a maximum of $20,000. This would change the balance sheet to the results in the "After Investing" column, resulting in a current ratio of 2:1.

b. Use the "After Investing" column and perform the calculations.

Current Ratio   = Current assets / Current liabilities
                = 30,000/15,000
                = 2.0

38. b.   Debt/Equity Ratio = Total liabilities / Stockholders' equity
                = 75,000/25,000
                = 3.0

    c.   Use the "After Net Income" column. The maximum dividend to maintain the 2:1 current ratio is $56,400.

39. **Comprehensive Review Problem**

Hawkeye Corporation
Common-Size Balance Sheets
December 31, 1999 and 1998

	1999	1998	Percent Change
Assets:			
Cash	4.3%	4.2%	0.1%
Marketable equity securities	0.2	0.5	(0.3)
Accounts receivable	17.1	16.6	0.5
Inventory	26.3	27.0	(0.7)
Other current assets	1.0	1.4	(0.4)
Land	13.5	12.8	0.7
Plant and equipment (net)	26.5	26.9	(0.4)
Intangible assets	11.1	10.6	0.5
Total assets	100.0%	100.0%	0.0%
Liabilities and stockholders' equity:			
Accounts payable	0.8%	1.2%	(0.4)%
Notes payable	3.0	4.5	(1.5)
Other accrued liabilities	1.2	1.0	0.2
Long-term debt	18.0	19.4	(1.4)
Deferred income taxes	6.5	6.1	0.4
Other long-term liabilities	5.8	4.6	1.2
Common stock	2.7	2.8	(0.1)
Retained earnings	62.0	60.4	1.6
Total liabilities and stockholders' equity	100.0%	100.0%	0.0%

Hawkeye Corporation
Common-Size Income Statements
For the Years Ended December 31, 1999 and 1998

	1999	1998	Percent Change
Net sales	100.0%	100.0%	0.0%
Cost of sales	(49.2)	(49.3)	(0.1)
Selling expenses	(25.3)	(25.8)	(0.5)
Administrative expenses	(21.0)	(20.7)	0.3
Interest expense	(0.6)	(0.6)	0.0
Interest income	0.2	0.2	0.0
Income before taxes	4.1	3.8	0.3
Income tax expense	1.2	1.2	0.0
Net income	2.9%	2.6%	0.3%

Hawkeye Corporation
Comparative Balance Sheets
December 31, 1999 and 1998

	1999	1998	Dollar Change	Percent Change
Assets:				
Cash	$ 159	$ 148	$ 11	7.4%
Marketable equity securities	8	17	(9)	(52.9)
Accounts receivable	632	585	47	8.0
Inventory	970	954	16	1.7
Other current assets	36	50	(14)	(28.0)
Land	500	450	50	11.1
Plant and equipment (net)	981	950	31	3.3
Intangible assets	409	375	34	9.1
Total assets	$3,695	$3,529	$166	4.7%
Liabilities and stockholders' equity:				
Accounts payable	$ 28	$ 43	$ (15)	(34.9)%
Notes payable	110	158	(48)	(30.4)
Other accrued liabilities	43	37	6	16.2
Long-term debt	665	685	(20)	(2.9)
Deferred income taxes	242	215	27	12.6
Other long-term liabilities	216	161	55	34.2
Common stock	98	98	0	0.0
Retained earnings	2,293	2,132	161	7.6
Total liabilities and stockholders' equity	$3,695	$3,529	$166	4.7%

Hawkeye Corporation
Comparative Income Statements
For the Years Ended December 31, 1999 and 1998

	1999	1998	Dollar Change	Percent Change
Net sales	$11,097	$10,613	$484	4.6%
Cost of sales	(5,462)	(5,227)	235	4.5
Selling expenses	(2,809)	(2,735)	74	2.7
Administrative expenses	(2,328)	(2,194)	134	6.1
Interest expense	(71)	(68)	3	4.4
Interest income	19	17	2	11.8
Income before taxes	$ 446	$ 406	$ 40	9.9
Income tax expense	134	125	9	7.2
Net income	$ 312	$ 281	$ 31	11.0%

Ratio	Formula	Calculations	Answer
	Profitability Ratios		
Return on Equity	Net income / Average stockholders' equity	312 / [(2,391 + 2,230) / 2]	0.135
Return on Assets	(Net income + Interest expense) / Average total assets	(312 + 71)/[(3,695 + 3,529) / 2]	0.106
Return on Sales	Net income / Net sales	312 / 11,097	0.028
Interest Coverage Ratio	Net income before Taxes / Interest expense	446 / 71	6.282
	Solvency Ratios		
Current Ratio	Current assets / Current liabilities	1,805 / 181	9.972
Quick Ratio	(Cash + Accounts receivable + Marketable securities) / Current liabilities	(159 + 632 + 8) / 181	4.414
	Activity Ratios		
Receivables Turnover	Net credit sales / Average accounts receivable	11,097 / [(632 + 585) / 2]	18.237
Inventory Turnover	Cost of goods sold / Average inventory	5,462 / [(970 + 954) / 2]	5.678
	Capitalization Ratios		
Financial Leverage	Return on equity - Return on assets	0.135 - 0.106	0.029
Debt / Equity	Total liabilities / Total stockholders' equity	1,304 / 2,391	0.545
	Market Ratios		
Earnings per Share	Net income / Average number of common shares outstanding	312 / 108	$ 2.89
Price / Earnings	Market price per share / Earnings per share	[(38 + 18) / 2] / 2.89	9.689
Dividend Yield	Dividends per share / Market price per share	0.75 / [(38 + 18) / 2]	0.027
Annual Return on Investment	(Ending market price - Beginning market price + Dividends) / Beginning market price	(35 - 30 + 0.75) / 30	0.192

Notes on Table of Key Ratios and Solutions

1. All answers in the ratio table are in decimal form, not in percentages.

2. Some ratios require an average amount. For example, return on assets uses average total assets as the denominator. These averages are calculated by adding the beginning and end-of-year balances and then dividing by two. The only exception to this rule is for average shares outstanding, which is simply given in the additional information.

3. Percentages may not total to 100% in the comparative and common-size financial statements due to slight rounding differences.

4. Common-size balance sheet amounts are computed by dividing each individual balance sheet account balance by total assets. For example, the 1999 common-size amount for accounts receivable divides December 31, 1999, accounts receivable by total assets. This is multiplied by 100 to convert to a percentage.

    [(\$632 / \$3,695) x 100 = 17.1 %]

5. Common-size income statement amounts are computed by dividing each individual income statement account balance by net sales. For example, the 1999 common-size amount for cost of sales divides 1999 cost of sales by net sales. This is multiplied by 100 to convert to a percentage.

    [(\$5,462 / \$11,097) x 100 = 49.2 %]

6. The "percent changes" in the common-size balance sheet and income statement are simply the 1999 percentages less the 1998 percentages.

7. The "dollar changes" in the comparative financial statements are the 1999 balances less the 1998 amounts for each account. The "percent changes" are the "dollar changes" divided by the 1998 balances. This is then multiplied by 100 to convert to a percentage. Refer to net sales in the comparative income statement as an example. The dollar change is calculated as:

    [\$11,097 - \$10,613 = \$484]

    The percent change is calculated as:

    [(\$484 / \$10,613) x 100 = 4.6 %]

CHAPTER 4

The Measurement Fundamentals of Financial Accounting

REVIEW OF KEY CONCEPTS

This chapter introduces the concepts underlying the measurement of economic events reported in the financial statements. Accounting concepts are usually categorized as assumptions, principles, and exceptions. In addition, the text discusses the valuation bases used to account for economic events and, in particular, the effect of an unstable monetary unit in interpreting financial statements prepared under a stable monetary unit assumption. If the dollar is stable across time, it can purchase the same quantity of every good at all points in time. If the dollar is unstable, interpreting changes in operating results must include factoring in the effect of changing prices.

A discussion of measurement valuation bases and the effect of inflation in interpreting financial statements is presented below. After completing this chapter, you should be familiar with the concepts underlying accounting and the relation between these concepts and the rules followed to account for transactions. You should also be able to describe the valuation bases for items on the balance sheet and the effect of inflation on the interpretation of financial statement data.

The Basis of Accrual Accounting: Revenue Recognition and Matching Principle

Revenue recognition is the process involving the measurement and timing of recording revenues. Recall that revenues are the increase in stockholders' equity resulting from the inflow of economic resources (typically cash or accounts receivable) accompanying selling the products or providing the services that represent the company's core business.

Revenue can be recorded when (1) the earnings process is substantially complete and (2) the net amount to be received from the transaction can be reasonably estimated. Notice that actually receiving cash from the customer is not a requirement. Instead, the company can still record a revenue if a promise to pay is received from the customer, and if the company can estimate any uncollectible portion (returns and bad debts). In this case the company must also be able to estimate costs to be incurred subsequent to the actual exchange (for example, if the product sold includes a warranty, the company estimates any future payments to repair or replace the item).

The **matching principle** determines the timing of recording expenses. Recall that expenses are the decrease in stockholders' equity resulting from the assets used or liabilities incurred accompanying selling the products or providing the services that represent the company's core business.

Ideally, expenses should be recorded in the same period that related revenues are recorded. Notice that a cash payment is NOT required in order to record an expense. Expenses represent the using up of assets (such as cash, inventory, or plant and equipment) or the incurring of liabilities (such as wage expense) in order to earn revenue. Expense recognition may follow the payment of cash (for example, inventory purchased earlier is sold) or precede payment of cash (for example, when employees are paid after they have provided the service). **Expense recognition follows revenue recognition, not the payment of cash.**

Example: Hercules sells weight-lifting equipment. The equipment is sold with a one-year warranty for repairs. Assume that 100 sets of weights are sold for $300 each and that each set cost Hercules $200. Half the money was collected immediately and half will be collected in six months. Hercules estimates no sets will be returned, but that $500 will not be collected. Hercules also estimates that $750 of warranty-related repair costs will be incurred.

Because Hercules has delivered the equipment, and can estimate uncollectible accounts and the cost of the warranty-related repairs, Hercules can record the $30,000 as sales. The journal entries to record the sale would be:

Cash (+A)	15,000	
Accounts Receivable (+A)	15,000	
Sales (R,+SE)		30,000
To record the sale.		
Cost of Goods Sold (E,-SE)	20,000	
Inventory (-A)		20,000
Bad Debt Expense (E,-SE)	500	
Allowance for Bad Debts (-A)		500
Warranty Expense (E,-SE)	750	
Warranty Liability (+L)		750
To record the sale related expenses.		

The company would report net income of $8,750 on the sale (Revenues - Expenses).

Measurement Valuation Bases

Fair Market Value

Businesses operate in both input and output markets. The goods or services that the company produces are marketed and sold in the output market. The price received for goods and services sold by the business is their fair market value and is recorded as revenue. Businesses purchase the raw materials and the labor required to produce goods and services in input markets. Businesses typically receive cash, accounts receivable, or notes receivable in exchange for the good or service sold to customers. Typically, the accounts receivable contract is informal, requiring payment of the amount due within 30 days. Usually, interest is not charged on accounts receivable if they are paid within the grace period. The amount due is usually the amount that would have been due if cash had been paid.

Present Value

Notes receivable are formal contracts that usually specify the exact timing of payment and the amount to be paid, including interest. Unlike a cash sale or sale on account, the amount recorded initially as an asset is not the total that will be paid by the customer over the life of the contract. A portion of the final payment amount is interest, which is the additional amount the customer pays for delaying payment. Interest is earned by the business as time passes. When the contract is initially signed, no time has passed, and therefore no interest is earned yet. The amount recorded at the time the contract is signed and the good or service is provided is the total contract payments less any interest included in the contract payments, or **the present value of the contract payments**. Alternatively, the present value of the contract payments is the amount that would be paid today in cash instead of signing the contract. The present value of the contract payments is the cash equivalent price of the good or service.

Example. James Mason purchases a car from a local dealer. The payment terms are $2,000 down and 24 payments of $612 each, beginning in one month. The interest rate charged for loans of similar risk and duration is 12 percent per year, or 1 percent per month. The total cash that Mr. Mason will pay for the car is $16,688 [$2,000 + ($612 x 24)]. However, a portion of the total cash paid is interest, which is earned by the dealer over the 24-month period. The amount earned by the dealer at the time the car is delivered to Mr. Mason is the $16,688 less the total interest included in this amount. To determine the amount earned at delivery, the present value of the cash flow stream is calculated using the techniques discussed in Appendix 4A in the text. This amount is $15,000 [$2,000 + ($612 x present value interest factor of an ordinary annuity where $i=1$ and $n=24$) (the factor is 21.2434)]. The car could have been purchased for $15,000 [$2,000 + $13,000] now instead of the payment terms under which the contract was written. Mr. Mason pays interest of $1,688 ($16,688 - $15,000). This is the cost of choosing this contract.

The dealer records sales revenue of $15,000 when the car is delivered to Mr. Mason. The dealer will record interest revenue of $1,688 over the life of the contract. The exact amount to be recorded each month is determined by the **effective interest method**, which is discussed in Chapter 11.

The present value is the basis for valuing most long-term liabilities. The payments made by the company to honor these contracts involve repayment of the amount originally borrowed plus interest. At a point in time, the accounting records should reflect the total amount owed, which includes the amount originally borrowed and interest which is owed according to the terms of the contract but unpaid to that date. The present value of the future cash flows required to be paid by the contract represents the amount owed at that point in time. Mortgages, leases, bonds, and pensions are examples of long-term liabilities which are valued using present value concepts.

Historical Cost

Businesses acquire labor, materials, equipment, buildings, and other factors used to produce goods and services in **input markets**. Like the price received for goods and services sold in the output market, the price paid for these **factors of production** depends upon the market mechanism.

These factors can be acquired by paying cash, exchanging other assets, incurring liabilities, or issuing common stock. Some factors are used up immediately in earning revenues and are immediately recorded as expenses. Other factors are acquired for use in earning revenues in one or more future time periods and are initially recorded as assets.

Different valuation bases may be used to account for an asset at various points in time before it is used to earn revenues. Initially, assets are usually accounted for using the historical cost principle. All costs necessary to ready the asset for its intended use are included in the cost of the asset on the balance sheet. As these costs are incurred, the asset account is increased. Some assets such as self-constructed buildings may take an extended period of time to complete. Several transactions may increase the value of the asset over time.

While the historical cost principle is usually applicable for asset valuation, assets are occasionally acquired and financed using long-term liabilities. As mentioned with respect to notes receivable, the long-term contracts specify the timing and amount of all future cash payments. The total of the cash payments satisfies the purchase obligation and interest incurred due to purchasing the asset on a long-term liability contract. Like the notes receivable case, the present value of the promised cash payments represents the initial cost of the asset. Usually, interest is not considered part of the original cost of an asset. The asset in such a case is valued at the present value of the future cash payments.

Example. Land is purchased in exchange for a long-term note. The note requires payment of $20,000 per year for four years. The first payment is due in one year. The total cash payments to satisfy the note's terms are $80,000 ($20,000 x 4). A portion of the $80,000 is payment for the land itself and a portion is the interest incurred from choosing this specific form of financing. If notes of similar risk and duration require a 10 percent interest rate, the present value of the note payments is $63,400 [20,000 x (the present value interest factor of an annuity where i=10 and n=4); (the factor is 3.17)]. The analysis suggests that the business could have paid cash of $63,400 instead of signing the long-term obligation. The business pays $16,600 ($80,000 - $63,400) in interest expense over the note's term. The land's book value is not increased by the interest payment under the historical cost principle. The interest is expensed as it is incurred with the passage of time.

After an asset is acquired in either the input or output market, its book value is periodically evaluated to ensure that the asset is not overvalued. The diverse nature of assets requires using different methods for this evaluation. This periodic review is an application of the **conservatism** concept. Conservatism states that when in doubt, financial statements should understate assets, overstate liabilities, accelerate recognition of losses, and delay recognition of gains.

Accounts receivable are evaluated by applying the **net realizable value** concept. The collectibility of accounts receivable is periodically reviewed. The book value of accounts receivable is reduced by the amount estimated to be uncollectible.

The **lower of cost or market** method is used to evaluate inventories periodically. If the price which would be paid to purchase the inventory in the input market (its **replacement cost**) is below its book value, the inventory's book value is reduced to replacement cost.

The book value of long-term productive assets, such as plant and equipment and intangibles, is typically not compared to fair market values because the asset often is not directly sold in an input market. These assets are used to produce other assets (inventory) or services which are then sold in output markets. These assets are valued at historical cost reduced by accumulated depreciation and amortization. Depreciation and amortization are unrelated to changes in the fair market value of the assets. Depreciation and amortization are allocations of cost over time.

Periodically, long-term productive assets' book values are reviewed to determine if obsolescence has occurred. For example, as new technologies improve the efficiency of a production process, some older plant assets may be replaced by the new technology. The company may choose to discard the assets by selling or scrapping them, or may use the assets in other production processes. In either case, the asset's value to the company's operations is impaired. If the book value is above this impaired value, the asset will be written down.

Inflation and Financial Statement Data Interpretation

The dollar's value to an individual depends upon the quantity of goods that can be purchased with the dollar. If the dollar is stable, it can purchase the same quantity of every good at all points in time. An underlying assumption of financial accounting is that the dollar is stable with respect to purchasing power. Unfortunately, this assumption is not a very good representation of the real world. The implication of this poor assumption is that the financial statement reader must factor in the effect of inflation when interpreting changes in the reported economic condition of the business.

For example, businesses sell products in output markets. The price received for goods is determined by the operating mechanism in that market. If the dollar's value deteriorates during a year, each dollar can purchase less of the good or service. In order to acquire a unit of the good or service, more dollars must be exchanged.

The business either reinvests the dollars received in goods or services from customers or distributes the dollars as dividends to stockholders. The dollars received or distributed can each purchase less of every good in the economy. The business and its owners are not as well off as they appear according to the financial statements because the purchasing power of every dollar is less.

Example. Maritime Inc. reports sales of $300,000 in 1997, $350,000 in 1998, and $400,000 in 1999. Maritime appears to be doing well. Growth in sales is 16.7 percent from 1997 to 1998, and 14.3 percent from 1998 to 1999. Assuming inflation is 10 percent in 1998, and 25 percent from 1997 to 1999, 1998 sales of $350,000 expressed in 1997 purchasing power are $318,182 [$350,000 / (1 + 0.10) (1998 inflation)]. 1999 sales expressed in 1997 purchasing power are $320,000 [$400,000 / (1 + 0.25)].

The real sales changes, after controlling for inflation, are 6.1 percent from 1997 to 1998, [($318,182 - $300,000) / $300,000] and 0.6 percent from 1998 to 1999 [($320,000 - $318,182) / $318,182]. Inflation-adjusted 1999 sales growth is relatively worse than when inflation is not controlled. Financial statement users must be aware of the effects of inflation so that they can make the necessary adjustments to arrive at numbers that are comparable across time.

QUESTIONS FOR YOUR REVIEW

1. The Hannah Corporation purchases 20,000 units of inventory for $1 each from various wholesalers on January 1, 1998. The inventory can be sold to customers for $1.50 each. If Hannah valued the inventory on its books at $30,000, what valuation basis was used?
   a. Historical cost
   b. Replacement cost
   c. Fair market value
   d. Present value

2. Referring to question (1), on January 1, 1999, 2,000 units of the 1998 purchase remain in inventory. If these units were purchased from wholesalers today they would cost $1.20, the inflation rate from 1998 to 1999 on the inventory is:
   a. 20% [(1.20-1.00) / 1.00]
   b. -20% [(1.20-1.50) / 1.50]
   c. - 4% average cost in 1998 [(1.00 + 1.50) / 2 = 1.25], inflation from 1998 to 1999 = [(1.20 - 1.25) / 1.25]
   d. 0%

3. Referring to questions (1) and (2), if Hannah was very efficient during 1999 and held all other costs equal to the 1998 levels, how much would Hannah need to charge per unit to earn the same gross profit percentage in 1999 as was earned in 1998?
   a. $1.40
   b. $1.50
   c. $1.70
   d. $1.80

4. Bradley Products purchased land in 1986 for $20,000 cash. The business has owned the land since that time. In 1999, Bradley purchased another tract of land for $20,000 cash. Assume that prices in general increased by 30 percent from 1986 to 1999. After the 1999 purchase, the *total* book value in the land account, using the stable dollar assumption, is:
   a. $20,000
   b. $40,000
   c. $46,000
   d. $52,000

5. Referring to question (4), if the stable dollar assumption is relaxed, the land account balance should be:
   a. $20,000
   b. $40,000
   c. $46,000
   d. $52,000

6.   The Alcott Company reported sales as follows:

1997	1998	1999
$100,000	$130,000	$160,000

Assuming the general inflation rate for 1997 through 1999 is 20 percent, what was the real increase in sales from 1997 to 1999?
a.   20 percent
b.   33 percent
c.   40 percent
d.   60 percent

7.   An example of an asset whose initial book value is determined by the output markets in which the business operates is:
a.   inventories
b.   plant and equipment
c.   accounts receivable
d.   goodwill

8.   Net income can be thought of as:
a.   the difference between cash received for goods or services sold and the cash paid to provide those goods or services.
b.   the difference between the prices received for goods or services in output markets and prices paid in input markets for factors of production used to create goods and services.
c.   the increase in stockholders' equity during a fiscal period.
d.   the increase in the difference between assets and liabilities during a fiscal period.

9.   An accounting process or principle which is justified by the fiscal period assumption is (are):
a.   accrual and deferral adjusting entries.
b.   conservatism.
c.   historical cost principle.
d.   stable monetary unit assumption.

10.   What is the main reason that historical cost is used to value most assets after acquisition?
a.   The replacement cost, fair market value, or present value bases are generally difficult to objectively determine compared to historical cost.
b.   The other valuation bases generally result in amounts close to historical cost, and historical cost is appropriate because the differences are not material.
c.   Matching and revenue recognition are only possible if historical cost is used.
d.   Accruals and deferrals are only possible if historical cost is used.

11.   For revenue to be recognized (i.e., recorded):
a.   revenue must be earned.
b.   revenue must be measurable.
c.   all material benefits given up (expenses) to earn revenues must be measurable.
d.   all the above.

12. An example of applying conservatism is:
    a. the lower of cost or market rule applied to inventories.
    b. the matching principle.
    c. the recognition of accumulated depreciation.
    d. the recording of accrual and deferral adjusting journal entries.

13. Expenses are usually recorded when:
    a. paid for.
    b. related revenues have been recorded.
    c. the tax law indicates that they are deductible.
    d. the fiscal period ends.

14. Most companies' fiscal year ends on December 31. Some companies choose non-December 31 year-ends because:
    a. the fiscal year-end is determined by the tax law.
    b. accruals and deferrals are not possible otherwise.
    c. their operating cycle is seasonal and financial reports are more meaningful if the entire operating cycle is included.
    d. this choice can reduce audit fees.

15. Amber Corporation purchased land using a long-term contract. Amber promises to pay $15,000 each year for the next 10 years. How should Amber record the land's acquisition?
    a. No entry should be made because no cash payment has been made.
    b. The land should be recorded at $150,000, since this is the total amount that Amber will pay to satisfy the purchase agreement's terms.
    c. The land should be recorded at some amount less than $150,000, since some interest is included in the future cash payments. The land's book value should not include interest.
    d. At some amount greater than $150,000, since real estate market prices will likely increase in the future.

    For questions 16-18, refer to the Time Value of Money Tables in the text.

16. What is the present value of $15,000, due in five years, discounted at 8 percent, compounded annually?
    a. $22,039
    b. $10,209
    c. $10,134
    d. $10,095

17. John is saving to purchase a new car four years from today. The bank pays interest at 6 percent, compounded annually. John is able to save $800 each year. John will make his first deposit at the end of the current year. How much will John have accumulated at the end of the four years?
    a. $3,000
    b. $3,200
    c. $3,500
    d. $3,600

18. John is purchasing a new car today for $14,000. The bank charges interest at 12 percent annual rate, compounded quarterly. John will make a cash down payment of $3,000 today. His first payment is at the end of the current quarter. The bank offers John a thirty quarter loan. What will be the amount of John's quarterly payments?
    a. $231
    b. $294
    c. $561
    d. $714

19. Amber Corporation purchased a piece of land on January 1, 1999, for $10,000. On December 31, 1999, Amber sold the land for $25,000.

    Required:
    a. Prepare the journal entries to record the purchase and sale of the land, assuming generally accepted accounting principles are followed.

    b. Assuming the general inflation rate from January 1, 1999 to December 31, 1999, is 15 percent, how much would Amber need to receive on the land's sale for the business to maintain the same level of purchasing power at the end of 1999 as it had at the beginning of 1999?

    c. Compute the return on investment in the land, assuming you use the reported gain.

19. d. What is the return on investment in the land, after controlling for general inflation?

    e. Mr. Amber notices the reported gain and suggests paying it out as a dividend. Given your analysis in parts (b), (c), and (d), and Mr. Amber's intention to maintain the same level of real investment in the business, how much of the gain is available for distribution as dividends?

20. Maroon Corporation is evaluating its policy of allowing customers to issue notes receivable in exchange for Maroon's products, which initially cost Maroon $500. Maroon charges the customers an annual interest rate of 4 percent, plus expected general inflation. The 4 percent is selected because that is how much Maroon typically earns on its assets over a year when inflation is zero.

    Tarragon Corporation purchased some of Maroon's merchandise on January 1, 1999, in exchange for a one-year note due December 31, 1999. Maroon anticipated inflation of 6 percent for 1999, so the interest rate on the note was set at 10 percent. If Tarragon paid cash for the merchandise, it would have paid $1,000.

    a. Prepare the journal entries for 1999 related to the Tarragon sale and the payment of the note receivable by Tarragon on December 31, 1999.

20. b. If the general inflation rate is 15 percent during 1999, how much would Maroon need to receive from Tarragon on December 31 to maintain the same purchasing power that was available on January 1?

   c. If the general inflation rate is 15 percent during 1999, considering that Maroon could have earned 4 percent on the $1,000 if Tarragon had paid cash for the sale, what interest rate would fully compensate Maroon for delaying receipt of the payment? Given this interest rate, what dollar amount would Tarragon pay Maroon at December 31, 1999?

   d. Given that Tarragon actually paid Maroon $1,100 at the end of 1999, is the interest revenue reported on the income statement an accurate reflection of the economic substance of the transactions? In real terms, did stockholder wealth increase or decrease?

CHAPTER 4-SOLUTIONS

1.	c	7.	c	13.	b
2.	a	8.	b	14.	c
3.	d	9.	a	15.	c
4.	b	10.	a	16.	b
5.	c	11.	d	17.	c
6.	b	12.	a	18.	c

19. a. 1/1/99   Land (+A)   10,000
                    Cash (-A)   10,000
                    Record the land purchase.

        12/31/99 Cash (+A)   25,000
                    Land (-A)   10,000
                    Gain on Sale of Land (Ga,+SE)   15,000
                    Record the land sale.

b. $10,000 + ($10,000 x 0.15) = $10,000 + $1,500 = $11,500. To maintain the same purchasing power at the end of the year as the business invested in the land at the beginning of the year, the land's value needs to increase by $1,500.

c. Return on investment using the reported gain:

[15,000 (reported gain)/10,000 (investment in the land)] x 100 = 150%.

d. Revised gain based upon investment in land adjusted for inflation:

$25,000 - $11,500 = $13,500.

Return on investment, controlling for general inflation:

($13,500/$11,500) x 100 = 117%.

While the return is still sizable, the return on investment is overstated if the financial statement gain is used.

e. In order for Mr. Amber to maintain the real investment in the business, the reported gain cannot be paid out as dividends. The company can pay $13,500 (the gain on the land sale after controlling for general inflation) in dividends and maintain its purchasing power.

20. a. 1/1/99 Note Receivable (+A)   1,000
                      Sales (R,+SE)   1,000

                  Cost of Goods Sold (E,-SE)   500
                      Inventory (-A)   500

     12/31/99 Cash (+A)   1,100
                      Note Receivable (-A)   1,000
                      Interest Revenue (R,+SE)   100

b. $1,000 + ($1,000 x 0.15) = $1,000 + $150 = $1,150.

c. If Maroon correctly estimated general inflation, the interest charged Tarragon would have been 0.15 + 0.04 = 0.19. Maroon would receive $1,190 at the end of the year [$1,000 + ($1,000 x 0.19)].

d. Maroon did not even maintain its purchasing power. In real terms, Maroon is worse off at the end of the period than at the beginning since it received only $1,100 instead of the $1,150 needed to maintain its purchasing power. Yet, its financial statements indicate that stockholders' wealth increased by $100.

    Investors might believe the $100 is available for dividends. Clearly, if the reported income of $100 was paid in dividends, the company's real investment would continue to deteriorate.

    When inflation is particularly high and difficult to estimate, businesses which allow customers to issue notes in exchange for merchandise run the risk of deteriorating owners' real investment in the business.

CHAPTER 5

The Mechanics of Financial Accounting

REVIEW OF KEY CONCEPTS

A modern business engages in thousands of economic events each day. The formal accounting system introduced in this chapter provides an organized and rational approach to analyzing the transactions using the **accounting model** and documenting the analysis. Information regarding the financial condition of the business at any point in time is available with relatively little extra effort when a formal accounting system is used. A well-designed, formal accounting system also reduces the possibility of undetected errors in recording the transactions.

Three critical points in the **accounting cycle** are discussed in detail below: (1) the **analysis of transactions** and the application of debit and credit rules to the analysis; (2) the **periodic adjustment process**; and (3) the **closing process**. A comprehensive problem is included at the end of the chapter, which provides an opportunity to go through the entire accounting cycle, including preparation of the financial statements. After completing the comprehensive problem, you will be more at ease with the mechanics of the formal accounting system and you will improve your understanding of financial accounting.

The Double-Entry Accounting System

The most widely used system of organizing economic transactions is the double-entry accounting system. The accounting equation is the basis of the system:

$$\textbf{Assets = Liabilities + Owners' Equity}$$

The owners' equity includes two basic components, the owners' original investments (common stock for a corporation) and the earnings retained in the business from successful past operations (retained earnings). The retained earnings amount is equal to revenues earned less expenses incurred less any dividends paid to the stockholders (the owners). The accounting equation can be expanded to include additional detail on these changes in the owners' equity as follows:

$$\textbf{Assets = Liabilities + Common Stock + Retained Earnings}$$
$$\textbf{+ Revenues - Expenses - Dividends}$$

Since this is an arithmetical relation, the elements can be rearranged by adding expenses and dividends to both sides:

$$\textbf{Assets + Expenses + Dividends = Liabilities + Common Stock}$$
$$\textbf{+ Retained Earnings + Revenues}$$

Notice that now all the elements of the equation are positive. Assets, expenses, and dividends are located on the left-hand side of the equation; liabilities, common stock, retained earnings, and revenues are located on the right-hand side.

At any point in time, the total of assets, expenses, and dividends is equal to the total of liabilities, common stock, retained earnings, and revenues. The economic interpretation of this relation is that the total of existing economic resources (assets), resources used thus far in the accounting period to earn revenues (expenses), and resources distributed to stockholders during the accounting period (dividends) must equal the sources of those existing, expired, and distributed resources (liabilities, common stock, retained earnings, and revenues).

The accounting system uses this expanded accounting model as the basis for recording transactions. The Latin terms debit and credit, which are translated left and right, are used to describe the physical writing of changes in account balances. Assets, expenses, and dividends balance increases are recorded with left-hand side entries on the books or debits. Decreases in assets, expenses, and dividends balances are recorded with right-hand side entries on the books or credits. Assets, expenses, and dividends typically have debit or left-hand side balances because the balances are usually positive.

Liabilities, common stock, retained earnings, and revenues balance increases are recorded with right-hand side entries on the books or credits. Decreases in liabilities, common stock, retained earnings, and revenues balances are recorded with left-hand side entries or debits. Liabilities, common stock, retained earnings, and revenues typically have credit or right-hand side balances because their balances are usually positive.

At any point in time, the sum of the balances of the accounts on the left-hand (debit) side of the equation (assets, expenses, and dividends) equals the sum of the balances on the right-hand (credit) side of the equation (liabilities, common stock, retained earnings, and revenues). An illustration which continues the Jewelbox, Inc., example from Chapter 1 follows:

Jewelbox, Inc.
Accounting Equation
August 1, 1999

Cash ($20,000) + Accounts Receivable ($30,000) + Inventory ($45,000) + Land ($40,000) + Expenses ($0) + Dividends ($0) =

Accounts Payable ($25,000) + Notes Payable ($30,000) + Common Stock ($30,000) + Retained earnings ($50,000) + Revenues ($0)

At August 1, 1999, Revenues, Expenses, and Dividends all have zero account balances, since no operating events have yet occurred. The following transactions take place during August 1999.

1.   Sold inventory which cost $15,000 for $22,000 cash.
2.   Collected $10,000 on accounts receivable.

3. Paid $500 of wages earned during the first two weeks of the month.
4. Sold inventory which cost $10,000 for $17,000 on account.
5. Purchased $30,000 of inventory on account.

The analysis of transactions uses the accounting equation and a few simple rules.

Assets + Expenses = Liabilities + Common Stock + Retained Earnings + Revenues

Rules to Conform with the Accounting System

1. Increases in assets, expenses, and dividends are recorded with debits (left-side entries). Decreases in assets, expenses, and dividends are recorded with credits (right-side entries).

2. Increases in liabilities, common stock, retained earnings, and revenues are recorded with credits (right-side entries). Decreases in liabilities, common stock, retained earnings, and revenues are recorded with debits (left-side entries).

	Account	**Category**	**Effect**
1a.	Cash	Asset	+ 22,000 debit
	Sales	Revenue	+ 22,000 credit
1b.	Cost of Goods Sold	Expense	+ 15,000 debit
	Inventory	Asset	- 15,000 credit
2.	Cash	Asset	+ 10,000 debit
	Accounts Receivable	Asset	- 10,000 credit
3.	Wage Expense	Expense	+ 500 debit
	Cash	Asset	- 500 credit
4a.	Accounts Receivable	Asset	+ 17,000 debit
	Sales	Revenue	+ 17,000 credit
4b.	Cost of Goods Sold	Expense	+ 10,000 debit
	Inventory	Asset	- 10,000 credit
5.	Inventory	Asset	+ 30,000 debit
	Accounts Payable	Liability	+ 30,000 credit

The analysis is formally recorded in the **general journal**. All transactions are recorded in this record in chronological order. The general journal follows the format shown below.

	Account Title and Explanation	Debit	Credit
1a.	Cash (+A)	22,000	
	Sales (R,+SE)		22,000
1b.	Cost of Goods Sold (E,-SE)	15,000	
	Inventory (-A)		15,000
2.	Cash (+A)	10,000	
	Accounts Receivable (-A)		10,000
3.	Wage Expense (E,-SE)	500	
	Cash (-A)		500
4a.	Accounts Receivable (+A)	17,000	
	Sales (R,+SE)		17,000
4b.	Cost of Goods Sold (E,-SE)	10,000	
	Inventory (-A)		10,000
5.	Inventory (+A)	30,000	
	Accounts Payable (+L)		30,000

After the transactions are recorded in the journal, the effect on the individual accounts is recorded by **posting** the journal entry effects to the **general ledger** accounts. The debit-side and credit-side of each account are totaled and the difference between the totals is the balance at that point in time. If the debit total exceeds the credit total, a debit balance exists. If the credit total exceeds the debit total, a credit balance exists. The **unadjusted trial balance** lists and totals the accounts with debit and credit balances separately to ensure that (1) the same dollar value of debits and credits are recorded in the ledger and (2) no obvious errors have been made (i.e., an asset, expense, or dividend account has a credit balance or a liability, stock, retained earnings, or revenue account has a debit balance). Typically, an unadjusted trial balance worksheet is used when many accounts exist. An example of such a worksheet appears on the next page.

Periodic Adjustments

The **accrual basis of accounting** provides a long-term perspective of the company's operating performance. Under accrual accounting, benefits are measured by revenues, and efforts are measured by expenses. The net income (revenues minus expenses) provides a measure of the profitability of the company's operating activities.

Under accrual accounting, **revenues are recorded when they are earned**. The company earns revenues by providing goods or services to its customers. The **matching principle** is employed to determine when expenses should be recorded. Expenses are a measure of the efforts employed to earn revenues. Under the matching principle, we wish to record expenses during the same accounting period in which we record the related, earned revenues.

Jewelbox, Inc.
Unadjusted Trial Balance
August 31, 1999

Account	Debit	Credit
Cash	51,500	
Accounts Receivable	37,000	
Inventory	50,000	
Land	40,000	
Cost of Goods Sold	25,000	
Wage Expense	500	
Dividends	0	
Accounts Payable		55,000
Notes Payable		30,000
Common Stock		30,000
Retained Earnings		50,000
Sales		39,000
	204,000	204,000

The difference between the performance measures provided by the cash and accrual bases is a matter of timing. Eventually, receipts from customers and payments to the company's employees and suppliers will be settled in cash. If all cash settlements were made in the same period during which revenues were earned and expenses incurred, the change in the company's cash position would be equal to its net income.

Preparing Periodic Adjustments

A company prepares its balance sheet and income statement using the accrual basis of accounting. Recall from the text that the company periodically records external exchange transactions as they occur. These journal entries include both cash and noncash transactions. However, these entries do not reflect the full accrual basis of accounting. The accounting records must be updated to a full accrual basis by preparing **adjusting journal entries** at the end of the accounting period.

Adjusting journal entries are used to record revenues earned or expenses incurred which are not the direct result of external transactions. These can be summarized into two general categories: **accrual adjustments** and **cost expiration adjustments** (sometimes referred to as **deferral adjustments**). Accruals and deferrals can arise relative to either revenues or expenses.

An accrual adjustment is necessary when revenue is earned (or an expense is incurred) through the passage of time. For example, a bank earns interest revenue each day for which it lends money to its customers (even though payments by customers are typically made on a less frequent basis). Similarly, the customer (borrower) incurs an interest expense with the passage of time. It may be useful for you to think of an accrual as a case where the cash receipt (cash payment) **follows** the revenue earning process (incurs an expense).

Deferrals (cost expirations) arise when the cash receipt or payment **precedes** the revenue or expense recognition. Magazine subscriptions provide a good example. The customer typically pays the publisher in advance for a one year (or longer) subscription. The customer has an asset, the right to receive future editions of the magazine, for which cash payment has been made. The customer cannot use the magazines until they are received; therefore, the cost only becomes an expense in future periods, when the magazines are received and used. The publisher has an obligation (a liability) to deliver future editions to the customer. The publisher has received a cash prepayment, but only earns revenue by providing its product to the customer during future time periods.

Recall from the text the following three characteristics of all adjusting journal entries:

1.   They are entered in the books at the end of the accounting period to achieve a matching of revenues and expenses in that and future time periods.
2.   They always involve at least one temporary (revenue, expense, or dividend) account and at least one permanent (asset or liability) account.
3.   They never involve the cash account.

The preparation of adjusting entries can be facilitated by answering the following three basic questions:

1.   What is the correct revenue or expense amount under the accrual basis of accounting?
2.   What amounts, if any, have previously been recorded? This requires an investigation of revenue and expense account balances, as well as any related asset and liability accounts.
3.   What is the entry required to bring the accounting records to the correct accrual basis amounts?

Example of a Cost Expiration Adjusting Entry for Revenues

The following example illustrates this three-step approach for a cost expiration adjusting entry. Inquiring Minds Magazine sells subscriptions to customers. During 1999, Inquiring Minds collected $48,000 from customers for advance payments on subscriptions. Inquiring Minds records cash collections for subscriptions as Unearned Subscriptions Revenue. By the end of the year, Inquiring Minds had mailed to customers monthly magazines having a total selling price of $27,000. The adjusting entry required for Inquiring Minds Magazine can be made as follows.

1. Inquiring Minds earned revenue of $27,000 by providing magazines to customers under its subscription obligations. Since $27,000 worth of magazines have already been provided to customers, the liability for future deliveries should now be only $21,000.

2. Inquiring Minds previously recorded a related liability (Unearned Subscriptions Revenue) of $48,000. To date, Inquiring Minds has recorded no revenue from these transactions.
3. Revenue must be increased (credited) for $27,000. The liability must be reduced (debited) for $27,000. The adjusting entry below leaves the correct balances in the revenue and liability accounts.

Unearned Subscriptions Revenue (-L)	27,000	
Subscriptions Revenue (R,+SE)		27,000

Example of a Cost Expiration Adjusting Entry for Expenses

Let's use the same transaction from the customer's perspective as an example illustrating the approach for a cost expiration expense adjustment. Assume Big City Hospital buys a subscription to place in its waiting room. In June 1999, Big City paid $480 for a one-year subscription. Big City records the cash payment for subscriptions as Prepaid Subscriptions Expense. By the end of the year, Big City has received one-half of the magazines under its subscription. The adjusting entry on Big City's records is made as follows.

1. Big City has incurred expense of $240 when it received magazines under its subscription. Since $240 worth of magazines have already been received, the asset for future deliveries should now be only $240.
2. Big City has previously recorded a related asset (Prepaid Subscriptions Expense) of $480. To date, Big City Hospital has recorded no expense from these transactions.
3. Expense must be increased (debited) for $240. The asset must be reduced (credited) for $240. The adjusting entry below leaves the correct balances in the expense and asset accounts.

Subscriptions Expense (E,-SE)	240	
Prepaid Subscriptions Expense (-A)		240

Example of an Accrual Adjusting Entry for Expenses

The Haka Corporation borrows $150,000 from the Last National Bank on July 1, 1999. The note requires Haka to repay the entire principal and accumulated interest on June 30, 2001. The interest rate is 12 percent per year. The required adjusting entry for the Haka Corporation on December 31, 1999 can be made as follows.

1. Haka has borrowed funds for a period of six months, thereby incurring an expense, even though cash payment was not required during the current year. The expense (the cost of borrowing) on an accrual basis would be $9,000. This is calculated by multiplying the interest rate (12 percent) times the amount borrowed ($150,000) times the period of time covered (6/12 of one year). Since an expense has been incurred and the amount has not yet been paid, Haka's accrual basis accounting records should include Interest Expense of $9,000 and a liability for Interest Payable of $9,000.

2. Haka originally recorded the borrowing by debiting the cash account and crediting a liability (Notes Payable) for $150,000. Haka has recorded no entry for the interest expense incurred.
3. Interest Expense must be increased (debited) by $9,000. Interest Payable must also be increased (credited) by $9,000. The adjusting entry places the correct accrual balances (as determined in step 1) on Haka's records.

Interest Expense (E,-SE)	9,000	
Interest Payable (+L)		9,000

Example of an Accrual Adjusting Entry for Revenues

The records of Last National Bank provide an example of a revenue accrual. The required adjusting entry for Last National on December 31, 1999 can be made as follows.

1. Last National has lent funds for a period of six months, thereby earning interest revenue, even though the cash receipt will not occur until June 30, 2001. The revenue on an accrual basis would be $9,000. Since a revenue has been earned and the amount has not yet been paid, Last National's accrual basis accounting records should include Interest Revenue of $9,000 and an asset for Interest Receivable of $9,000.
2. Last National originally recorded the borrowing by debiting the note receivable asset account and crediting the cash account in the amount of $150,000. Last National has recorded no entry for the interest revenue earned.
3. Interest Revenue must be increased (credited) for $9,000. Interest Receivable must also be increased (debited) by $9,000. The adjusting entry places the correct accrual balances (as determined in step 1) on Last National's records.

Interest Receivable (+A)	9,000	
Interest Revenue (R,+SE)		9,000

Completion of the Accounting Cycle

Periodic adjustments represent entries which "fine tune" the account balances to ensure that all the accounts fairly present the financial position of the business at the end of the accounting period. Adjustments are recorded in the same way as any other transaction. Journal entries are prepared and posted to the general ledger accounts.

Another trial balance, the adjusted trial balance, is prepared after the adjusting journal entries are posted to ensure that the debit balance and credit balance accounts total the same number. The financial statements are then prepared. If a manual system is used, the accountant prepares the income statement, which includes revenues and expenses and the statement of stockholders' equity, which lists changes in common stock and retained earnings due to additional investments, dividends (withdrawals by owners), and net income (loss) for the period. Finally, the balance sheet is prepared. The asset, liability, and stock account balances are all copied from the ledger balances. The balance in retained earnings is copied from the statement of stockholders' equity. The beginning retained earnings balance plus net income (revenues minus expenses) minus dividends equals the ending retained earnings balance.

Closing Entries

After the financial statements have been completed, **closing entries** are prepared. These are journal entries which transfer the revenue, expense, and dividend balances into the retained earnings account. After the transfer, the revenue, expense, and dividend accounts have zero balances. Transactions related to operations for the next period can now be recorded and an income statement summarizing the operating results for that period alone can be prepared. This process facilitates presenting comparative income statements to be used in financial statement analysis.

Since zero balances are required, the closing process requires that debit balance accounts are credited for the balance and **Income Summary** is debited. Credit balance accounts are debited and Income Summary is credited.

Income Summary has a credit balance if credits (revenues) exceed debits (expenses). Obviously, a net income exists in this circumstance. The income summary account has a debit balance if debits (expenses) exceed credits (revenues), a net loss situation.

Income Summary is closed by debiting its total (in the event of income) and crediting Retained Earnings. The reverse is true in the event of a loss.

The dividend account is closed directly into Retained Earnings without an intermediate step. Recall that dividends differ from expenses. Expenses represent resources consumed in the process of earning revenues. The difference between revenues and expenses represents the change in stockholders' wealth due to operations. Dividends do not represent consumption of resources, but a distribution of the business resources to the stockholders. While the wealth invested in the business is reduced, individual stockholder wealth is the same. The stockholders' investment in the company declines, but they receive cash which can be used for whatever purpose the stockholders wish.

After completing the closing process, the balance in the general ledger retained earnings account should agree with the balance sheet retained earnings account.

QUESTIONS FOR YOUR REVIEW

1. The purpose of a trial balance is to:
    a. make certain the accounts have correct balances.
    b. make certain the debits equal the credits.
    c. meet a legal requirement.
    d. replace the income statement and balance sheet.

2. Which of the following accounts usually has a nonzero balance after closing entries have been posted to the general ledger account?
   a. Retained Earnings
   b. Dividends
   c. Income Summary
   d. Salaries Expense

3. The revenue, expense, gain, and loss accounts are closed at the end of the financial statement time interval because:
   a. assets would otherwise be incorrectly presented on the balance sheet.
   b. the income statement could not be prepared otherwise.
   c. the next period's income statement could not otherwise be easily prepared.
   d. the balance sheet for the current period could not be prepared since the retained earnings balance can not be calculated without closing entries.

4. Aardvark Pet Store sold 25 parrots for $100 cash each. Each parrot initially cost Aardvark $70. The journal entry(ies) to record the sale is (are):

   a. Cash (+A)   2,500
          Sales (R,+SE)   2,500
       Cost of Goods Sold (E,-SE)   1,750
          Inventory (-A)   1,750

   b. Cash (+A)   2,500
          Revenue (R,+SE)   750
          Inventory (-A)   1,750

   c. Cash (+A)   2,500
          Gain on Parrot Sale (Ga,+SE)   750
          Inventory (-A)   1,750

   d. Cash (+A)   2,500
          Sales (R,+SE)   2,500
       Cost of Goods Sold (E,-SE)   1,750
          Accounts Payable (+L)   1,750

5. A debit balance in which of the following accounts indicates an error has occurred in either analyzing or recording a transaction?
   a. Retained Earnings
   b. Income Summary
   c. Dividends
   d. Sales Revenue

6. The journal entry to record the sale of land for $27,000 cash that initially cost the company $30,000 is:

a. Retained Earnings (-SE)	3,000	
Cash (+A)	27,000	
Land (-A)		30,000

b. Cash (+A)	27,000	
Land (-A)		27,000

c. Cash (+A)	27,000	
Sales Expense (E,-SE)	3,000	
Land (-A)		30,000

d. Cash (+A)	27,000	
Loss on Sale of Land (Lo,-SE)	3,000	
Land (-A)		30,000

Questions 7 and 8 refer to the following information.

The following accounts and balances are taken from Proust Brewery Inc.'s ledger at December 31, 1999, the company's fiscal year-end. All the accounts have normal balances.

Cash	$ 29,000	Equipment	$50,000
Beer sales	600,000	Notes payable	30,000
Accounts receivable	75,000	Prepaid expenses	3,000
Dividends	10,000	Retained earnings	60,000
Cost of goods sold	450,000	Salary expense	70,000
Interest expense	4,000	Land	9,000

7. Net income for 1999 is:
   a. $63,000
   b. $66,000
   c. $73,000
   d. $76,000

8. Total assets on the balance sheet are:
   a. $176,000
   b. $173,000
   c. $166,000
   d. $163,000

9. Which of the following transactions is normally recorded as a capital expenditure?
   a. Wages paid to manufacturing employees
   b. Wages paid to management employees
   c. Electric utility charges
   d. Purchase of a new delivery vehicle

10. Which of the following transactions is normally recorded as an expense?
    a. Purchase of merchandise for resale
    b. Wages paid to management employees
    c. A twelve-month prepayment on a fire insurance policy
    d. Purchase of a new delivery vehicle

11. Which of the following items is most properly classified as an accrual?
    a. Depreciation expense
    b. Expiration of prepaid insurance
    c. Interest expense
    d. Usage of office supplies

12. Which of the following items is most properly classified as a cost expiration?
    a. Depreciation expense
    b. Wage expense
    c. Interest expense
    d. Purchase of a new delivery vehicle

13. Brown Company had accounts receivable on January 1 of $33,000 and $40,000 at January 31. Sales revenues during January were $100,000. How much cash was collected from Brown's customers during January?
    a. $100,000
    b. $7,000
    c. $133,000
    d. $93,000

14. Pete's Sandwich Shop had prepaid rent of $70,000 at the beginning of 1999 and a zero balance in this account at the end of the year. During 1999, Pete paid $220,000 in cash for rent. What is Pete's rent expense for 1999?
    a. $290,000
    b. $220,000
    c. $150,000
    d. $70,000

15. Office supplies on hand were $24,000 at the end of the year. Purchases during the year totaled $36,000. Supplies used during the year were $45,000. What was the amount of office supplies on hand at the beginning of the year?
    a. $45,000
    b. $36,000
    c. $33,000
    d. $24,000

16. Jim's Hardware pays for all merchandise purchases in cash. Jim's inventory on July 1 was $42,000, and $46,000 on July 31. Jim recorded cost of goods sold during July of $86,500. How much did Jim pay for purchases in July?
    a. $132,500
    b. $128,500
    c. $90,500
    d. $88,000

17. The following comprehensive problem will allow you to work through the entire accounting cycle (excluding periodic adjusting entries). You will analyze transactions; prepare journal entries; post those entries to ledger accounts; prepare a trial balance; prepare the financial statements; prepare the closing entries and post those to the ledger; and prepare the final trial balance. When you successfully finish this problem, your understanding of the mechanics of the formal accounting system will be considerably improved.

    Suggestion: We recommend tearing out this section of the study guide to enable you to freely move through the steps with all the schedules readily available to you.

    Step One. On the following page is the final trial balance at August 31, 1999, for Lopez Sporting Goods, Inc. Use the T-accounts provided and record the beginning balances for September (which are the ending balances of August). Notice that the only types of accounts with balances are Assets, Liabilities, Common Stock, and Retained Earnings. August's revenue, expense, and dividend accounts have been closed into Retained Earnings.

    Step Two. Prepare the analysis and journal entries for each of the given transactions using the analysis and journal entry schedules provided. We suggest writing down on a separate piece of paper or index card the debit and credit rules. Refer to these rules as you fill out the analysis schedule.

    Step Three. Post the journal entries to the T-accounts. Use the blank T-accounts provided for any accounts that are included in the journal entries but not in the final trial balance for August.

    Step Four. After posting all the entries to the T-accounts, determine each account's balance by adding debit (left-hand side) entries together and credit (right-hand side) entries together. Subtract the debit total from the credit total. Draw a line across the T-account after the last entry and enter the balance on the appropriate side. If the debit total exceeds the credit total, a debit balance for the difference exists. The opposite is true if credits exceed debits.

Step Five. Using the account balances from step four, prepare the trial balance in the space provided. Are the debit and credit side totals equal? Do the balances appear correct? Do asset and expense accounts have debit balances? Do liabilities, common stock, retained earnings, and revenues have credit balances? If you answer no to any of these questions, recheck the analysis, journal entries, and posting to T-accounts to identify your mistake.

Step Six. Prepare the income statement, statement of retained earnings, and balance sheet from the trial balance. You must select the accounts which are appropriately included in each.

Step Seven.
a. Using the trial balance, identify the revenue, expense, and dividend accounts. Prepare the closing journal entries using the account titles and balances identified.
b. Post the closing journal entries to the T-accounts.
c. Using the T-account balances after closing, prepare the final trial balance.

Lopez Sporting Goods, Inc.
Final Trial Balance
August 31, 1999

	Debit	Credit
Cash	200,000	
Accounts Receivable	500,000	
Inventory	800,000	
Land	150,000	
Accounts Payable		600,000
Notes Payable		100,000
Common Stock		400,000
Retained Earnings		550,000
Totals	1,650,000	1,650,000

The following transactions occurred during September 1999:

1. Sept. 1   Inventory which cost $50,000 is sold for $70,000 cash.
2. Sept. 1   Accounts receivable collected, $40,000.
3. Sept. 1   Bought land for $60,000, $20,000 cash and $40,000 note payable, due in one year. The interest rate on this note and the $100,000 note outstanding at the beginning of the month is 12 percent annually, 1 percent paid at the end of each month.
4. Sept. 10 Declared and paid dividends of $20,000. A dividend account is used as discussed in the chapter in the textbook.
5. Sept. 15 Inventory which cost $150,000 is sold for $240,000; $120,000 cash and a $120,000 accounts receivable are received.
6. Sept. 15 Paid S. Faber, sales clerk, $4,000 salary and commission for the first half of September.
7. Sept. 20 Paid accounts payable, $50,000.

8. Sept. 25 Collected accounts receivable, $150,000.
9. Sept. 30 Interest on the notes paid, $1,400 [($100,000 + $40,000) x 0.01].
10. Sept. 30 S. Faber, sales clerk, is owed $4,000 for the second half of September, but this amount is unpaid at September 30.
11. Sept. 30 A telephone bill of $2,000 is owed but unpaid at September 30.

Transaction Analysis

	Account	Category	Effect
1a.			
1b.			
2.			
3.			
4.			
5a.			
5b.			
6.			
7.			
8.			

9.			
10.			
11.			

General Journal

	Account Title	Debit	Credit
1a.			
1b.			
2.			
3.			
4a.			
4b.			
5.			
6.			
7.			
8.			
9.			

10.			
11.			

Cash	Accounts Receivable

Inventory	Land

Accounts Payable	Notes Payable

Common Stock	Retained Earnings

Lopez Sporting Goods, Inc.
Trial Balance
September 30, 1999

<u>**Debit**</u>   <u>**Credit**</u>

Lopez Sporting Goods, Inc.
Income Statement
For the Month Ended September 30, 1999

Lopez Sporting Goods, Inc.
Statement of Retained Earnings
For the Month Ended September 30, 1999

Lopez Sporting Goods, Inc.
Balance Sheet
September 30, 1999

General Journal (Closing entries)

	Account Title and Explanation	Debit	Credit

Lopez Sporting Goods, Inc.
Final Trial Balance
September 30, 1999

<u>Debit</u>   <u>Credit</u>

18. Presented below is an unadjusted trial balance for Colonel Ward's Fried Chicken, Inc., as of December 31, 1999. Using the additional information provided, prepare any required adjusting journal entries.

	Debit	Credit
Cash	20,000	
Accounts Receivable	45,000	
Chicken and Cole Slaw Inventory	65,000	
Prepaid Rent	4,000	
Restaurant Supplies	8,000	
Restaurant Fixtures and Equipment	275,000	
Accumulated Depreciation		82,500
Accounts Payable		50,000
Long-term Note Payable		80,000
Common Stock		100,000
Retained Earnings		105,500
Sales		255,000
Cost of Goods Sold	155,000	
Supplies Expense	16,000	
Salary Expense	44,000	
Advertising Expense	24,000	
Interest Expense	0	
Utilities and Other Operating Expense	12,000	
Dividends	5,000	
	673,000	673,000

a. On December 1, Colonel Ward paid $24,000 to a local television station for some new advertising spots. The advertising was to be equally spaced and aired throughout the months of December and January. The cost was expensed when paid.

b. On May 1, Colonel Ward signed a lease for storage space in an adjoining building. Colonel Ward paid $4,000 to cover the first ten months rent and capitalized this amount.

c.   The restaurant fixtures and equipment are depreciated on a straight-line basis over a 20-year useful life.

d.   Colonel Ward borrowed $80,000 on January 1, 1997. The interest rate is 12 percent, and payments of interest only are to be made on January 1 of each year. The original borrowing plus the final year's interest is due on January 1, 2003.

e.   All restaurant supplies purchased during the year were charged to Supplies Expense. A physical count revealed that $3,200 in restaurant supplies were still on hand at December 31.

f.   Employees were owed $1,040 in unpaid wages for work performed since the last payroll date on December 28.

19. Using the information in question 18, prepare an income statement for Colonel Ward's Fried Chicken, Inc., for the year ended December 31, 1999.

20. Prepare adjusting journal entries, as required, for each of the following independent situations. In all cases, the fiscal year ends on December 31.

    a. Fixed assets costing $150,000 have an estimated life of 15 years. The company uses the straight-line method of depreciation.

    b. On July 1, the company purchased a three-year fire insurance policy for $72,000 in cash. The $72,000 was charged to insurance expense.

    c. The company's supplies inventory balance was $15,000 on January 1. Supplies purchased during the year totaled $24,000. These amounts were capitalized throughout the year. A count at year end reveals that $15,750 are still on hand.

    d. The company pays rent at the end of every three months, in the amount of $2,000 per month. The rent was last paid on October 31.

    e. The company borrowed $30,000 on September 1 at a rate of 6 percent per year. The entire balance, including interest, is due to be repaid in March of next year.

CHAPTER 5-SOLUTIONS

1.	b	6.	d	11.	c
2.	a	7.	d	12.	a
3.	c	8.	c	13.	d
4.	a	9.	d	14.	a
5.	d	10.	b	15.	c
				16.	c

17. **Steps 1 and 2.** Transaction analysis.

	Account	Category	Effect	
1a.	Cash	Asset	+ 70,000	debit
	Sales	Revenue	+ 70,000	credit
1b.	Inventory	Asset	- 50,000	credit
	Cost of Goods Sold	Expense	+ 50,000	debit
2.	Cash	Asset	+ 40,000	debit
	Accounts Receivable	Asset	- 40,000	credit
3.	Land	Asset	+ 60,000	debit
	Cash	Asset	- 20,000	credit
	Notes Payable	Liability	+ 40,000	credit
4.	Cash	Asset	- 20,000	credit
	Dividend	Dividend	+ 20,000	debit
5a.	Cash	Asset	+ 120,000	debit
	Accounts Receivable	Asset	+ 120,000	debit
	Sales	Revenue	+240,000	credit
5b.	Inventory	Asset	- 150,000	credit
	Cost of Goods Sold	Expense	+ 150,000	debit

	Account	Category	Effect	
6.	Cash	Asset	- 4,000	credit
	Salaries Expense	Expense	+ 4,000	debit
7.	Cash	Asset	- 50,000	credit
	Accounts Payable	Liability	- 50,000	debit
8.	Cash	Asset	+ 150,000	debit
	Accounts Receivable	Asset	- 150,000	credit
9.	Cash	Asset	- 1,400	credit
	Interest Expense	Expense	+ 1,400	debit
10.	Salary Expense	Expense	+ 4,000	debit
	Salary Payable	Liability	+ 4,000	credit
11.	Utility Expense	Expense	+ 2,000	debit
	Utility Payable	Liability	+ 2,000	credit

General Journal

	Account Title	Debit	Credit
1a.	Cash (+A)	70,000	
	Sales (R, +SE)		70,000
1b.	Cost of Goods Sold (E,-SE)	50,000	
	Inventory (-A)		50,000
2.	Cash (+A)	40,000	
	Accounts Receivable (-A)		40,000
3.	Land (+A)	60,000	
	Cash (-A)		20,000
	Notes Payable (+L)		40,000
4.	Dividends (-SE)	20,000	
	Cash (-A)		20,000

	Account Title	Debit	Credit
5a.	Cash (+A)	120,000	
	Accounts Receivable (+A)	120,000	
	Sales (R, +SE)		240,000
5b.	Cost of Goods Sold (E,-SE)	150,000	
	Inventory (-A)		150,000
6.	Salary Expense (E,-SE)	4,000	
	Cash (-A)		4,000
7.	Accounts Payable (-L)	50,000	
	Cash (-A)		50,000
8.	Cash (+A)	150,000	
	Accounts Receivable (-A)		150,000
9.	Interest Expense (E,-SE)	1,400	
	Cash (-A)		1,400
10.	Salary Expense (E,-SE)	4,000	
	Salary Payable (+L)		4,000
11.	Utility Expense (E,-SE)	2,000	
	Utility Payable (+L)		2,000

Steps 3, 4, and 7b. Posting to the T-accounts (ledger accounts).

	Cash					Accounts Receivable			
B.B.	200,000	(3)	20,000		B.B.	500,000	(2)	40,000
(1a)	70,000	(4)	20,000		(5a)	120,000	(8)	150,000
(2)	40,000	(6)	4,000					
(5a)	120,000	(7)	50,000		E.B.	430,000		
(8)	150,000	(9)	1,400					
E.B.	484,600							

	Inventory					Land			
B.B.	800,000	(1b)	50,000		B.B.	150,000		
		(5b)	150,000		(3)	60,000		
E.B.	600,000				E.B.	210,000		

Accounts Payable

(7)	50,000	B.B.	600,000
		E.B.	550,000

Notes Payable

	B.B.	100,000
	(3)	40,000
	E.B.	140,000

Common Stock

	B.B.	400,000
	E.B.	400,000

Retained Earnings

Div.	20,000	B.B.	550,000
		Inc.	98,600
		E.B.	628,600

Sales

		(1a)	70,000
		(5a)	240,000
To close	310,000	E.B.	310,000
		Post-closing balance	0

Cost of Goods Sold

(1b)	50,000	
(5b)	150,000	
E.B.	200,000	To close	200,000
Post-closing balance	0	

Interest Expense

(9)	1,400	
E.B.	1,400	To close	1,400
Post-closing balance	0	

Salary Expense

(6)	4,000	
(10)	4,000	
E.B.	8,000	To close	8,000
Post-closing balance	0	

Utility Expense

(11)	2,000		
E.B.	2,000	To close	2,000
Post-closing balance	0		

Dividends

(4)	20,000		
E.B.	20,000	To close	20,000
Post-closing balance	0		

Salary Payable

		(10)	4,000
		E.B.	4,000

Utility Payable

		(11)	2,000
		E.B.	2,000

Income Summary

CGS	200,000	Sales	310,000
Int. Exp.	1,400		
Sal. Exp.	8,000		
Util.Exp.	2,000		
To close	8,600	E.B.	98,600
		Post-closing balance	0

Step 5. Preparation of the trial balance.

Lopez Sporting Goods, Inc.
Trial Balance
September 30, 1999

	Debit	Credit
Cash	484,600	
Accounts Receivable	430,000	
Inventory	600,000	
Land	210,000	
Accounts Payable		550,000
Notes Payable		140,000
Common Stock		400,000
Retained Earnings		550,000
Sales		310,000
Cost of Goods Sold	200,000	
Interest Expense	1,400	
Salary Expense	8,000	
Utility Expense	2,000	
Dividends	20,000	
Salary Payable		4,000
Utility Payable		2,000
	1,956,000	1,956,000

Step 6. Preparation of the financial statements.

Lopez Sporting Goods, Inc.
Income Statement
For the Month Ended September 30, 1999

Sales		$310,000
Less expenses:		
Cost of goods sold	$200,000	
Salary expense	8,000	
Utility expense	2,000	
Interest expense	1,400	211,400
Net income		$ 98,600

Lopez Sporting Goods, Inc.
Statement of Retained Earnings
For the Month Ended September 30, 1999

Retained earnings-August 31, 1999	$550,000
Add: Net income for September	98,600
Less: Dividends	(20,000)
Retained earnings-September 30, 1999	$628,600

Lopez Sporting Goods, Inc.
Balance Sheet
September 30, 1999

Assets:		Liabilities and Stockholders' Equity:	
Cash	$ 484,600	Notes payable	$ 140,000
Accounts receivable	430,000	Accounts payable	550,000
Inventory	600,000	Utility payable	2,000
Land	210,000	Salary payable	4,000
		Total liabilities	$ 696,000
		Common stock	$ 400,000
		Retained earnings	628,600
		Total stockholders' equity	$1,028,600
		Total liabilities and	
Total assets	$1,724,600	stockholders' equity	$1,724,600

Step 7. Closing journal entries, posting to T-accounts, and final trial balance.

General Journal (Closing Entries)

Account Title and Explanation	Debit	Credit
Sales	310,000	
Income Summary		310,000
To close revenue accounts.		
Income Summary	211,400	
Cost of Goods Sold		200,000
Salary Expense		8,000
Utility Expense		2,000
Interest Expense		1,400
To close expense accounts.		
Income Summary	98,600	
Retained Earnings		98,600
To close income summary.		
Retained Earnings	20,000	
Dividends		20,000
To close dividends.		

Lopez Sporting Goods, Inc.
Final Trial Balance
September 30, 1999

	Debit	Credit
Cash	484,600	
Accounts Receivable	430,000	
Inventory	600,000	
Land	210,000	
Accounts Payable		550,000
Notes Payable		140,000
Salary Payable		4,000
Utility Payable		2,000
Common Stock		400,000
Retained Earnings		628,600
	1,724,600	1,724,600

			Debit	Credit
18.	a.	Prepaid Advertising (+A)	12,000	
		Advertising Expense (E,-SE)		12,000
	b.	Rent Expense (E,-SE)	3,200	
		Prepaid Rent (-A)		3,200
	c.	Depreciation Expense (E,-SE)	13,750	
		Accumulated Depreciation (-A)		13,750
	d.	Interest Expense (E,-SE)	9,600	
		Interest Payable (+L)		9,600
	e.	Supplies Expense (E,-SE)	4,800	
		Restaurant Supplies (-A)		4,800
	f.	Salary Expense (E,-SE)	1,040	
		Salary Payable (+L)		1,040

19. You may wish to begin by preparing an adjusted trial balance. Post the adjusting entries made in question 18. The accounts highlighted in bold type were added during the adjustment process.

Colonel Ward's Fried Chicken, Inc.
Adjusted Trial Balance
December 31, 1999

	Debit	Credit
Cash	20,000	
Accounts Receivable	45,000	
Chicken and Cole Slaw Inventory	65,000	
Prepaid Rent	800	
Prepaid Advertising	**12,000**	
Restaurant Supplies	3,200	
Restaurant Fixtures and Equipment	275,000	
Accumulated Depreciation		96,250
Accounts Payable		50,000
Salary Payable		**1,040**
Interest Payable		**9,600**
Long-term Note Payable		80,000
Common Stock		100,000
Retained Earnings		105,500
Sales		255,000
Cost of Goods Sold	155,000	
Supplies Expense	20,800	
Salary Expense	45,040	
Advertising Expense	12,000	
Interest Expense	9,600	
Rent Expense	**3,200**	
Depreciation Expense	**13,750**	
Utilities and Other Operating Expense	12,000	
Dividends	5,000	
	697,390	697,390

Colonel Ward's Fried Chicken, Inc.
Income Statement
For the Year Ended December 31, 1999

Sales	$255,000
Less: Cost of goods sold	155,000
Gross margin	$100,000
Less expenses:	
Supplies expense	$ 20,800
Salary and wage expense	45,040
Advertising expense	12,000
Interest expense	9,600
Rent expense	3,200
Depreciation expense	13,750
Utilities and other operating expenses	12,000
Total expenses	$116,390
Net income (loss)	($ 16,390)

20.	a.	Depreciation Expense (E,-SE)	10,000	
		Accumulated Depreciation (-A)		10,000
	b.	Prepaid Insurance (+A)	60,000	
		Insurance Expense (E,-SE)		60,000
	c.	Supplies Expense (E,-SE)	23,250	
		Supplies Inventory (-A)		23,250
	d.	Rent Expense (E,-SE)	4,000	
		Rent Payable (+L)		4,000
	e.	Interest Expense (E,-SE)	600	
		Interest Payable (+L)		600

CHAPTER 6

The Current Asset Classification, Cash, and Accounts Receivable

REVIEW OF KEY CONCEPTS

The Basics of Accounting for an Asset

The next several chapters are devoted to a more detailed study of accounting for various types of assets. There are three accounting questions to be considered in accounting for all assets.

1. How should the asset be recorded at acquisition?
2. How should the asset and any related revenue or expense be accounted for during the period the asset is held (the holding period)?
3. How should the asset be accounted for at disposition?

Questions (1) and (3) can be answered with very general rules. Looking first at **acquisitions**, all assets are originally recorded at their **historical cost**. The historical cost of an asset includes the initial purchase price plus any additional costs required to bring the asset to the location and condition for its intended use in the business.

A general rule can also be applied to asset **dispositions**. When disposing of an asset, the selling price is compared to the **book value** (or recorded amount in the company books) of the asset. The difference between selling price and book value is recorded as a gain or loss on disposition of the asset. When an asset is first purchased, the book value is the asset's historical cost. For some assets, this cost may be adjusted from time to time during the holding period. These cases will be considered in the discussion of individual assets over the next few chapters.

The rules for asset accounting during the **holding period** vary across different types of assets. Holding period accounting will be discussed for individual assets, including the issue of how assets are to be reported (classified) in the company's financial statements.

The Current Asset Classification

Current assets are those assets which are intended to be converted into cash within one year, or a company's **operating cycle**, whichever is longer. The current asset classification includes cash, short-term notes and accounts receivable, inventory, short-term investments in marketable securities, and prepaid expenses. A company's operating cycle is the normal time taken to complete a cycling of cash. Cash originally received from investors is used to purchase inventory, which is then sold to customers, and cash is eventually collected from the customers. This chapter discusses accounting for cash and receivables; problems unique to accounting for inventories and marketable securities are discussed in later chapters.

Current assets provide a measure of the company's short-term **solvency** (liquidity). Since these assets are intended to be converted to cash, they indicate the availability of cash to meet short-term obligations and liabilities as these become due.

Cash

Cash is the most liquid of all assets. Liquidity is normally a measure of how quickly an asset can be converted into cash. Due to its liquidity, cash requires considerable safeguarding and control. Adequate amounts of cash on hand are essential to permit companies to pay obligations as they become due, which is critical for a company to stay in business for an extended period of time.

Accounts Receivable

Accounts Receivable arise from credit sales to customers. In the normal course of business, customers will pay the amounts owed in cash. Accounts receivable represent an asset, because the company will derive a future benefit from the receipt of cash. Typical journal entries to record credit sales and subsequent collections are as follows:

Accounts Receivable (+A)	385	
Sales (R,+SE)		385
To recognize a credit sale.		

Cash (+A)	385	
Accounts Receivable (-A)		385
Collected cash on account.		

Uncollectible Accounts Receivable

Unfortunately, not all customers pay their accounts. If some customers fail to pay, then the asset balance for Accounts Receivable will be overstated (a portion of the future benefit will not be realized or converted into cash). When credit is extended to a customer, a company cannot determine which customers will fail to pay. (If they could, they would never have sold to these customers on a credit basis!)

The cost of **uncollectible accounts receivable** is a **selling expense**. It arises from the decision to sell on credit, which is a tool companies use to generate additional sales beyond sales restricted to cash payment only. A proper matching of expenses (Uncollectible Accounts Expense) with the related generated revenue (Sales) is required under accrual accounting. The uncollectible accounts expense should be recorded in the same period that the related revenue appears in the income statement. This is accomplished through the use of the **allowance method** and an adjusting entry.

Allowance for Uncollectible Accounts

Under the allowance method, a company estimates the amount of uncollectible accounts and makes an adjusting entry to ensure the proper matching of expenses with revenues. At a later date, when it is finally determined that the customer is unable to pay, the account receivable balance will be written off. The approach is facilitated by setting up the **Allowance for Uncollectible Accounts**, which is a contra asset account. (This account is also known as the Allowance for Doubtful Accounts or the Allowance for Bad Debts).

Assume that on December 31, 1998, a company estimates that $500 of outstanding accounts receivable will become uncollectible. On March 18, 1999, John Jones' account in the amount of $115 is written off. The basic entries are as follows:

12/31/98	Uncollectible Accounts Expense (E,-SE)	500	
	Allowance for Uncollectible Accounts (-A)		500
	Estimated uncollectible accounts.		
3/18/99	Allowance for Uncollectible Accounts (+A)	115	
	Accounts Receivable (-A)		115
	Wrote off John Jones' account as uncollectible.		

Allowance for Uncollectible Accounts will appear as a deduction from Accounts Receivable on the balance sheet. After deducting the allowance, the net amount of Accounts Receivable is the amount expected to be received in the future, or the **net realizable value**. Note that the adjusting entry matches the estimated expense from uncollectible accounts with the related revenues recognized in the year the sale was made. The actual write-off of an account in a subsequent year does not change the total net realizable value of accounts receivable. In addition, the entry to write off an account does not affect net income in the year the account becomes uncollectible. The expense was already estimated and recorded in the year of the sale.

Recoveries of Accounts Previously Written Off

In some cases a customer will repay an account after the account has been written off. These recoveries of previously written off accounts are recorded by essentially reversing the entry from the write-off date and then recording the receipt like any other collection of a receivable. For example, suppose that John Jones has recovered from his financial difficulties and pays the owed balance on February 1, 2001. The collection is recorded as follows:

2/1/01	Accounts Receivable (+A)	115	
	Allowance for Uncollectible Accounts (-A)		115
	Reinstated John Jones' account.		
	Cash (+A)	115	
	Accounts Receivable (-A)		115
	Received cash on reinstated account.		

Estimating Uncollectible Accounts Receivable

A company estimates uncollectible accounts based on past experience, either with its own customers or from a more general information source. For example, a company may choose to look at collection experiences of other companies in the same industry. Two basic approaches are used to make the estimate for the resulting adjusting entries.

The first estimation approach is based on a **percentage of credit sales** made during the period. Note that Credit Sales is an **income statement** account. The amount estimated under the percentage of credit sales approach is the correct balance for another income statement account, Uncollectible Accounts Expense. Assume that a retail appliance company has recorded $500,000 in Credit Sales during 1998. Based on the industry average over the past five years, appliance retailers typically experience losses of one percent on total credit sales. The company would estimate its uncollectible accounts expense as $5,000 (1% x $500,000). Any existing balance in Allowance for Uncollectible Accounts is ignored. The adjusting entry to record the estimated uncollectible accounts is simply:

Uncollectible Accounts Expense (E,-SE)	5,000	
Allowance for Uncollectible Accounts (-A)		5,000

A second estimation approach is to compute the estimate based on the outstanding balance of **Accounts Receivable**. Note that Accounts Receivable is a **balance sheet** account. The amount estimated under this approach is the correct balance for another balance sheet account, Allowance for Uncollectible Accounts. Assume that our retail appliance company has recorded $500,000 in Credit Sales during 1998. Of this amount, $24,000 in accounts receivable have not yet been collected on December 31. The company's Allowance for Uncollectible Accounts has a credit balance of $150 on December 31. Based on the industry average over the past five years, appliance retailers typically experience losses of five percent on outstanding accounts receivable. The company would estimate its required Allowance for Uncollectible Accounts as $1,200 (5% x $24,000). Any existing balance in Allowance for Uncollectible Accounts must be considered. As a result, the amount to be expensed is $1,050 ($1,200 - $150). The adjusting entry to record the estimated uncollectible accounts in this example is:

Uncollectible Accounts Expense (E,-SE)	1,050	
Allowance for Uncollectible Accounts (-A)		1,050

A variation of the balance sheet approach is known as an **aging of accounts receivable**. Aging accounts receivable results in a better estimate of uncollectibles by looking at how long an account has been outstanding, not just the total accounts receivable outstanding at a point in time. For example, if we sold to one customer on December 30, but payment is not due until January 30, we would not be concerned that the balance had not been paid on December 31. We would be much more uncertain about collecting from a customer whose balance was six months past due on December 31. The aging approach takes this uncertainty into account by assigning different percentages, depending on the length of time that an account is overdue. Once again, the percentages used in making the estimate would be based on past experience. The aging approach is likely to provide a more accurate estimate than the other approaches described above. Assume that our appliance retailer provides a more detailed breakdown of the $24,000 in outstanding accounts receivable at December 31, as follows:

Age	Receivable Amount	Percent Uncollectible	Estimated Amount Uncollectible
Current	$14,000	1%	$ 140
1 - 30 days past due	4,000	5%	200
31 - 60 days past due	2,000	10%	200
61 - 90 days past due	2,500	20%	500
Over 90 days past due	1,500	50%	750
Totals	$24,000		$1,790

Recall that the allowance has a credit balance of $150 prior to adjustment. The required adjusting entry based on the aging schedule of accounts receivable is:

Uncollectible Accounts Expense (E,-SE)	1,640	
Allowance for Uncollectible Accounts (-A)		1,640

QUESTIONS FOR YOUR REVIEW

1. Companies often offer their customers a purchase discount. Under what circumstances should the customer take advantage of the discount?
   a. When their borrowing rate exceeds the annual rate provided by the discount.
   b. When their borrowing rate is less than the annual rate provided by the discount.
   c. Whenever they can pay in cash without borrowing.
   d. Purchase discounts should never be taken.

2. Robin's Pet Shelter Inc. purchased feed and supplies from Karl's Kat Foods on June 15, 1999. The total cost was $2,400 and Karl offered terms of 2/10, n/30. If Karl uses the gross method to record receivables and receives payment on July 14, what is the correct journal entry?

   a. Cash (+A)   2,400
        Accounts Receivable (-A)   2,400

   b. Cash (+A)   2,352
        Accounts Receivable (-A)   2,352

   c. Cash (+A)   2,352
       Sales Discounts (-R,-SE)   48
        Accounts Receivable (-A)   2,400

   d. Cash (+A)   2,400
       Sales Discounts (R,+SE)   48
        Accounts Receivable (-A)   2,352

3. Karl's Kat Foods sold $1,300 of supplies to Robin's Pet Shelter on October 11, under Karl's normal terms of 2/10, n/30. Karl received Robin's payment on October 20. The correct entry for Karl to record this receipt under the gross method is:

    a.   Cash (+A)   1,300

           Accounts Receivable (-A)   1,300

    b.   Cash (+A)   1,274

           Accounts Receivable (-A)   1,300

           Sales Discounts (R,+SE)   26

    c.   Cash (+A)   1,274

           Accounts Receivable (-A)   1,274

    d.   Cash (+A)   1,274

           Sales Discounts (-R,-SE)   26

           Accounts Receivable (-A)   1,300

4. Which of the following items would be excluded in calculating a company's quick ratio?
    a.   Cash
    b.   Marketable securities
    c.   Accounts payable
    d.   Inventory

5. Which of the following items would be excluded in calculating a company's current ratio?
    a.   Cash
    b.   Marketable securities
    c.   Land
    d.   Inventory

6. Choose the best definition of a company's operating cycle from the following list.
    a.   The twelve-month period that a firm uses as its fiscal year
    b.   The average time required to sell a firm's inventory
    c.   The average time required to collect accounts receivable from a firm's customers
    d.   Total time between the date inventory is originally purchased and the date cash is eventually collected from customers

7. Short-term accounts receivable from customers should be included on a company's balance sheet based on:
    a.   the total price of credit sales.
    b.   net realizable value.
    c.   present value of the expected future cash flows.
    d.   present value of the expected future cash flows, adjusted for expected inflation up to the maturity date of the receivables.

8. Larry's Lawn Service accepted a $2,000 note receivable from a customer on June 1. The note includes interest at 6 percent annually, and matures on September 30. How much interest revenue will Larry earn on this note?
   a. $40
   b. $60
   c. $120
   d. $180

9. Which of the following should be excluded in determining a company's working capital?
   a. Accounts payable
   b. Accounts receivable
   c. Allowance for doubtful accounts
   d. Prepaid premiums on a three-year insurance policy

10. Which of these is most useful in measuring a company's short-term liquidity?
    a. Current ratio and quick ratio
    b. Current ratio and return on total assets
    c. Current ratio and dividend payout ratio
    d. Quick ratio and dividend payout ratio

11. Venus Candy Company reported accounts receivable balances of $130,000 and $115,500 on January 1 and December 31, 1999, respectively. Credit sales in 1999 totaled $658,000. What is the average collection period for accounts receivable?
    a. 72 days
    b. 64 days
    c. 57 days
    d. 67 days

12. John's Deli uses the allowance method to account for uncollectible accounts. Which of the following describes the impact of writing off a customer's account under this approach?
    a. The carrying value of accounts receivable will be increased during the year in which the account is written off.
    b. The carrying value of accounts receivable will be decreased during the year in which the account is written off.
    c. The carrying value of accounts receivable will be unaffected during the year in which the account is written off.
    d. John's net income will decrease during the year in which the account is written off.

13. Which of the following statements describes the reason for the preference for the allowance methods over the direct write-off method?
    a. The allowance method results in the lowest cost.
    b. The allowance method provides the best matching of uncollectible accounts expense and credit sales revenue.
    c. The allowance method is easier to use.
    d. The allowance method has been shown to minimize the number of accounts which must be written off.

14. High Flyers Advertising Company reported a credit balance of $21,000 in Allowance for Doubtful Accounts on January 1, 1999. Based on prior experience, High Flyers estimates that 2 percent of receivables eventually become uncollectible. During 1999, customer accounts totaling $14,500 were written off. The balance in Accounts Receivable was $683,000 on December 31, 1999. What is High Flyers' uncollectible accounts expense for 1999?
    a. $14,500
    b. $13,660
    c. $7,160
    d. $6,500

15. Which of the following methods is likely to produce the most reliable estimate for an allowance for doubtful accounts?
    a. Percentage of cash sales
    b. Percentage of credit sales
    c. Percentage of outstanding accounts receivable
    d. Aging of accounts receivable

16. Gordon's Pottery uses an aging method to estimate uncollectible accounts. Gordon has assembled the following information as of December 31, 1999.

Age of Accounts	Balance	Percent Collectible
Current	$400,000	97
1 - 30 days overdue	150,000	92
31 - 60 days overdue	100,000	90
61 - 90 days overdue	50,000	80
Over 90 days overdue	30,000	75

On January 1, Gordon's books indicated a debit balance of $625,000 in Accounts Receivable and a credit balance of $22,000 in Allowance for Doubtful Accounts. During the year, Gordon wrote off customer accounts totaling $1,650 as uncollectible.

Required:

a. Prepare the Accounts Receivable Aging Schedule for December 31, 1999.

16. b.   Prepare the entry to record uncollectible accounts expense for 1999.

 c.   What is the correct balance in Allowance for Doubtful Accounts on December 31, 1999?

17. Notsohonest John's Original Vermont Maple Syrup Company purchased 200,000 gallons of "raw materials" from a Canadian supplier on November 1, 1999. John agreed to pay the supplier in equal amounts over the coming three months, with payments due on December 1, January 1, and February 1. John is not required to pay any interest charges. The total payments under the contract amount to 450,000 Canadian dollars. Exchange rates are provided below. John's fiscal year ends on December 31.

Date	U.S. Dollars per Canadian Dollar
11/1	$0.85
12/1	0.80
12/31	0.84
1/1	0.84
2/1	0.82

Required: Prepare all journal entries on John's books related to the purchase and eventual cash payment.

18. Doug's Home Appliance Company reports a balance in Accounts Receivable of $56,350 on January 1, 1999. Allowance for Doubtful Accounts has a credit balance of $1,165 on the same date. Prepare summary journal entries to reflect the following activities during 1999.

   a. Accounts receivable from customers in the amount of $2,050 were written off during the year.

   b. Sales in 1999 totaled $361,500, of which $350,000 was on credit.

   c. A customer account in the amount of $700, which had been written off during 1997, was finally collected.

   d. Collections on accounts receivable, in addition to the above $700, totaled $326,500.

   e. Based on an aging of accounts receivable on December 31, Doug estimates that $2,610 of customer accounts will be written off in future periods.

19. Spartan Electric Products enters into the following transactions during the year ended December 31, 1999. Prepare all required journal entries and adjusting journal entries related to these transactions. Spartan does not recognize any discounts on its note transactions.

   a. On March 15, Spartan sold merchandise for $75,000, accepting a two-year, 10 percent note from the customer.

   b. On July 31, Spartan accepted a $10,000, six-month note from a customer on an open account receivable. The stated interest rate was 12 percent.

   c. On August 15, Spartan accepted a one-year, $12,000 note from a customer on an open account receivable. The stated interest rate was 12 percent.

   d. On November 30, Spartan sold merchandise for $60,000, accepting a one-year, 10 percent note from the customer.

e. On December 15, the customer paid the balance due on the note signed on August 15.

f. Prepare any required adjusting entries on December 31.

CHAPTER 6-SOLUTIONS

1.	a	5.	c	9.	d	13.	b
2.	a	6.	d	10.	a	14.	c
3.	d	7.	b	11.	d	15.	d
4.	d	8.	a	12.	c		

16.a.

Gordon's Pottery
Accounts Receivable Aging Schedule

Accounts Receivable	Percent Uncollectible	Uncollectible Amount
$400,000	0.03	$12,000
150,000	0.08	12,000
100,000	0.10	10,000
50,000	0.20	10,000
30,000	0.25	7,500
$730,000		$51,500

b.
Uncollectible Accounts Expense (E,-SE)	31,150	
Allowance for Doubtful Accounts (-A)		31,150

c. The correct balance is a credit of $51,500.

17.
Nov. 1	Purchases (E,-SE)(or Inventory)		382,500	
	Accounts Payable (+L)			382,500
Dec. 1	Accounts Payable (-L)		120,000	
	Cash (-A)			120,000
Dec. 31	Accounts Payable (-L)		10,500	
	Exchange Gain (Ga,+SE)			10,500
Jan. 1	Accounts Payable (-L)		126,000	
	Cash (-A)			126,000
Feb. 1	Accounts Payable (-L)		126,000	
	Cash (-A)			123,000
	Exchange Gain (Ga,+SE)			3,000

18. a.
Allowance for Doubtful Accounts (+A)	2,050	
Accounts Receivable (-A)		2,050

18. b.   Accounts Receivable (+A)   350,000
         Cash (+A)   11,500
             Sales Revenue (R,+SE)   361,500

    c.   Accounts Receivable (+A)   700
             Allowance for Doubtful Accounts (-A)   700

         Cash (+A)   700
             Accounts Receivable (-A)   700

    d.   Cash (+A)   326,500
             Accounts Receivable (-A)   326,500

    e.   Uncollectible Accounts Expense (E,-SE)   2,795
             Allowance for Doubtful Accounts (-A)   2,795

The December 31 balance in the allowance account is a *debit* balance of $185. The initial balance was a credit of $1,165. Entries made to the allowance account to reflect transactions during the year included (a) a debit of $2,050, and (c) a credit of $700. A credit of $2,795 is required to bring the allowance account to its desired ending credit balance of $2,610.

19. a.   Notes Receivable (+A)   75,000
             Sales (R,+SE)   75,000

    b.   Notes Receivable (+A)   10,000
             Accounts Receivable (-A)   10,000

    c.   Notes Receivable (+A)   12,000
             Accounts Receivable (-A)   12,000

    d.   Notes Receivable (+A)   60,000
             Sales (R,+SE)   60,000

    e.   Cash (+A)   12,480
             Notes Receivable (-A)   12,000
             Interest Revenue (R,+SE)   480

    f.   Interest Receivable (+A)   6,937.50
             Interest Revenue (R,+SE)   6,937.50

Adjusting entry for interest earned, but not yet received on December 31, 1999.

CHAPTER 7

Merchandise Inventory

REVIEW OF KEY CONCEPTS

Inventory is a key asset for manufacturers, wholesalers, and retailers. Specific issues related to inventory accounting by manufacturers are discussed in courses in management accounting. The focus in introductory financial accounting is on inventory accounting by retailers and wholesalers. Inventory is initially recorded as an asset when purchased (it is **capitalized**). Later on, when benefits are provided to the company through sales, a portion of the inventory becomes an expense, namely, **Cost of Goods Sold**. Inventory accounting impacts both the balance sheet and income statement of a company. Eventually, all transactions are settled in cash (including credit purchases and sales of inventory), so inventory accounting also impacts a company's statement of cash flows.

There are several important concepts reviewed here. First, as with any asset, the company must account for inventory acquisitions, holding period activity, and inventory disposition. The company must make a choice to adopt either a **periodic** or a **perpetual** inventory system. In addition, most companies will also choose a **cost flow assumption**. Finally, inventory values may fluctuate over time. If the value of inventory declines significantly (below its historical cost), then the asset balance will be overstated. This potential problem is handled by making a **lower of cost or market** adjustment as needed.

Recording Inventory Acquisitions

The cost to record any asset is the acquisition price plus all costs incurred to bring the asset to the location and condition for its intended use. In the case of inventory, the recorded cost of the asset normally includes the purchase price plus any shipping charges (**freight in**) less any **cash discounts** offered by the supplier.

Recording Inventory Sales and Dispositions

The asset inventory provides **future benefits** to the company in the form of **sales revenues** when the inventory is sold to customers. Proper **matching** requires that we associate an expense (**Cost of Goods Sold**) with the earned revenue. The expense is the cost of the item sold. This can be easily understood conceptually using the **specific identification method**. The company keeps track of all individual items in inventory and their historical cost. The cost of goods sold is the historical cost of each item actually sold. As a practical matter, this approach becomes rather cumbersome (and costly) when there are large numbers of inventory items being sold. This approach is used only when individual inventory items have large dollar values and can be easily identified (e.g., by a serial number stamped on the item).

To alleviate record keeping problems (and costs), most companies adopt a cost flow assumption. Cost flow assumptions minimize record keeping and associated costs. The cost flow assumption is a simplification. Actual physical flow of goods need not (and generally does not) match the cost flow assumption adopted. The three cost flow assumptions are: (1) first in, first out (**FIFO**), (2) last in, first out (**LIFO**), and (3) **average cost**.

A Comprehensive Example. The following example, while a very simple one, highlights the financial statement impact of the choice of an inventory method (i.e., periodic versus perpetual) and a cost flow assumption (i.e., FIFO, LIFO, or average cost). The choices impact the balance sheet in the valuation of the reported amount for the ending inventory. The reported net income is affected because the choices may produce different amounts for Cost of Goods Sold. Remember that total inventory-related costs will be the same under all choices. The choices determine how cost is allocated between the balance sheet (Ending Inventory) and the income statement (Cost of Goods Sold).

The following information is available for the month of June:

Date	Transaction	Units	Unit Cost	Total Cost
6/ 1	Beginning inventory	20	$10	$200
6/10	Purchase	10	15	150
6/20	Sale	10		

Periodic Inventory System

Assume first that the company adopts a periodic inventory system. The following calculations illustrate the computation of ending inventory and cost of goods sold under the various cost flow assumptions. Consider the physical flow of units during June. There were a total of 30 units which could have been sold (goods available for sale), having a total cost of $350. Ten units were sold and twenty remain in the ending inventory. The objective is to allocate the total cost between an asset which will benefit future periods (ending inventory) and an expense of the current period (cost of goods sold).

First-In, First-Out (FIFO). Under this assumption, the units sold were those purchased FIRST, costing $10 each. Total cost of goods sold is, therefore, $100. The remaining units in ending inventory include 10 units costing $10 each and 10 units costing $15 each, for a total of $250.

Last-In, First-Out (LIFO). Under this assumption, the units sold were those purchased LAST, costing $15 each. Total cost of goods sold is, therefore, $150. The remaining units in ending inventory include 20 units costing $10 each, for a total of $200.

Average Cost. Under this assumption, all units have the same cost, i.e., the average cost [$350 / 30 units]. The units sold cost $11.67 each. Total cost of goods sold is, therefore, $116.67. The remaining units in ending inventory include 20 units costing $11.67 each, for a total of $233.40.

Specific Identification. Recall that specific identification is not a cost flow assumption. Under this method, the cost allocation must match the actual physical flow of goods. We include this method here for completeness. Under specific identification, there are any number of possible combinations.

For example, the company may have sold seven of the units from beginning inventory and three of the units from the June 10 purchase. This would produce a cost of goods sold of $115 [7 units @ $10 + 3 units @ $15] and an ending inventory valuation of $235 [13 units @ $10 + 7 units @ $15]. Alternatively, the company might have sold five of the units from beginning inventory and five of the units from the June 10 purchase. This would produce a cost of goods sold of $125 [5 units @ $10 + 5 units @ $15] and an ending inventory valuation of $225 [15 units @ $10 + 5 units @ $15].

Perpetual Inventory System

Assume now that the company adopts a perpetual inventory system. Note that the physical flow of units during June is unaffected. There were still a total of 30 units which could have been sold, having a total cost of $350. Ten units were sold and twenty remain in the ending inventory.

First-In, First-Out (FIFO). Under this assumption, the units sold were those purchased FIRST, costing $10 each. Total cost of goods sold is, therefore, $100. The remaining units in ending inventory include 10 units costing $10 each and 10 units costing $15 each, for a total of $250. Note that these amounts are identical to those calculated under the periodic system. This will always be the case with the FIFO cost flow assumption.

Last-In, First-Out (LIFO). Under this assumption, the units sold were those purchased LAST, costing $15 each. Total cost of goods sold is, therefore, $150. The remaining units in ending inventory include 20 units costing $10 each, for a total of $200. Once again, note that these amounts are identical to those calculated under the periodic system. This will NOT always be the case with the LIFO cost flow assumption. These calculations depend on the timing of purchases and sales within the accounting period.

Average Cost. Under this assumption, all units have the same cost, i.e., the average cost [$350 / 30 units]. The units sold cost $11.67 each. Total cost of goods sold is, therefore, $116.67. The remaining units in ending inventory include 20 units costing $11.67 each, for a total of $233.40. Once again, note that these amounts are identical to those calculated under the periodic system. This will NOT always be the case with the average cost flow assumption. These calculations are also dependent on the timing of purchases and sales within the accounting period.

The Impact of the Timing of Purchases and Sales within the Period

As noted above, the timing of purchases and sales within the period has an impact on the calculation of the values for ending inventory and cost of goods sold. Let's modify the original example, reversing the dates of the purchase and sale during June.

Date	Transaction	Units	Unit Cost	Total Cost
6/ 1	Beginning inventory	20	$10	$200
6/10	Sale	10		
6/20	Purchase	10	15	150

LIFO Perpetual Inventory System

Under this assumption, the units sold were those purchased LAST as of the date of the sale (June 10), and cost $10 each. Total cost of goods sold is, therefore, $100. The remaining units in ending inventory include 10 units costing $10 each and 10 units costing $15 each, for a total of $250. Note how the timing has changed the amounts for ending inventory and cost of goods sold.

LIFO Average Cost

Under this assumption, all units have the same cost, i.e., the average cost. When the sale takes place on June 10, the only units available for sale are those from the beginning inventory. The units sold cost $10 each [$200 / 20 units]. Total cost of goods sold is, therefore, $100. The remaining units in ending inventory include 20 units costing an average of $12.50 each [10 units @ $10 + 10 units @ $15], for a total of $250. Once again, note how the timing has changed the amounts for ending inventory and cost of goods sold.

As noted above, the calculations under the periodic system will not be affected by the timing of transactions within the accounting period. This is also true of the perpetual system/FIFO combination. You may wish to check these for understanding.

Accounting for Inventory During the Holding Period

The Lower-of-Cost-or-Market Adjustment

Over time, the value of the inventory may decline due to physical obsolescence, changing technology, or changing styles and tastes of customers. Recall that inventory is carried on the balance sheet at its historical cost. Should the value of the inventory decline below its cost, then the asset balance will be overstated and requires an adjustment. The adjusting entry is an easy one:

Loss on Inventory Write-Down (E,-SE)   xxx
      Inventory (-A)   xxx

There are four basic steps to determine the amount of the adjustment, if any: (1) determine the cost of the ending inventory, by applying the company's chosen cost flow assumption; (2) determine the market value of the ending inventory; (3) compare the cost and market values; and (4) adjust *only* if market is *less* than cost. When market is greater than cost, no adjustment is required.

There are three possible amounts which can be used for the market value of inventory. The **replacement cost** is the historical cost of repurchasing or reproducing the inventory. The **ceiling** price is the **net realizable value** (i.e., the estimated selling price) of inventory. The **floor** price is the ceiling less a normal profit margin. (A normal profit margin might be the average profit earned by the company.) When these three values are ranked from highest to lowest, the **market value** will always be the middle value.

QUESTIONS FOR YOUR REVIEW

1. Which of the following items would be excluded in determining Gold Company's December 31 ending inventory?
   a. Goods in transit sold FOB destination that have been shipped, but not yet received by the customer.
   b. Goods in transit purchased FOB shipping point that were shipped by the supplier on December 28, but not yet received by Gold.
   c. Goods that Gold holds for sale on consignment, received from Silver Corporation.
   d. Goods that Silver Corporation sells on consignment for Gold that remain unsold at December 31.

2. Which costs should not be included in determination of ending inventory?
   a. Freight-in
   b. Freight-out
   c. Import duties paid on purchased goods
   d. Wages paid to workers in the receiving department

3. Which of the following is not a benefit of a perpetual inventory costing system?
   a. Provides more timely and useful information for management
   b. Provides more timely and useful information for financial statement users
   c. Provides greater control over inventory ordering and storage costs
   d. Provides reduced bookkeeping costs

4. Identify the type of firm for which specific identification would be an appropriate inventory method.
   a. Hardware store
   b. Retail grocery
   c. Fine arts gallery
   d. Paper manufacturer

5. Which inventory cost flow assumption reports the most current inventory values on a company's balance sheet?
   a. FIFO
   b. LIFO
   c. Weighted average cost
   d. Moving average cost

6. Which inventory cost flow assumption reports the most current inventory values on a company's income statement?
   a. FIFO
   b. LIFO
   c. Weighted average cost
   d. Moving average cost

7. Which inventory cost flow assumption best approximates current replacement cost for the ending inventory?
   a. FIFO
   b. LIFO
   c. Weighted average cost
   d. Moving average cost

8. Handy Andy uses a periodic inventory system. What is the financial statement impact of an understatement of ending inventory?
   a. The current year's net income will be overstated.
   b. The next year's net income will overstated.
   c. The next year's ending inventory will be understated.
   d. The next year's ending inventory will be overstated.

9. Choose the true statement about calculation of net purchases from the following list.
   a. Gross purchases less returns and allowances less purchase discounts
   b. Gross purchases plus returns and allowances plus purchase discounts
   c. Gross purchases plus returns and allowances less purchase discounts
   d. Gross purchases less returns and allowances less purchase discounts plus freight-in

10. Al's Hardware recorded net purchases of $12,000 during June. Al's beginning inventory was $9,000, which was $1,000 higher than the ending inventory. Al's cost of goods sold for June was:
    a. $21,000
    b. $20,000
    c. $13,000
    d. $ 3,000

Answer questions 11 through 16 using the following information.

Date	Transaction	Units	Unit Cost	Total
7/ 1	Beg. inv.	400	$ 12	$ 4,800
7/ 6	Purchase	600	13	7,800
7/10	Sale	500	?	?
7/14	Purchase	200	14	2,800
7/16	Sale	500	?	?
7/21	Purchase	200	14	2,800
7/26	Purchase	400	15	6,000
7/28	Sale	400	?	?

11. Assume that the company uses a periodic inventory system and a FIFO cost flow assumption. What is the cost of goods sold for July?
    a. $24,200
    b. $19,400
    c. $18,822
    d. $18,200

12. Assume that the company uses a periodic inventory system and a LIFO cost flow assumption. What is the cost of goods sold for July?
    a. $24,200
    b. $19,400
    c. $18,822
    d. $18,200

13. Assume that the company uses a periodic inventory system and an average cost flow assumption. What is the cost of goods sold for July?
    a. $24,200
    b. $19,400
    c. $18,822
    d. $18,200

14. Assume that the company uses a periodic inventory system and a LIFO cost flow assumption. What is the cost of ending inventory on July 31?
    a. $6,000
    b. $5,200
    c. $4,800
    d. $3,000

15. Assume that the company uses a perpetual inventory system and a FIFO cost flow assumption. What is the cost of goods sold for July?
    a. $24,200
    b. $19,400
    c. $18,822
    d. $18,200

16. Assume that the company uses a perpetual inventory system and a LIFO cost flow assumption. What is the cost of ending inventory on July 31?
    a. $6,000
    b. $5,200
    c. $4,800
    d. $3,000

17. Madeline's Catering reported sales of $55,800 and cost of sales of $34,200 for 1999. Madeline's beginning inventory was $15,000, and ending inventory totaled $21,000. Purchases were $40,200 during 1999. What was Madeline's inventory turnover ratio in 1999?
    a.   1.90
    b.   2.28
    c.   1.63
    d.   3.10

18. Cindy's Kitchens is a leading retailer for replacement kitchen cabinets. At December 31, 1999, Cindy noted the following information concerning ending inventory: historical cost, $32,300; net realizable value, $40,000; current replacement cost, $35,600; and normal profit margin, $5,700. What value should Cindy use in reporting ending inventory on her December 31, 1999, balance sheet?
    a. $32,300
    b. $40,000
    c. $35,600
    d. $34,300

19. Cindy's Kitchens noted the following information concerning ending inventory at December 31, 2000: historical cost, $37,100; net realizable value, $41,500; current replacement cost, $36,700; and normal profit margin, $6,000. What value should Cindy use in reporting ending inventory on her December 31, 2000, balance sheet?
    a. $37,100
    b. $41,500
    c. $36,700
    d. $35,500

20. An accounting clerk errs in calculating the cost of ending inventory for 1999, overstating the amount by $36,000. What is the impact on 1999 and 2000 net income?

	1999 Net Income	**2000 Net Income**
a.	$36,000 overstated	$36,000 overstated
b.	$36,000 overstated	$36,000 understated
c.	$36,000 understated	$36,000 overstated
d.	$36,000 understated	$36,000 understated

21. Janet's Gym, selling home exercise and fitness equipment, opened for business on May 1. Record the following transactions for Janet's Gym, assuming that Janet uses a periodic inventory system.

    May 2   Purchases three stationary bicycles for $150 each, four rowing machines for $200 each, and five stair steppers for $175 each, agreeing to pay the supplier within 60 days.

    May 9   Sells one rowing machine for $400 cash.

May 14   Purchases 20 copies of Slim Jim's latest exercise video tape for $10 each, agreeing to pay the supplier within 30 days.

May 19   Sells one stationary bicycle for $420. The purchaser agrees to pay in 30 days.

May 24   Sells four video tapes for $20 cash each.

May 26   Purchases five Miracle Machines for $1,750 each, agreeing to pay the supplier within 60 days. The Miracle Machine enables the user to sit at home, watch sports on television, eat lots of snacks, and maintain peak physical condition.

May 28   Customers flock to the Gym. Janet sells all five Miracle Machines for $4,000 cash each. Thousands of other customers express an interest in buying the new machines when they become available. Two of the Miracle Machine purchasers feel that more is always better, and each purchases a copy of the video tape for $22 in cash to view while enjoying the Miracle Machine.

May 30   Janet finishes cleaning up the debris left by customers on the 28th and counts up the remaining inventory. Her count finds zero Miracle Machines, three rowing machines, two stationary bicycles, five stair steppers, and 12 video tapes.

22. Repeat question (21), but now assume that Janet's Gym uses the perpetual inventory system.

    May 2   Purchases three stationary bicycles for $150 each, four rowing machines for $200 each, and five stair steppers for $175 each, agreeing to pay the supplier within 60 days.

    May 9   Sells one rowing machine for $400 cash.

    May 14   Purchases 20 copies of Slim Jim's latest exercise video tape for $10 each, agreeing to pay the supplier within 30 days.

    May 19   Sells one stationary bicycle for $420. The purchaser agrees to pay in 30 days.

    May 24   Sells four video tapes for $20 cash each.

    May 26   Purchases five Miracle Machines for $1,750 each, agreeing to pay the supplier within 60 days. The Miracle Machine enables the user to sit at home, watch sports on television, eat lots of snacks, and maintain peak physical condition.

May 28   Customers flock to the Gym. Janet sells all five Miracle Machines for $4,000 cash each. Thousands of other customers express an interest in buying the new machines when they become available. Two of the Miracle Machine purchasers feel that more is always better, and each purchases a copy of the video tape for $22 in cash to view while enjoying the Miracle Machine.

May 30   Janet finishes cleaning up the debris left by customers on the 28th and counts up the remaining inventory. Her count finds: zero Miracle Machines, three rowing machines, two stationary bicycles, five stair steppers, and 12 video tapes.

23. Presented below are inventory transactions for Carpet City for the month of June. Calculate both ending inventory and cost of goods sold for June under the various cost flow assumptions.

June 1   Beginning inventory of 30 carpets costing $60 each.
June 3   Sold 10 carpets for $100 each.
June 8   Purchased 15 carpets for $50 each.
June 12 Sold 12 carpets for $120 each.
June 19 Purchased 10 carpets for $70 each.
June 24 Sold 15 carpets for $120 each.
June 29 Purchased 10 carpets for $75 each.

a.   Carpet City uses a periodic, FIFO system.

b.   Carpet City uses a periodic, LIFO system.

c.   Carpet City uses a perpetual, FIFO system.

d.   Carpet City uses a perpetual, LIFO system.

e.   Carpet City uses a periodic, average cost system.

24. The following partial information has been taken from the accounting records of Dave's Discount Store.

	12/31/95	12/31/96	12/31/97
Beginning inventory	$50,000	$62,500	(e)
Purchases	25,000	30,000	$ 37,500
Purchase discounts	(a)	(d)	(f)
Cost of goods sold	5,000	22,500	40,000
Cost of goods available for sale	67,500	(c)	90,000
Ending inventory	(b)	67,500	(g)
Sales	26,300	61,240	104,600

Required:

a.   Compute the missing amounts.

b. Assume that Dave uses a periodic inventory system. Prepare the closing entry to recognize ending inventory and cost of goods sold for each year.

25.   The Toy Store reported the following amounts on December 31, 1999: ending inventory (based on a physical count), $275,000 and accounts payable, $81,000. The Toy Store uses a periodic inventory system. A review of the records revealed the additional information presented below.

Required:

a. Prepare the required adjusting entry, if any, for each of the items below.

b. Calculate ending balances for Inventory and Accounts Payable on December 31.

   (1) The Toy Store ordered $12,000 of merchandise from a supplier on December 28, with terms FOB shipping point. The merchandise was shipped on December 29 and received on January 4.

   (2) The Toy Store had ordered $7,000 of merchandise from a supplier on December 29, with terms FOB destination. The merchandise was shipped on December 29 and received on January 2.

(3) The Toy Store had shipped $17,000 of merchandise to a customer on December 29, with terms FOB destination. The merchandise originally cost $9,000. The merchandise was received on January 2.

(4) The physical inventory count included $14,500 of merchandise that was held on consignment for Marx Brothers Manufacturing.

(5) The physical inventory count included $4,300 of merchandise that was received late on December 31, but not recorded in Accounts Payable until January 2.

(6) The Toy Store ordered $28,000 of merchandise from a supplier on December 22, with terms FOB destination. The merchandise was shipped on December 24 and received on December 28.

CHAPTER 7 - SOLUTIONS

1.	c	6.	b	11.	d	16.	b
2.	b	7.	a	12.	b	17.	a
3.	d	8.	b	13.	c	18.	a
4.	c	9.	d	14.	c	19.	c
5.	a	10.	c	15.	d	20.	b

21. May 2   Purchases (E,-SE)   2,125
    Accounts Payable (+L)   2,125

  May 9   Cash (+A)   400
    Sales (R,+SE)   400

  May 14 Purchases (E,-SE)   200
    Accounts Payable (+L)   200

  May 19 Accounts Receivable (+A)   420
    Sales (R,+SE)   420

  May 24 Cash (+A)   80
    Sales (R,+SE)   80

  May 26 Purchases (E,-SE)   8,750
    Accounts Payable (+L)   8,750

  May 28 Cash (+A)   20,044
    Sales (R,+SE)   20,044

  May 30 Inventory (+A)   1,895
    Cost of Goods Sold (E,-SE)   9,180
    Purchases (E,-SE)   11,075

Purchases: $2,125 + $200 + $8,750 = $11,075

Ending Inventory: (3 x $200) + (2 x $150) + (5 x $175) + (12 x $10) = $1,895

	Beginning inventory	$ 0
+	Purchases	11,075
	Cost of goods available for sale	$11,075
-	Ending inventory	(1,895)
	Cost of goods sold	$ 9,180

22. May 2   Inventory (+A)   2,125
                 Accounts Payable (+L)   2,125

     May 9   Cash (+A)   400
                 Sales (R,+SE)   400

              Cost of Goods Sold (E,-SE)   200
                 Inventory (-A)   200

     May 14   Inventory (+A)   200
                 Accounts Payable (+L)   200

     May 19   Accounts Receivable (+A)   420
                 Sales (R,+SE)   420

              Cost of Goods Sold (E,-SE)   150
                 Inventory (-A)   150

     May 24   Cash (+A)   80
                 Sales (R,+SE)   80

              Cost of Goods Sold (E,-SE)   40
                 Inventory (-A)   40

     May 26   Inventory (+A)   8,750
                 Accounts Payable (+L)   8,750

     May 28   Cash (+A)   20,044
                 Sales (R,+SE)   20,044

              Cost of Goods Sold (E,-SE)   8,770
                 Inventory (-A)   8,770

If all of the above entries are posted to the T-accounts for Inventory and Cost of Goods Sold, the ending balances will be $1,915 and $9,160, respectively. However, if Cost of Goods Sold is calculated (see next page), the amount should be $9,180. The difference is due to an inventory shortage (theft, damages, etc.). Janet purchased 20 video tapes, 6 were sold, but only 12 remain in inventory. Two tapes ($20 total cost) were lost. Note that this amount was simply included in Cost of Goods Sold under the periodic system. The required adjusting entry is:

     May 30   Inventory Shortage (E,-SE)   20
                 Inventory (-A)   20
Purchases: $2,125 + $200 + $8,750 = $11,075

Ending inventory: (3 x $200) + (2 x $150) + (5 x $175) + (12 x $10) = $1,895

	Beginning inventory	$ 0
+	Purchases	11,075
	Cost of goods available for sale	$11,075
-	Ending inventory	(1,895)
	Cost of goods sold	$ 9,180

23. Begin this problem by accounting for the physical units of inventory and determining cost of goods available for sale.

The beginning inventory was 30 units and purchases totaled 35 units. A total of 37 units were sold, leaving an ending inventory of 28 units. Note that the accounting for the physical units is unaffected by the choice of inventory system or cost flow assumption.

Cost of Goods Available for Sale

		Units	Unit Cost	Total Cost
6/1	Beginning inventory	30	$60	$1,800
6/8	Purchase	15	50	750
6/19	Purchase	10	70	700
6/29	Purchase	10	75	750
	Goods available for sale	65		$4,000

a.   FIFO, periodic (ending inventory is 28 units)

		Units	Unit Cost	Total Cost
6/8	Purchase	8	$50	$ 400
6/19	Purchase	10	70	700
6/29	Purchase	10	75	750
	Ending inventory	28		$1,850

$$\text{CGS} = \text{CGAS} - \text{EI}$$
$$= \$4,000 - \$1,850$$
$$= \$2,150$$

23.   b.   LIFO, periodic (ending inventory is 28 units)

		Units	Unit Cost	Total Cost
6/1	Beginning inventory	28	$60	$1,680
	Ending inventory	28		$1,680

$$\text{CGS} = \text{CGAS} - \text{EI}$$
$$= \$4,000 - \$1,680$$
$$= \$2,320$$

c. FIFO, perpetual (ending inventory is 28 units). You may wish to work this out, but it is easier to simply recall that FIFO yields identical amounts under the periodic and perpetual systems. The answers are therefore the same as in part (a).

d. The perpetual inventory records must be maintained to determine LIFO inventory and cost of goods sold. Units are in parentheses.

		Inventory		**Cost of Goods Sold**		
6/ 1	Beg. inventory (30)	30	@ $60	-		
6/ 3	Sale (10)	20	@ $60	10	@	$60
6/ 8	Purchase (15)	20	@ $60	-		
		15	@ 50			
6/12	Sale (12)	20	@ $60	12	@	$50
		3	@ 50			
6/19	Purchase (10)	20	@ $60	-		
		3	@ 50			
		10	@ 70			
6/24	Sale (15)	18	@ $60	10	@	$70
				3	@	50
				2	@	60
6/29	Purchase (10)	18	@ $60	-		
		10	@ 75			

The ending inventory is the units remaining on June 29. The total cost is $1,830 (18 x $60 and 10 x $75). Cost of goods sold is obtained by either adding up the total entries made to the account, or subtracting the ending inventory from cost of goods available for sale. Cost of goods sold is $2,170.

e. Average cost, periodic (ending inventory is 28 units). The average cost amounts can be computed using the initial calculation made for cost of goods available for sale. There were 65 units available at a total cost of $4,000. This gives an average cost of $61.54 (rounded). Using the average cost:

Ending inventory = 28 units x $61.54 = $1,723.12

Cost of goods sold = 37 units x $61.54 = $2,276.98

24. a. It is easiest to solve for the missing amounts by recalling the basic conceptual relations among these variables, and then applying simple algebraic techniques.

    (a) BI   +   P   -   PD   =   CGAS
          $50,000 + $25,000 -   PD   = $67,500
          PD   = $7,500

    (b) CGAS   -   EI   =   CGS
          $67,500 -   EI   = $5,000
          EI   = $62,500

    (c) CGAS   -   EI   =   CGS
          CGAS   - $67,500 = $22,500
          CGAS   = $90,000

    (d) BI   +   P   -   PD   =   CGAS
          $62,500 + $30,000 -   PD   = $90,000
          PD   = $2,500

    (e) BI(2000) =   EI (1999)
          BI(2000) = $67,500

    (f) BI   +   P   -   PD   =   CGAS
          $67,500 + $37,500 -   PD   = $90,000
          PD   = $15,000

    (g) CGAS   -   EI   =   CGS
          $90,000 -   EI   = $40,000
          EI   = $50,000

24.b.   Closing entries

	1998	**1999**	**2000**
Account	**Debit (Credit)**	**Debit (Credit)**	**Debit (Credit)**
Cost of Goods Sold (E,-SE)	5,000	22,500	40,000
Inventory (ending) (+A)	62,500	67,500	50,000
Purchase Discounts (E,-SE)	7,500	2,500	15,000
Inventory (beginning) (-A)	(50,000)	(62,500)	(67,500)
Purchases (-E,+SE)	(25,000)	(30,000)	(37,500)

25.a.   (1)   Inventory (+A)   12,000
             Accounts Payable (+L)   12,000

      (2)   No adjustment required.

      (3)   Inventory (+A)   9,000
             Cost of Goods Sold (-E,+SE)   9,000

      (4)   Cost of Goods Sold (E,-SE)   14,500
             Inventory (-A)   14,500

      (5)   Cost of Goods Sold (E,-SE)   4,300
             Accounts Payable (+L)   4,300

      (6)   No adjustment required.

b.   The correct ending balances for Inventory and Accounts Payable are easily computed by preparing T-accounts and posting the adjusting entries.

Inventory		Accounts Payable	
275,000	14,500		81,000
12,000			12,000
9,000			4,300
281,500			97,300

CHAPTER 8

Investments in Equity Securities

REVIEW OF KEY CONCEPTS

Investments in equity securities represent assets to the investor. Therefore, we must be concerned here with the basic questions faced in accounting for assets in the earlier chapters. The same basic rules apply in accounting at acquisition, disposal, and during the holding period. You should focus on differences in accounting for this type of asset as compared to other assets.

Companies make investments in equity securities issued by other companies for two primary reasons. In the first case, cash is simply being invested to earn a return in the form of dividends and/or price appreciation (capital gains). Management will convert these investments back into cash whenever the need arises to pay current liabilities as they come due. Such investments are appropriately classified as current assets on the balance sheet. An investment is classified as a **trading security** if the investment is primarily held in order to sell it in the near future to profit from short-term price fluctuations. Trading securities are always classified as current assets. Other marketable security investments are classified as **available-for-sale securities**. Depending upon management's intent regarding their holding period, available-for-sale securities may be classified as current or long-term assets.

In the second case, management may wish to invest in another firm so as to establish an ability to *significantly influence* or *control* the financial and operating decisions of the investee firm. For example, management may wish to invest in a major supplier in order to guarantee a steady source of needed raw materials. Such investments are properly classified as noncurrent (long-term) assets on the balance sheet. An **equity security** investment represents an ownership interest in another firm. Equity securities include common and preferred stocks, as well as rights or options to obtain or sell such securities. (As in the text, our discussion will emphasize investments in common stocks.) The balance sheet classification (current or noncurrent) of an equity investment is thus dependent on the intentions of management. Accounting for investments during the holding period will be affected by the balance sheet classification of the investment.

Recording Acquisitions

The cost to record any asset is the acquisition price plus all costs incurred to bring the asset to the location and condition for its intended use. Typical additional costs encountered in purchasing equity securities include brokerage commissions, exchange fees, and transfer taxes. These costs are appropriately added to the purchase price to record investment acquisitions. As an example, assume that Spartan Corporation purchases 200 shares of the common stock of Small Company for $25 per share. Additional commissions and fees total $132. Assuming the investment is properly recorded as a trading security, the purchase is recorded as follows:

Trading Securities (+A)	5,132	
Cash (-A)		5,132

Lump Sum Purchase

A company may purchase several equity securities in a single transaction. The total cost of a lump sum (or basket) purchase is allocated among the assets acquired, based on their relative fair market values. Assume that Spartan Corporation acquires 5,000 shares of the common stock and 2,000 shares of the preferred stock of Johnson, Inc., a new corporation, for $200,000. The estimated value of the shares is $30 per share for common and $50 per share for preferred. Assuming the investments are both trading securities, the journal entry to record the purchase is:

Trading Securities-Common (+A)	120,000	
Trading Securities-Preferred (+A)	80,000	
Cash (-A)		200,000

Accounting for Investments at Disposition

At some point in time the company may choose to sell its investments. This presents no particular accounting problems. The company will record the receipt of cash or other assets received from the sale. The equity securities being sold must be removed from the accounting records. A gain or loss on sale is recorded, based on any difference between the selling price and the book value (carrying value) of the investment.. Assume that Spartan later sells the preferred stock of Johnson acquired in the last example. The stock is sold for $92,000. The journal entry to record the sale is:

Cash (+A)	92,000	
Trading Securities-Preferred (-A)		80,000
Realized Gain on Sale of Mark. Sec. (Ga,+SE)		12,000

The book value (carrying value) of an investment will *not* always be equal to its original cost because of accounting procedures applied during the **holding period**.

Accounting for Investments in Equity Securities During the Holding Period

Accounting for equity securities during the holding period is dependent on their balance sheet classification (trading, available-for-sale, or other long-term) and the accounting method employed. All trading and available-for-sale (whether considered current or long-term) investments are accounted for using the **cost method**. When an investment is accounted for under the cost method, firms are generally also required to make an adjustment to reflect the market value at the balance sheet date. In addition to applying the cost method to available-for-sale securities classified as long-term investments, the **equity method** and the preparation of **consolidated financial statements** may be appropriate to account for long-term equity investments under certain circumstances which are discussed later in the chapter. All the alternative accounting methods record acquisitions and dispositions in the same manner, as previously described. The choice among the alternative accounting methods directly affects only accounting during the holding period. The choice will indirectly affect accounting for dispositions due to changes in the carrying value of investments during the holding period.

Recognition and Realization

Two accounting concepts are important to understanding the differences among the alternative accounting methods for investments. The first, **recognition**, means that an item is formally recorded in the accounting records. The amount of such item affects the amounts reported in the company's financial statements. **Realization** indicates that an amount has been confirmed in an exchange transaction. For example, suppose that you purchase an asset for $500. At a later date, you sell that asset for $600. You have realized a gain as a result of the price appreciation and sale of the asset. Alternatively, suppose that you do not sell the asset, but simply observe that it has increased in market value to $600. Although you may be economically better off, the gain due to price appreciation has not been realized in an exchange transaction.

As a general rule, all realized gains and losses are recognized. In the following sections, we will review situations where **unrealized gains** or **losses** are sometimes recognized as well.

Current Investments in Marketable Equity Securities

Investments classified as current assets are properly accounted for using the cost method, with an adjustment to mark them to their market value (i.e., **mark-to-market**). Under the cost method, the investor will recognize income earned on the investment as it is received in the form of *dividends*. Assume that Beta Company owns 1,000 shares of Max Inc. and receives a dividend of $1.20 per share on December 15. The receipt would be recorded with the following journal entry:

Cash (+A)   1,200
    Dividend Income (R,+SE)   1,200

The above entry recognizes the increase in cash and the revenue earned on the investment under the cost method. Notice that the entry has no impact on the book value of the investment. This is the only type of entry normally made during the holding period for investments carried under the cost method. However, an additional entry is needed when the cost method is modified to include the mark-to-market (MTM) adjustment.

Mark-to-Market Method

The MTM adjustment is made when preparing financial statements. *SFAS No. 115* requires a mark-to-market adjustment for all securities (debt and equity) carried under the cost method for which a fair value can be determined. Nonmarketable securities are carried at historical cost with no market adjustment. *SFAS No.115* provides for separate and different treatments of investments classified as trading versus available-for-sale.

The general approach is to compare the cost and market value of each security investment at each balance sheet date. If the security is classified as a trading security and market is *more* than cost, the investment account is increased or debited so that the market value at the balance sheet date is reflected in the asset account. The corresponding credit is to *Unrealized Gain on Trading Securities*. If the market value is less than cost, the trading security account is decreased (or credited) and *Unrealized Loss on Trading Securities* is debited. The unrealized gain or loss is included in the income statement under the *Other Revenue and Expense* classification.

Example: Southwest Company, which began operations in 1998, had the following investments appropriately classified as trading securities at the end of 1998 and 1999.

December 31, 1998:

Company	Cost	Market Value	Unrealized Gain (Loss)
Alder Corporation	$ 20,000	$ 16,000	$(4,000)
Michaels Corporation	60,000	52,000	(8,000)
Chilly Company	40,000	46,000	6,000
Totals	$120,000	$114,000	$(6,000)

December 31, 1999:

Company	Book Value	Market Value	Unrealized Gain (Loss)
Alder Corporation	$ 16,000	$ 20,000	$4,000
Michaels Corporation	34,667	30,000	(4,667)
Chilly Company	46,000	54,000	8,000
Delaney Corporation	28,000	24,000	(4,000)
Totals	$124,667	$128,000	$3,333

Since cost exceeds market, the required 1998 year-end adjusting entry is:

Trading Securities (Chilly) (+A)	6,000	
Unrealized Loss on Trading Securities (Lo,-SE)	12,000	
Unrealized Gain on Trading Securities (Ga,+SE)		6,000
Trading Securities (Alder) (-A)		4,000
Trading Securities (Michaels) (-A)		8,000

The unrealized gain and loss will appear on Southwest's 1998 income statement.

During 1999, Southwest sold a third of its shares of Michaels for $26,000. Southwest has classified the investments as current.

The entry to record the sale of Michaels Corp. investment is:

Cash (+A)	26,000	
Trading Securities (Michaels) (-A)		17,333
Realized Gain on Sale of Trading Sec. (Ga,+SE)		8,667

Since the Michaels investment was written down to $52,000 at the end of 1999, the book value of the investment sold was $52,000 \div 3 = \$17,333$.

The adjusting entry for 1999 is:

Trading Securities (Alder) (+A)	4,000		
Trading Securities (Chilly) (+A)	8,000		
Unrealized Loss on Trading Securities (Lo,-SE)	8,667		
Unrealized Gain on Trading Securities (Ga,-SE)		12,000	
Trading Securities (Michaels) (-A)		4,667	
Trading Securities (Delaney) (-A)		4,000	

Available-for-Sale Security Investments

If the security is classified as available-for-sale, the investment may be classified as current or long-term, depending upon management's intention. The investment is accounted for under the cost method. An adjustment is made at the balance sheet date to mark the investment to market. Like the trading security mark-to-market result, the carrying value of the asset becomes its market value after the adjustment. Unlike trading securities, the unrealized gains and losses resulting from applying mark-to-market are recorded in unrealized price increases (decreases) accounts, which are shown directly in the stockholders' equity section of the balance sheet. When securities are sold, the realized gain (loss) on the investment sale is the difference between the securities original cost and its sale price.

Example: Using the Southwest Company example, the 1998 adjusting entry would be:

Available-for-Sale Securities (Chilly) (+A)	6,000		
Unrealized Price Decreases on AFS Securities (-SE)	12,000		
Unrealized Price Increases on AFS Sec. (+SE)			6,000
AFS Securities (Alder) (-A)		4,000	
AFS Securities (Michaels) (-A)		8,000	

The Unrealized Price Increase (Dec.) appears as an addition to (reduction of) stockholders' equity.

The entry to record the sale of Michaels Corp. investment is:

Cash (+A)	26,000		
Trading Securities (Michaels) (-A)		17,333	
Unrealized Price Decreases on AFS Securities (+SE)			2,667
Realized Gain on Sale of AFS Sec. (Ga,+SE)		6,000	

Since the Michaels investment was written down to $52,000 at the end of 1998, the book value of the investment sold was $52,000 ÷ 3 = $17,333. Unrealized Price Decreases contains the $8,000 Michaels write down. $2,667 of this amount relates to the one-third sold. As a result, the total amount credited is $20,000 ($17,333 + $2,667), the original cost. As a result, the realized gain amounts to $6,000, the difference between the sales price and the original cost.

The adjusting entry for 1999 is:

AFS Securities (Alder) (+A)	4,000	
AFS Securities (Chilly) (+A)	8,000	
Unrealized Price Decreases on AFS Sec. (-SE)	8,667	
Unrealized Price Decreases on AFS (+SE)		12,000
AFS Securities (Michaels) (-A)		4,667
AFS Securities (Delaney) (-A)		4,000

Other Long-Term Equity Investments

There are three different accounting methods available for long-term equity investments: (1) the *cost method*, (2) the *equity method*, and (3) *consolidation*. The choice of method depends on the degree of control exercised by the investor. The cost method is used when the investor exercises no control or significant influence over the investee. These securities are classified as available-for-sale. A rule of thumb is to use the cost method whenever an investor holds less than 20 percent of the investee's outstanding shares. The equity method is used to account for long-term investments in common stock in which the investor exercises significant influence over the investee. This method is normally used when an investor owns between 20 percent and 50 percent of the investee's outstanding shares. Consolidation is used when the investor owns a **controlling interest** in the investor. This method will normally be used when the investor owns more than 50 percent of the investee's outstanding shares.

The Equity Method

Under the equity method, the investor recognizes a proportionate share of the investee's earned net income as investment revenue and as an increase in the book value of the investment. Additionally, the investment account balance is reduced for any dividends received.

Example: On January 2, 1998, ABC Company purchased 30,000 shares of the common stock of Brown Corporation, a closely held company, for $450,000. During 1998 and 1999, Brown had 200,000 common shares outstanding. Brown reported net income of $400,000 and $300,000 in 1998 and 1999, respectively. Dividends paid by Brown were $160,000 in 1998 and $120,000 in 1999. Since ABC owns 15 percent of Brown's outstanding shares, ABC will recognize 15 percent of dividends and income each year.

Assuming that the investment allows ABC to exert significant influence over the operating and financing policies of Brown, prepare journal entries for ABC related to the investment in Brown for 1998 and 1999.

Equity Method Entries

1/02/98	Investment in Equity Securities (+A)	450,000	
	Cash (-A)		450,000
	Purchased 30,000 shares of Brown stock at $15.		
12/31/98	Investment in Equity Securities (+A)	60,000	
	Income from Equity Investments (R,+SE)		60,000
	Recognized 15% of Brown's 1998 net income.		
12/31/98	Cash (+A)	24,000	
	Investment in Equity Securities (-A)		24,000
	Received dividends from Brown.		
12/31/99	Investment in Equity Securities (+A)	45,000	
	Income from Equity Investments (R,+SE)		45,000
	Recognized 15% of Brown's 1999 net income.		
12/31/99	Cash (+A)	18,000	
	Investment in Equity Securities (-A)		18,000
	Received dividends from Brown.		

If Brown had incurred a net loss during the year, ABC must adjust its equity method entry accordingly. For example, assume that Brown incurred a net loss of $100,000 in 1998. The entry becomes:

12/31/98	Income from Equity Investments (Lo,-SE)	15,000	
	Investment in Equity Securities (-A)		15,000
	Recognized 15% of Brown's 1998 net loss.		

Consolidated Financial Statements

If an investor purchases a controlling interest in another company's equity securities (i.e., more than 50 percent of the outstanding shares), then we prepare financial statements as if the combined companies were a single reporting entity. This process is known as the preparation of consolidated financial statements. Your text (including the appendix) provides some examples on consolidated reporting. This topic is covered in more detail in courses in advanced financial accounting.

QUESTIONS FOR YOUR REVIEW

1. Which of the following accounting methods is not used for short-term investments in equity securities?
    a. Equity method
    b. Cost method
    c. Mark-to-market
    d. Any of these methods might be used.

2. Which of the following accounting methods is used for long-term investments in equity securities?
    a. Equity method
    b. Consolidation method
    c. Mark-to-market
    d. Any of these methods might be used.

3. A company received dividend payments of $500 from an investment appropriately carried under the equity method of accounting. Which of the following statements is true?
    a. Dividend Income is debited for $500.
    b. Dividend Income is credited for $500.
    c. The investment account is debited for $500.
    d. The investment account is credited for $500.

4. A company received dividend payments of $500 from an investment appropriately carried under the cost method of accounting. Which of the following statements is true?
    a. Dividend Income is debited for $500.
    b. Dividend Income is credited for $500.
    c. The investment account is debited for $500.
    d. The investment account is credited for $500.

5. The cost method should be used to account for an investment in equity securities when:
    a. the investor lacks any ability to control or significantly influence the operating activities of the investee.
    b. the investor can control the operating activities of the investee.
    c. the investor lacks the ability to control but can significantly influence the operating activities of the investee.
    d. the investor owns a majority interest in the investee's common stock.

6. The equity method should be used to account for an investment in equity securities when:
    a. the investor lacks any ability to control or significantly influence the operating activities of the investee.
    b. the investor can control the operating activities of the investee.
    c. the investor lacks the ability to control but can significantly influence the operating activities of the investee.
    d. the investor owns a majority interest in the investee's common stock.

7. Which of the following is not an equity security?
   a. Common stock
   b. Stock warrant
   c. Convertible bond
   d. Stock option

8. Which of the following is used to determine whether an equity security should be classified as a current or a noncurrent asset?
   a. The maturity date.
   b. Any investments held over six months must be classified as noncurrent assets.
   c. Any investments costing over $10,000 must be classified as noncurrent assets.
   d. The classification is based on the intentions of management.

9. Investments in available-for-sale equity securities, carried under the cost method, require a mark-to-market adjustment. Which of the following statements is true regarding unrealized price changes?
   a. Only unrealized price changes not deemed to be permanent will affect reported net income.
   b. Only unrealized price changes on trading securities investments affect reported net income.
   c. Only unrealized losses reduce reported net income.
   d. Only unrealized price changes on available-for-sale investments affect reported net income.

10. Which of the following investments would most likely be reported using the equity method of accounting?
    a. The investor owns 35 percent of the investee's preferred stock.
    b. The investor owns 35 percent of the investee's common stock.
    c. The investor owns 65 percent of the investee's preferred stock.
    d. The investor owns 65 percent of the investee's common stock.

11. Byrd's Basketballs Inc. purchased 20 percent of the outstanding common shares of the Magic Company on January 1, 1999, for $60,000 cash. During 1999, Magic reported net income of $40,000 and paid dividends of $10,000. Assuming that this investment is appropriately carried under the cost method, what is the amount of investment income that would appear on Byrd's 1999 income statement?
    a. $2,000
    b. $8,000
    c. $10,000
    d. $40,000

12. Byrd's Basketballs Inc. purchased 20 percent of the outstanding common shares of the Magic Company on January 1, 1999, for $60,000 cash. During 1999, Magic reported net income of $40,000 and paid dividends of $10,000. Assuming that this investment is appropriately carried under the equity method, what is the amount of investment income that would appear on Byrd's 1999 income statement?
   a. $2,000
   b. $8,000
   c. $10,000
   d. $40,000

13. Byrd's Basketballs Inc. purchased 20 percent of the outstanding common shares of the Magic Company on January 1, 1999, for $60,000 cash. During 1999, Magic reported net income of $40,000 and paid dividends of $10,000. Assuming that this investment is appropriately carried under the equity method, what is the correct ending balance of the investment account that would appear on Byrd's 1999 balance sheet?
   a. $60,000
   b. $66,000
   c. $68,000
   d. $70,000

14. Which of the following uses the mark-to-market rule?
   a. Equity method
   b. Long-term nonmarketable equity securities
   c. The cost method for available-for-sale investments
   d. Consolidation method

Use the following information to answer questions 15 through 17.

Carolina Corporation holds the following securities in its current portfolio of trading securities.

		Market Value at December 31	
Company	Cost	1998	1999
Sparky, Inc.	$5,000	$5,200	$4,800
Rover, Inc.	2,500	2,200	2,200

Assume Sparky is properly classified as a trading security and Rover as an available-for-sale security.

15. The required adjustment at December 31, 1998 for the investment in Sparky is:
   a. Trading Securities (+A)   200
         Unrealized Gain on Trading Sec. (Ga, +SE)   200
   b. Trading Securities (+A)   200
         Unrealized Price Inc. on Trading Sec. (+SE)   200
   c. Trading Securities (+A)   200
         Realized Gain on Trading Sec. (Ga,+SE)   200
   d. Trading Securities (+A)   200
         Realized Price Inc. on Trading Sec. (+SE)   200

16. Which of the following adjusting entries is required at December 31, 1998, for the Rover investment?

a.	Unrealized Loss on AFS Securities (Lo,-SE)	300	
	Available-for-Sale Sec. (-A)		300
b.	Unrealized Price Dec. on AFS Securities (-SE)	300	
	Available-for-Sale Sec. (-A)		300
c.	Realized Loss on AFS Securities (Lo,-SE)	300	
	Available-for-Sale Sec. (-A)		300
d.	Realized Price Dec. on AFS Securities (-SE)	300	
	Available-for-Sale Sec. (-A)		300

17. Assume that during 1999, Carolina sells its investment in Rover for $2,100. The entry to record the sale is:

a.	Unrealized Loss on AFS Sale (Lo,-SE)	400	
	Cash(+A)	2,100	
	Available-for-Sale Sec. (-A)		2,200
	Unrealized Price Decrease (+SE)		300
b.	Realized Loss on AFS Sale (Lo,-SE)	400	
	Cash(+A)	2,100	
	Available-for-Sale Sec. (-A)		2,200
	Unrealized Price Decrease (+SE)		300
c.	Realized Loss on AFS Sale (Lo,-SE)	100	
	Cash(+A)	2,100	
	Available-for-Sale Sec. (-A)		2,200
d.	Unrealized Price Decrease on AFS (Lo,-SE)	100	
	Cash(+A)	2,100	
	Available-for-Sale Sec. (-A)		2,200

Use the following information to answer questions 18 through 19.

On January 1, 1999, Spartan Corporation made long-term investments in Hoosier and Buckeye Companies. Information on those investments and their 1999 income and dividends follows:

Company	Hoosier	Buckeye
Total price	$400,000	$250,000
Ownership percent	15%	30%
Net income	$100,000	$45,000
Dividends	$30,000	$12,500

18. Assuming that Spartan had no other investments, what amount of dividend income will it report for 1999?
    a. $42,500
    b. $30,000
    c. $8,250
    d. $4,500

19. On January 1, 2000, what is the total book value of Spartan's portfolio (assuming that there were no changes in the market value of the investments)?
    a. $651,000
    b. $659,750
    c. $700,000
    d. $719,500

20. On July 1, 1999, the Nittany Corporation made the following trading security investment:

    200 shares of Wolverine Company for $4,000

    On December 31, 1999, the market price for Wolverine Company was $30 per share. What entry (if any) is necessary when Nittany closes their books on December 31, 1999?
    a. Trading Securities (+A)   2,000
         Unrealized Gain on Trad. Sec. (Ga,+SE)   2,000
    b. Trading Securities (+A)   2,000
         Unrealized Price Inc. on Trad. Sec. (+SE)   2,000
    c. Trading Securities (+A)   2,000
         Realized Gain on Trad. Sec. (Ga,+SE)   2,000
    d. No entry is necessary.

21. Jayhawk Corporation had the following transactions related to its investments in available-for-sale equity securities during 1999. Jayhawk had no securities investments prior to 1999. All securities are correctly classified as current assets, and none of the investments are large enough to allow significant operating influence. Prepare all required journal entries and adjusting entries.

    1/5   Purchased 5,000 shares of Wildcat Company for $15 each.

    3/13   Purchased 1,000 shares of Gopher Inc. for $20 each.

    4/25   Sold 500 shares of Wildcat Company for $18 each.

6/30   Received dividends from Gopher Inc. in the amount of $1,200.

9/2   Purchased 500 shares of Hawkeye Corporation for $30 per share.

12/15   Received notice that Gopher Inc. had declared a dividend of $1.50 per share, to be paid on January 6, 2000.

12/31   Noted the following market values per share:
    Wildcat Company $21
    Gopher Inc.   10
    Hawkeye Corporation 32

22. During 1998, Buffalo Corporation made the following trading security investments in stock:

   10 shares of Beta Company common at $30 per share
   25 shares of Chuckie Company common at $20 per share

At the end of the fiscal year, Beta Company stock was selling for $40 per share and Chuckie Company for $15 per share.

During 1999, Buffalo sold 10 shares of Chuckie Company for $23 per share. Buffalo also purchased 20 shares of Delta Company for $14 per share.

At the end of 1999, Buffalo's stock had the following market values:

   Beta Company $35 per share
   Chuckie Company $25 per share
   Delta Company $10 per share

Required: Record all transactions related to Buffalo's investments during 1998 and 1999. Also prepare any required year-end adjusting entries.

23. Anthony Industries Inc. made the following available-for-sale investments during 1998:

   100 shares of Clement Corporation for $62 per share
   325 shares of Lion Corporation for $27 per share

At the end of 1998, market prices for the stock were:

   Clement $70 per share
   Lion $22 per share

During 1999 Anthony made no other investments. The end of the year market prices for the stock were:

   Clement $71 per share
   Lion $25 per share

Required: Record all transactions related to Anthony's investments during 1998 and 1999. Also prepare any required year-end adjusting entries.

24. Hawkeye Corporation purchased the following long-term investments in 1999:

   200 shares, or 45 percent of Badger Company for $100 per share
   600 shares, or 30 percent of Illini Industrials for $20 per share

Year-end information on the investments is:

Company	Badger	Illini
Market price per share	$145	$37
Net income	$42,392	$56,436
Dividends per share	$0.27	$1.21

Required: Record all of the journal entries Hawkeye will make regarding its long-term investments.

CHAPTER 8-SOLUTIONS

1.	a	6.	c	11.	a	16.	b
2.	d	7.	c	12.	b	17.	b
3.	d	8.	d	13.	b	18.	d
4.	b	9.	b	14.	c	19.	b
5.	a	10.	b	15.	a	20.	a

21. 1/5   AFS Securities (+A)   75,000
          Cash (-A)   75,000
          Purchased 5,000 shares of Wildcat
          Company for $15 each.

     3/13 AFS Securities (+A)   20,000
          Cash (-A)   20,000
          Purchased 1,000 shares of Gopher
          Inc. for $20 each.

     4/25 Cash (+A)   9,000
          AFS Securities (-A)   7,500
          Realized Gain on Sale of Mark. Sec. (Ga,+SE)   1,500
          Sold 500 shares of Wildcat
          Company for $18 each.

     6/30 Cash (+A)   1,200
          Dividend Income (R,+SE)   1,200
          Received dividends from Gopher
          Inc. in the amount of $1,200.

     9/ 2 AFS Securities (+A)   15,000
          Cash (-A)   15,000
          Purchased 500 shares of Hawkeye
          Corporation for $30 per share.

     12/15 Dividends Receivable (+A)   1,500
          Dividend Income (R,+SE)   1,500
          Received notice that Gopher Inc.
          had declared a dividend of $1.50
          per share, to be paid on January 6, 2000.

12/31	AFS Securities (Wildcat) (+A)	27,000	
	Unrealized Price Increase on AFS Sec. (+SE)		27,000
12/31	Unrealized Price Decrease on AFS Sec. (-SE)	10,000	
	AFS Securities (Gopher) (-A)		10,000
	AFS Securities (Hawkeye) (+A)	1,000	
	Unrealized Price Increase on AFS Sec (+SE)		1,000
	Mark-to-market adjustment.		

22.   <u>1998</u>

Trading Securities (+A)	300	
Cash (-A)		300
Purchased 10 shares of Beta		
Company common at $30/share.		
Trading Securities (+A)	500	
Cash (-A)		500
Purchased 25 shares of Chuckie		
Company common at $20/share.		

<u>December 31, 1998</u>

<u>Company</u>	<u>Cost</u>	<u>Market</u>
Beta Company	$300	$400
Chuckie Company	<u> 500</u>	<u> 375</u>
Totals	<u>$800</u>	<u>$775</u>

Trading Securities (Beta) (+A)	100	
Unrealized Loss on Trad. Sec. (Lo,-SE)	25	
Trading Securities (Chuckie) (-A)		125

<u>1999</u>

Cash (+A)	230	
Trading Securities (-A)		150
Realized Gain on Sale of Mark. Sec. (R,+SE)		80
Sold 10 shares of Chuckie Company		
common at $23/share.		

Trading Securities (+A)	280	
Cash (-A)		280

Purchased 20 shares of Delta Company
common at $14/share.

December 31, 1999

Company	Cost	Market
Beta Company	$400	$350
Chuckie Company	225	375
Delta Company	280	200
Totals	$905	$925

Trading Securities (Chuckie) (+A)	150	
Unrealized Gain on Trad. Sec. (Ga,+SE)		20
Trading Securities (Beta) (-A)		50
Trading Securities (Delta) (-A)		80

23. <u>1998</u>

AFS Securities (Clement) (+A)	6,200	
Cash (-A)		6,200

Purchased 100 shares of Clement
Corporation for $62/share.

AFS Securities (Lion) (+A)	8,775	
Cash (-A)		8,775

Purchased 325 shares of Lion
Corporation for $27/share.

Company	Cost	1998	1999
Clement	$ 6,200	$ 7,000	$ 7,100
Lion	8,775	7,150	8,125
Totals	$14,975	$14,150	$15,225

December 31, 1998

AFS Sec. (Clement) (+A)	800	
Unrealized Price Increase on AFS Sec.(+SE)		800
Unrealized Price Decrease on AFS Sec. (-SE)	1,625	
AFS Sec. (Lion) (-A)		1,625

December 31, 1999

AFS Sec. (Clement) (+A)	100	
Unrealized Price Increase on AFS Sec.(+SE)		100
AFS Sec. (Lion) (+A)	975	
Unrealized Price Increase on AFS Sec.(+SE)		975

24.
Investment in Equity Securities (+A)	20,000.00	
Cash (-A)		20,000.00

*Purchased 200 shares of Badger Company
for $100/share.*

Investment in Equity Securities (+A)	12,000.00	
Cash (-A)		12,000.00

*Purchased 600 shares of Illini
Industrials for $20/share.*

Investment in Equity Securities (+A)	19,076.40	
Income from Equity Investments (R,+SE)		19,076.40

Recognized 45% of Badger net income.

Investment in Equity Securities (+A)	16,930.80	
Income from Equity Investment (R,+SE)		16,930.80

Recognized 30% of Illini net income.

Cash (+A)	54.00	
Investment in Equity Securities (-A)		54.00

Received dividends from Badger.

Cash (+A)	726.00	
Investment in Equity Securities (-A)		726.00

Received dividends from Illini.

CHAPTER 9

Long-Lived Assets

REVIEW OF KEY CONCEPTS

This chapter discusses accounting for a group of productive assets. The basic principles discussed in previous chapters still apply. The long-lived assets discussed here differ primarily in that they are used to produce goods and services provided by the business over future time periods. These are *operating assets*. The value in future periods is derived from operating activities; management does not intend to sell these assets in the normal course of business. We discuss accounting for asset acquisition and disposal, as well as accounting during the holding period. Due to the economic nature and long life of these assets, holding period accounting is critically important.

There are several major types of long-lived assets. **Land** is often owned as a location for the company's operating activities. **Fixed assets** include buildings, machinery, furniture, and equipment used in the daily operations of the company. **Intangible assets** are long-lived assets that have value in the rights conveyed to the company, rather than in their physical substance. Examples in this category include patents, copyrights, trademarks, and goodwill. Observe that the physical value of the paper on which a patent is printed is of little value. However, the 17-year exclusive right to produce a product protected by the government's patent may produce significant future revenues for the company. **Natural resources** such as rights to extract coal, petroleum, timber, or other minerals are a significant source of revenues in many industries. The final category of long-lived assets is **deferred costs**. Deferred costs are a miscellaneous type of long-lived asset and could include long-term prepaid expenses, organization costs, and similar items. Accounting for these different groups of long-lived assets is virtually identical. There are only minor differences in details of calculations and identification of these categories on the balance sheet.

Recording Long-Lived Asset Acquisitions

Recall the basic rule in accounting for acquisition of assets. *Assets are recorded based on their historical cost, which includes the purchase price plus all costs to get the asset into the condition and location for its intended use.* There are no particular problems in accounting for acquisitions of long-lived assets. The only differences from other assets we have studied are in the types of additional costs included in the recorded amounts for these assets.

For example, a company acquires land on which it intends to construct a new retail store. Land should be recorded at its cost plus all costs to get the asset into the condition and location for its intended use. These additional costs for a land purchase include legal fees, title search costs, surveying costs, and other closing costs. If the land has an existing structure which must be removed, then demolition costs are added to the land account. If the company can salvage the old building materials, then any proceeds from sales of salvage material should be netted (credited) against the balance in the land account. If a company purchases machinery for use in a factory, it may face significant additional costs for delivery and installation. These costs are considered a part of the total cost of the machinery and should be *capitalized*. Recall that to capitalize a cost means to add it to the balance in an asset account and amortize the cost over future time periods benefited by use of the asset.

Lump-sum purchases are common for fixed assets. Often a company will purchase land and an existing building. Allocation of the lump-sum purchase price is important, since land has an indefinite life. Land, therefore, is not amortized. It is important to assign a reasonable amount to the building account, as amortization of this asset will impact net income in future periods.

Example: Gopher Corporation purchases an existing bookstore operation. Gopher pays $300,000 for the land, building, store fixtures and equipment, and existing inventory. Gopher must use estimated fair market values for these assets in order to make the proper allocation to the balance sheet accounts. Gopher estimates the fair market values of the purchased assets as follows:

Land	$100,000
Building	200,000
Inventory	50,000
Fixtures and equipment	50,000
	$400,000

The allocation of the cost is based on the assets' relative fair market values.

Asset	Allocation Formula	Allocated Cost
Land	($100,000 ÷ $400,000) x $300,000	$ 75,000
Building	($200,000 ÷ $400,000) x $300,000	150,000
Inventory	($50,000 ÷ $400,000) x $300,000	37,500
Fixtures	($50,000 ÷ $400,000) x $300,000	37,500
		$300,000

Accounting During the Holding Period

Operating assets provide benefits to the company over future periods of time. These assets are used to produce revenues over their estimated useful life. Proper application of the matching principle requires that the cost of these assets be allocated over the time periods to be benefited. The cost allocation process produces annual amortization expense, which is the cost allocated to a specific time period due to the use of long-lived assets. Accountants use special terms to identify the amortization of various types of assets.

Buildings, equipment, and other physical assets used in the business are often referred to as either fixed assets or property, plant, and equipment. Amortization arising from the use of these assets is known as depreciation expense. There is no external transaction that creates depreciation expense. Depreciation expense is recorded using an adjusting journal entry, as follows:

Depreciation Expense (E,-SE)	XXX	
Accumulated Depreciation (-A)		XXX

Estimates Required in Accounting for Long-Lived Assets

Long-lived assets provide benefits for many future time periods. For example, a factory building may be used for 20 years or more. One can never be certain of the physical or economic life of such an asset. For accounting purposes, it is necessary to estimate the useful economic life, which may differ from the asset's physical life. It may take over 100 years for a modern concrete and steel building to physically collapse. However, that building may only be useful as an efficient production facility for say, twenty years. It is this productive life that constitutes the building's *economic useful life*. Proper application of the matching principle would allocate the cost of this building to the twenty years over which it is expected to provide revenues from the manufacture of the company's products. Since technology is constantly changing, often rapidly, management can do no better than to estimate the building's economic life.

It is also necessary to estimate the **salvage value** or **residual value** of productive assets. This is the amount at which the asset can be sold, once it has outlived its usefulness to the company. A company should not allocate the total cost of an asset purchased for $500,000 as an expense if the company can sell it at a later date (the end of its estimated economic useful life) for $300,000.

Depreciation Methods and Computations

Chapter 9 of your text provides a good description of alternative depreciation methods. The focus in the study guide is on the basic concepts and limits examples to the straight-line method. There are several exercises to allow you to practice computations from the alternative methods that you have learned from the text. It is worthwhile to take some time to explore the conceptual basis for the various **accelerated depreciation** methods.

Straight-Line Method

The simplest method to calculate depreciation expense is the straight-line method. Under the straight-line method, the annual expense is calculated by dividing the **depreciation base** by the estimated useful life of the asset. The depreciation base is simply the amount to be depreciated; it is calculated by subtracting the salvage value from the asset's historical cost.

Example. Spartan Construction purchases a piece of heavy equipment for $370,000. In addition, Spartan pays delivery costs of $6,000 and installation costs of $11,000. The equipment is estimated to have a useful life, under normal operating conditions, of ten years. At the end of its normal life, Spartan estimates it can sell the used equipment for $40,000.

The historical cost for the equipment is $387,000, the total cost to purchase the asset and get it into the condition and location for its intended use. The depreciation base for the equipment is $347,000, the historical cost less the estimated salvage value. Under the straight-line method, the annual depreciation expense is $34,700. The adjusting entry to record the depreciation is:

Depreciation Expense (E,-SE)   34,700
      Accumulated Depreciation (-A)   34,700

Accelerated Depreciation Methods

Accelerated depreciation methods are illustrated in the text. These methods charge a greater depreciation expense in the early years of an asset's life than that obtained using the straight-line method. However, in later years, these methods will result in a lower expense than the straight-line method. All depreciation methods will result in the same total depreciation expense over the life of the asset. The asset's total cost is allocated over its total life. The alternative methods affect only the amounts charged in individual years.

Accelerated depreciation methods attempt to provide a smoothing of total operating expense over the life of an asset. If you purchase a new automobile, you are likely to experience very low maintenance and repair costs in the first few years of its life (perhaps even zero if you have a good warranty). As the vehicle ages, repair costs increase. If you depreciate the vehicle using the straight-line method, you would record a higher total operating expense (depreciation expense plus repair and maintenance expense) in the later years. If you use accelerated depreciation, the lower depreciation expense of later years is combined with the higher repair costs to yield approximately equal total operating expense over each year of the asset's life.

Amortization of Other Long-Lived Assets

If you have carefully followed your text, you should realize that amortization of long-lived assets other than fixed assets is accomplished in an almost identical manner. Accountants employ different terms for the expense. For example amortization of an intangible asset is referred to as amortization expense and amortization of a natural resource is referred to as depletion expense. The methods used to calculate amortization also differ to reflect underlying economic differences in the way in which these assets generate future revenues. Accelerated amortization methods are rarely used for intangible assets. Depletion expense is normally calculated using the production method. These are only minor differences in terminology and details. The basic amortization or cost allocation concept is identical for all long-lived assets.

Betterments versus Maintenance Expense

Long-lived assets differ from assets discussed in previous chapters in that a company will often make additional expenditures related to the asset over its extended useful life. These expenditures fall into two categories: betterments and maintenance. Maintenance costs are routine costs to maintain the asset in proper working order. For example, changing the engine oil and other minor repairs would be considered maintenance for a personal automobile. Maintenance costs are expensed in the period in which they are incurred.

Betterments are expenditures made to improve the long-lived asset. Betterments are capitalized costs. The cost of a betterment is added to the asset account balance and depreciated over the remaining life of the asset. A betterment is an expenditiure that (1) increases the useful life of the asset, (2) increases the quality of the asset's output, (3) increases the quantity of the asset's output, or (4) reduces the operating costs of the asset.

Example. Return to the last example, and assume that Spartan made the following expenditures during the third year of the asset's life. Spartan paid $20,000 for a new computerized control panel. The new part will allow the machine to operate more smoothly and will increase its output by 20 percent. The smoother operating control will also increase the life of the equipment by two years. Spartan also paid $1,200 to lubricate the machine. Lubrication is required approximately every three years. Spartan makes the following entries during the year.

Maintenance Expense (E,-SE)	1,200	
Cash (-A)		1,200
Recognized ordinary lubrication costs.		
Equipment (+A)	20,000	
Cash (-A)		20,000
Recognized betterment control panel.		
Depreciation Expense (E,-SE)	29,760	
Accumulated Depreciation (-A)		29,760
Recognized depreciation based on the betterment.		

Depreciation is calculated as follows. The betterment cost is added to the historical cost of the asset, bringing total cost up to $407,000. The salvage value is deducted to arrive at the revised depreciation base of $367,000. However, only $297,600 of the depreciation base remains to be depreciated, since depreciation expense in the first two years of operations totaled $69,400. The estimated useful life is extended two years by the betterment. The equipment has a remaining life of ten years. The depreciation calculation is made by taking the remaining depreciation base and dividing it by the revised remaining estimated life ($297,600/10 years = $29,760 per year).

This provides a general rule for changes in accounting estimates. Accounting estimate changes are only accounted for in current and future periods. Prior periods' revenues and expenses are unaffected. In the case of changes related to the depreciation expense estimate, current and future depreciation will be calculated by expensing the *revised remaining depreciation base* over the *revised remaining useful life* of the asset.

Disposal of Long-Lived Assets

The basic accounting entry to record disposal of a long-lived asset is no different from that of any other asset. The selling company will record the asset received in the exchange and eliminate the existing asset from its accounts. Any difference between selling price and book value (or carrying value) is recorded as a gain or loss on the sale.

For example, Hawkeye Corporation purchased land on which it intended to build a storage facility. Hawkeye paid $250,000 for the land. Hawkeye's plans have now changed, and it sells the land for $270,000. The journal entry to record the sale is:

Cash (+A)	270,000	
Land (-A)		250,000
Gain on Sale (Ga,+SE)		20,000
Sold land for gain.		

If the asset has been depreciated, then the company must also remove the related accumulated depreciation balance when the asset is sold. For example, assume Hawkeye Corporation sold equipment which originally cost $150,000 for $80,000. Up to the date of the sale, Hawkeye has recorded total depreciation expense of $50,000. The journal entry to record the sale is:

Cash (+A)	80,000	
Accumulated Depreciation (+A)	50,000	
Loss on Sale (Lo,-SE)	20,000	
Equipment (-A)		150,000
Sold equipment for loss.		

The loss on sale (or gain on sale) of long-lived assets is included as a component of operating expense on the company's income statement.

QUESTIONS FOR YOUR REVIEW

1. Which of the following long-lived assets is not subject to amortization?
    a. A copyright on a science fiction novel
    b. A patent for an underwater camera
    c. A trademark
    d. A long-term investment in marketable equity securities

2. Hoosier Corporation purchased a delivery truck on October 30, 1999. The following costs were incurred with the purchase of the truck.

Purchase price	$40,000
Sales tax on purchase price	800
Interest on the loan to buy	2,000
Spare parts inventory	800
Freight charges on delivery	500

    How much should Hoosier debit to the truck account?
    a. $40,800
    b. $41,300
    c. $42,800
    d. $44,100

3.   The book value of an asset reported on the balance sheet is a measure of:
     a.   estimated fair market value.
     b.   estimated replacement cost.
     c.   realizable value.
     d.   historical cost less depreciation expense taken to date.

4.   Which of the following costs should be excluded from the asset account for the purchase of factory production equipment?
     a.   Building improvements
     b.   Freight charges
     c.   Installation charges
     d.   Sales tax paid on the equipment

5.   The primary purpose of depreciation expense is to:
     a.   provide a cash reserve for replacement when the asset becomes obsolete.
     b.   match costs with revenues.
     c.   inform investors of asset replacement cost.
     d.   reflect changes in the fair market value of an asset.

6.   The allocation of the cost of natural resources is termed:
     a.   amortization expense.
     b.   depreciation expense.
     c.   depletion expense.
     d.   production expense.

7.   Which of the following costs is excluded from the land account for land purchased for use in a manufacturing process?
     a.   Demolition of an existing building
     b.   Real estate broker's commissions and fees
     c.   Interest on a mortgage loan made to purchase the land
     d.   Appraisal fees, survey fees, and other real estate closing costs

8.   The portion of a lump-sum purchase of $600,000 allocated to Land when the land is appraised at $180,000 and the building on the land is appraised at $540,000 is:
     a. $60,000
     b. $150,000
     c. $180,000
     d. $200,000

9.   Land and a building are purchased for $300,000. The appraised values of the land and building are $45,000 and $180,000, respectively. The building should be recorded at:
     a. $60,000
     b. $180,000
     c. $225,000
     d. $240,000

10. A gain on sale of a long-lived asset is recorded when:
    a. selling price exceeds the book value of the asset sold.
    b. selling price exceeds the historical cost of the asset sold.
    c. book value exceeds the selling price of the asset sold.
    d. selling price exceeds the fair market value of the asset sold.

11. Which depreciation method produces the highest depreciation expense for the first year of an asset's life?
    a. Straight-line
    b. Sum-of-the-year's-digits
    c. Double-declining-balance
    d. It's impossible to tell without more information.

12. Nittany Company acquired a new machine at a cost of $76,000, with an expected salvage value of $4,000 and estimated life of eight years. Using the sum-of-the-years'-digits method, depreciation expense for the *second year* of the asset's life is:
    a. $4,000
    b. $4,222
    c. $14,000
    d. $14,788

13. Nittany Company acquired a new machine at a cost of $76,000, with an expected salvage value of $4,000 and estimated life of eight years. What is depreciation expense for the *second year*, using the double-declining balance method?
    a. $13,500
    b. $14,250
    c. $19,000
    d. $25,000

14. Nittany Company acquired a new machine at a cost of $76,000, with an expected salvage value of $4,000 and estimated life of eight years. Assuming Nittany depreciated this machine using the straight-line method, what would be the accumulated depreciation after the third year?
    a. $18,000
    b. $19,000
    c. $27,000
    d. $28,500

15. Johnson Inc. sells a building that cost $75,000 on June 1, 1996. At that time it was estimated that the building would have a useful life of ten years with a salvage value of $15,000. The building was sold on June 1, 1999, for $54,000. If the straight-line depreciation method was used, what is the gain or loss on disposal?
    a. $12,000 gain
    b. $12,000 loss
    c. $3,000 loss
    d. $3,000 gain

16. On January 1, 1999, the Holland Brewing Corporation purchased new equipment costing $270,000 with an estimated useful life of five years. Salvage value was estimated to be $30,000. Using the sum-of-the-years'-digits method of depreciation, what would be depreciation expense for the year ending December 31, 1999?
    a. $16,000
    b. $48,000
    c. $80,000
    d. $90,000

17. On January 1, 1995, Boilermakers Inc. purchased a new boiler for $1,000,000. The boiler had an expected life of nine years and an expected salvage value of $100,000. On January 1, 1999, Boilermakers spent $240,000 for a renovation to the boiler, which extended the useful life by five years (14 years total). Salvage value is unchanged. If Boilermakers uses the straight-line method of depreciation, what is the depreciation expense for 1999?
    a. $84,000
    b. $74,000
    c. $60,000
    d. $50,000

Use the following information to answer questions 18 through 20.

On January 1, 1999, Eagle Corporation purchased new equipment at a total cost of $88,000. Eagle expects to use the equipment for five years with a salvage value of $8,000 after the fifth year.

18. What is depreciation expense for the fourth year using the sum-of-the-years'-digits method of depreciation?
    a. $10,667
    b. $11,732
    c. $21,332
    d. $23,468

19. What is the book value after two years using the straight-line method of depreciation?
    a. $40,000
    b. $48,000
    c. $52,000
    d. $56,000

20. After two years, Eagle revised the useful life from five to six years. Salvage value is unchanged. What is depreciation expense for year 3 using the straight-line method? (Assume straight-line had been used in the previous two years. Round answer to nearest whole dollar).
    a. $9,600
    b. $12,000
    c. $13,332
    d. $14,668

21. On January 1, 1999, Raven Construction purchased new equipment costing $920,000. The equipment was expected to be in service for ten years after which it would be worth $40,000. Raven's fiscal year ends on December 31.

    Raven is considering three alternative depreciation methods for the new equipment. Raven's management would like to choose the method which will provide the maximum total depreciation expense over the first three years of the life of the new equipment. Calculate depreciation expense for years 1 through 3, using the following methods.

    a.   Straight-line method

    b.   Sum-of-the-years'-digits method

    c.   Double-declining-balance method

22. Chanticleer Corporation purchased a retail outlet for $600,000 on January 1, 1999. The price included land, building, and equipment. A professional appraiser estimates the land is worth $225,000, the building $360,000, and the equipment $315,000. Chanticleer depreciates all assets using the straight-line method. Salvage value is estimated as 10 percent of an asset's historical cost. Chanticleer estimates that a building will normally last 20 years and equipment must be replaced every ten years.

    Required: Prepare all required journal entries and adjusting entries related to the purchased assets for the year ended December 31, 1999.

23. A piece of equipment that cost $16,200 and on which $9,000 of accumulated depreciation had been recorded was disposed of an January 2, the first day of business of the current year.

    a. What is the correct journal entry if the equipment was scrapped?

    b. What is the correct journal entry if the equipment was sold for $3,000 cash?

c.   What is the correct journal entry if the equipment was sold for $9,000 cash?

d.   The equipment is traded in on other equipment having a list price of $24,000. A $7,800 trade-in is allowed and the balance is paid in cash. What is the correct journal entry? (Gains and losses are to be recognized.)

e.   The equipment is traded in on other equipment having a list price of $24,000. A $3,600 trade-in is allowed and the balance is paid in cash. What is the correct journal entry? (Gains and losses are to be recognized.)

f.   The equipment is traded in on other equipment having a list price of $24,000. A $3,600 trade-in is allowed and the balance is paid in cash. What is the correct journal entry? (Gains and losses are not recognized.)

24. Big Time Publishing Company purchased the copyright to a basic accounting textbook for $50,000. The usual life of a textbook is about five years. However, the copyright will remain in effect for another 75 years. Prepare the journal entry to record the annual amortization expense on the copyright?

25. Michigan Mining Corporation purchased land containing an estimated 10 million tons of iron ore for a cost of $4,400,000. The land without the iron ore is estimated to be worth $1,800,000. The company expects that all the usable iron can be mined in ten years. Buildings costing $600,000 with an estimated useful life of twenty years were erected on the site. Equipment costing $700,000 with an estimated useful life of ten years was installed. Because of the remote location, neither the buildings nor the equipment has an estimated residual value. During its first year of operations, Michigan Mining mined and sold one million tons of iron ore.

    a. Prepare the journal entry to record the depletion expense for the first year of operations?

    b. What is the amount of annual depreciation expense for the buildings if Michigan Mining wishes to make it *proportional* to the depletion expense?

CHAPTER 9-SOLUTIONS

1.	d	6.	c	11.	c	16.	c
2.	b	7.	c	12.	c	17.	b
3.	d	8.	b	13.	b	18.	a
4.	a	9.	d	14.	c	19.	d
5.	b	10.	a	15.	c	20.	b

21. a. Straight-line method
    Depreciation Base = Cost - Salvage value
    $$= \$920,000 - \$40,000$$
    $$= \$880,000$$

    Depreciation Expense = Depreciation base $\div$ Estimated life
    $$= \$880,000 / 10 \text{ years}$$
    $$= \$88,000 \text{ per year}$$

    Total Depreciation Expense-Years 1 through 3 = \$264,000

   b. Sum-of-the-years'-digits method
    Sum of the years' digits = $10 + 9 + \ldots + 1 = 55$
    Depreciation expense = Depreciation base x factor
    The factor changes over time. The denominator will be the sum of the years' digits. The numerator will be the number of years of estimated life remaining as of the beginning of the current year.

    Year 1: Depreciation Expense = \$880,000 x 10/55 =   \$160,000
    Year 2: Depreciation Expense = \$880,000 x 9/55 =   144,000
    Year 3: Depreciation Expense = \$880,000 x 8/55 =   128,000
         Total Depreciation Expense =   \$432,000

   c. Double-declining-balance method
    The estimated useful life is ten years. This gives a straight-line rate of 10 percent per year for Depreciation Expense. Double-declining balance depreciation expense is calculated by multiplying the book value of an asset times the declining balance rate. The book value (carrying value) of an asset is its cost less accumulated depreciation taken to date. Since the straight-line rate is 10 percent, the double-declining balance rate will be 20 percent.

    Year 1: \$920,000 x 0.20   =   \$184,000
    Year 2: (\$920,000 - \$184,000) x 0.20   =   147,200
    Year 3: (\$920,000 - \$184,000 - \$147,200) x 0.20   =   117,760
         Total Depreciation Expense   =   \$448,960

22. | | | |
|---|---|---|
| Land (+A) | 150,000 | |
| Building (+A) | 240,000 | |
| Equipment (+A) | 210,000 | |
| Cash (-A) | | 600,000 |

Purchased fixed assets.

Asset	Allocation Formula	Allocated Cost
Land	($225,000 ÷ $900,000) x $600,000	$150,000
Building	($360,000 ÷ $900,000) x $600,000	240,000
Equipment	($315,000 ÷ $900,000) x $600,000	210,000
		$600,000

Depreciation Expense (E,-SE)	10,800	
Accumulated Depreciation (-A)		10,800

Recognized annual depreciation on building.
[($240,000 - $24,000) x 1/20]

Depreciation Expense (E,-SE)	18,900	
Accumulated Depreciation (-A)		18,900

Recognized annual depreciation on equipment.
[($210,000 - $21,000) x 1/10]

23. a.
Accumulated Depreciation (+A)	9,000	
Loss on Retirement (E,-SE)	7,200	
Equipment (-A)		16,200

Disposed of asset with no salvage value.

b.
Cash (+A)	3,000	
Accumulated Depreciation (+A)	9,000	
Loss on Retirement (E,-SE)	4,200	
Equipment (-A)		16,200

Disposed of asset with $3,000 salvage value.

c.
Cash (+A)	9,000	
Accumulated Depreciation (+A)	9,000	
Equipment (-A)		16,200
Gain on Retirement (R,+SE)		1,800

Disposed of asset with $9,000 salvage value.

d.
Equipment (+A)	24,000	
Accumulated Depreciation (+A)	9,000	
Equipment (-A)		16,200
Cash (-A)		16,200
Gain on Retirement (R,+SE)		600

Traded asset with $7,800 trade-in allowance.

e. Equipment (+A)   24,000
    Accumulated Depreciation (+A)   9,000
    Loss on Retirement (E,-SE)   3,600
        Equipment (-A)   16,200
        Cash (-A)   20,400
    Traded asset with $3,600 trade-in allowance.

f. Equipment (+A)   27,600
    Accumulated Depreciation (+A)   9,000
        Equipment (-A)   16,200
        Cash (-A)   20,400
    Traded asset with $3,600 trade-in allowance.

24. Amortization Expense (E,-SE)   10,000
        Copyright (-A)   10,000
    Amortized intangible asset.

Amortization should be based on the estimated useful life of the copyright, not its legal life. Amortization is therefore based on the five-year life.

25. a. Depletion Expense (E,-SE)   260,000
            Accumulated Depletion (-A)   260,000
        Recognize depletion based on first-year production.
        Total cost of property $4,400,000
        Less: Residual value   (1,800,000)
        Depletion base $2,600,000

    Depletion rate: $2,600,0000 ÷ 10,000,000 tons = $0.26 per ton

    1,000,000 tons x $0.26 per ton = $260,000

b. Cost of Buildings $600,000
    Base   10,000,000 tons

    Depreciation rate = $600,000 ÷ 10,000,000 tons = $0.06 per ton

    Depreciation expense = 1,000,000 tons x $0.06 per ton = $60,000

CHAPTER 10

Introduction to Liabilities:
Economic Consequences, Current Liabilities, and Contingencies

REVIEW OF KEY CONCEPTS

The last few chapters have emphasized accounting for various categories of assets. In Chapters 10 and 11, the focus shifts to the other side of the balance sheet to discuss accounting for liabilities. Liabilities are divided into two general categories: *current liabilities* and *long-term liabilities*. This chapter discusses the accounting for liabilities in general, as well as focusing on current liabilities and contingent liabilities. Long-term liabilities are discussed in Chapter 11.

Liabilities are defined as "probable future sacrifices of economic benefits arising from present obligations of a particular entity, to transfer assets or provide services to other entities in the future as a result of past transactions or events." In other words, liabilities are amounts that are owed by the company and must be settled in some future time period.

Accounting for Liabilities

As was the case with assets, there are three basic accounting problems to be addressed for liabilities. Liabilities must be originally recorded, ultimately settled or discharged, and accounted for in the interim period.

A simple accounts payable example illustrates the initial accounting and discharge of a liability. A company purchases merchandise on credit for $450, and pays the supplier within thirty days. The following journal entries are required:

Merchandise Inventory (+A)	450	
Accounts Payable (+L)		450

Recorded liability from a credit purchase.

Accounts Payable (-L)	450	
Cash (-A)		450

Paid supplier for credit purchase.

Although the example is a simple one, it represents the basic concepts of recording and settling liabilities.

Current Liabilities

Current liabilities are liabilities that are expected to require the use of current assets or incur other current liabilities in settlement of the initial current liability.

The ratio of current assets divided by current liabilities, the **current ratio**, is an important indicator of a company's short-term solvency or liquidity. Even if a company is highly profitable, if it does not have sufficient current assets on hand to pay its liabilities when they become due, the company will not survive.

Current liabilities can be divided into two broad categories: *determinable current liabilities* and *contingent liabilities*.

Determinable Liabilities

Determinable liabilities have terms of payment which are contractually fixed and therefore easily measured both in amount and as to their due date. Included in this category are accounts and notes payable (or short-term debts), dividends payable, unearned revenues, third-party collections, and accrued liabilities. Most of these liabilities have already been introduced earlier in the text. In this chapter, we will discuss liabilities that you have not encountered before.

Short-term debts or notes payable are liabilities arising out of a formal borrowing agreement, normally with a bank. A common type of notes payable is where the borrower repays the face value of the note and accumulated interest at a specified future date. For example, Twins, Inc. borrows $10,000 from Third National Bank on January 1, 1999. The note is due in six months and the interest rate is 8 percent. Normally, the quoted interest rate is an annual rate, so Twins is actually paying 4 percent for the six months of loan term. At the end of six months, Twins pays $10,400 to the bank; the initial amount borrowed, $10,000, and $400 ($10,000 x 0.08 x 6/12) interest expense.

The journal entries to account for the note are:

1/1/99	Cash (+A)	10,000	
	Notes payable (+L)		10,000
6/30/99	Notes payable (-L)	10,000	
	Interest expense (E, -SE)	400	
	Cash (-A)		10,400

Another type of note payable is a note issued at a discount. In this case, the borrower initially receives less than the face value of the note, but must repay the higher face value. The difference between the amount borrowed and the amount repaid is the cost of borrowing or the interest expense.

Example. Buckeye Corporation borrows $15,000 from the Hoosier National Bank on June 1. Buckeye signs a three-month note with a face value of $15,225. The $225 difference between the amount borrowed and the face value is a discount on notes payable. The discount is originally recorded as a contra-liability (an account which has a debit balance and is subtracted from the amount of the note payable on the balance sheet). Each month a portion of the discount will be amortized, i.e., converted to interest expense through an adjusting journal entry. The journal entries over the term of the note are as follows:

Cash (+A)	15,000	
Discount on Notes payable (-L)	225	
Notes Payable (+L)		15,225

Issued short-term note payable for cash.

Interest Expense (E,-SE)	75	
Discount on Notes Payable (+L)		75

*Recognized accrual of interest on
 the note ($225 ÷ 3 months).*

The above entry is repeated at the end of each of the three months.

Notes Payable (-L)	15,225	
Cash (-A)		15,225

Paid face value on the note.

Note that initially, the net note payable is $15,000, $15,225 (Notes Payable, a credit balance account) - $225 (Discount on Notes Payable, a debit balance account). Observe that just prior to the repayment of $15,225, the discount on notes payable has been reduced to a zero balance by the three adjusting entries so that the net note payable is $15,225 (the total amount owed). Over the term of the note, Buckeye has recognized interest expense in the amount of $225. The payment of $15,225 includes the repayment of the $15,000 borrowed plus the $225 of interest expense.

Third-Party Collections

Companies often serve as collecting agents for the government, and sometimes for other companies as well. A common example is sales tax. If a firm sells a product for $100, and the state levies a 5 percent sales tax, then the company must collect $105 from the customer. Of this amount, $5 will be held (normally until month's end) and then remitted to the state government. Payroll tax withholding is another third-party collection for a governmental unit. Third-party collections for other companies might include union dues and employee health or life insurance premiums. Accounting for these types of collections is illustrated using the sales tax example.

Cash (+A)	105	
Sales (R,+SE)		100
Sales Tax Payable (+L)		5

Sold merchandise and collected 5% sales tax.

Sales Tax Payable (-L)	5	
Cash (-A)		5

Paid sales tax to the state government.

Accrued Liabilities

Accrued liabilities are obligations created when an expense is incurred prior to a cash payment. *Normal accrued liabilities* arise from common transactions, such as wages payable, interest payable, and rent payable, and are recorded through adjusting entries. These accruals were discussed in Chapter 4. *Contingent accrued liabilities* are dependent on a future event, and therefore cannot be as precisely measured. Contingent accrued liabilities require estimation by management. For example, businesses (and some individuals) are required to make income tax payments to the federal government during the year, usually every three months (quarterly). Such income taxes payments can only be calculated by using estimates of taxable income. The final tax settlement for the year is based on actual net taxable income.

Contingencies and Contingent Liabilities

A *contingency* is an existing condition which may (or may not) give rise to a future gain or loss to the company. Lawsuits are a frequently encountered example. Depending on the final settlement, a company may incur a loss in a suit filed against them, or realize a gain if a suit filed against another party is successful.

Gain contingencies usually do not appear in either the financial statements or the footnotes until the gain is actually realized (i.e. when the lawsuit is settled). This practice is justified by the concept of conservatism.

The same concept of conservatism requires that **loss contingencies** be disclosed or accrued under certain circumstances before it is realized. Two criteria are applied to determine whether a loss contingency should be accrued. The contingency must be *highly probable* and *estimable*. When both conditions are met, then the loss contingency is accrued; i.e., the contingent liability appears on the balance sheet and a loss appears on the income statement. Significant loss contingencies which meet one (but not both) criterion must be disclosed in the financial statement footnotes. As a rule, companies will normally disclose all significant loss contingencies in the footnotes, even when neither criteria is met. The criteria are highly subjective, require management discretion, and typically require the assistance of outside legal counsel.

The required entries to record a contingent liability are straightforward, once management has determined that both criteria have been met. The contingency is initially recorded using management's best estimate of the likely outcome. An adjustment may be required when the issue is finally resolved. For example, assume that Shady Company has been sued by a customer for $2 million. At December 31, 1998, I.M. Sharp, attorney at law, estimates that the suit will probably be settled for $500,000. The suit is finally settled on June 30, 1999, for $600,000. The following journal entries are required.

12/31/98	Contingent Loss (Lo,-SE)	500,000	
	Contingent Liability (+L)		500,000
	Recorded contingent loss due to lawsuit.		

6/30/99	Contingent Loss (Lo,-SE)	100,000	
	Contingent Liability (-L)	500,000	
	Cash (-A)		600,000
	Record final settlement of lawsuit.		

Other Loss Contingencies

Lawsuits are not the only type of loss contingencies recorded by companies. Companies often offer a warranty or a guarantee to their customers for products or services sold. The precise terms of such warranties vary widely, but all represent a contingency which should be accrued. Although companies strive to maintain high quality control standards over production, manufacturing processes are not perfect. Some products will be defective and require repair or replacement under the customer's warranty. Managers can look at past performance and develop reliable estimates of future costs under warranty and guarantee obligations. Since, warranties are offered to customers to promote sale of the company's products, proper matching requires that the estimated future warranty costs be recorded as an expense in the same period that the company records the sales revenues; this may be earlier than when the actual return or repair occurs.

Example. Spartan Manufacturing Company was formed on January 1, 1999. Spartan sells a line of golf balls which are guaranteed to fly straight up the middle of the fairway. If the balls fail to meet expectations, customers may return them for a full cash refund. During 1999, Spartan sold 500,000 balls for $10 each. Also during 1999, customers returned 10,000 balls and received their promised refunds. Spartan estimates that approximately 10 percent of the balls will be returned by the customers. Spartan would make the following journal entries during 1999.

Cash or Accounts Receivable (+A)	5,000,000	
Sales (R,+SE)		5,000,000
Sold 500,000 golf balls for $10 each.		

Warranty Expense (E,-SE)	500,000	
Contingent Warranty Liability (+L)		500,000
Recognized contingent liability		
(ten percent of sales).		

Contingent Warranty Liability (-L)	100,000	
Cash (-A)		100,000
Paid warranty liability on balls		
returned by customers.		

The above entries will leave an ending balance of $400,000 in Contingent Warranty Liability. This will cover future estimated returns of golf balls sold during 1999.

QUESTIONS FOR YOUR REVIEW

1. Which of the following is *not* a contingent accrued liability?
    a. Dividends Payable
    b. Bonus Liability
    c. Vacation Pay Liability
    d. Income Taxes Payable

2. Which of the following is an accrued loss contingency?
    a. Sales Tax Payable
    b. Warranty Liability
    c. Accounts Payable
    d. All the above are accrued loss contingencies.

3. Which of the following would most likely *not* be recorded as a contingent liability?
    a. Warranty Liability
    b. Lawsuit Liability
    c. Vacation Pay Liability
    d. Accounts Payable to Attorneys

4. Spartan Corporation is the issuer of a $10,000, 6-month, 10 percent note. Which of the following is *true* regarding the recording of the transaction?
    a. Notes Payable should be credited for $10,500.
    b. Notes Payable should be credited for $11,000.
    c. Notes Payable should be credited for $10,000.
    d. Cash should be credited for $10,500.

Questions 5 and 6 refer to the following information.

On November 1, 1998, Hoosier Corporation signed an 8-month, 6 percent, $25,000 note payable with principal and interest due at maturity.

5. If the fiscal year ends on December 31, which of the following is *true* at year-end?
    a. Interest Expense is $250.
    b. Interest Expense is $375.
    c. Notes Payable is $25,250.
    d. Notes Payable is $26,500.

6. What is Hoosier's total liability on the note as of July 1, 1999?
    a. $25,000
    b. $26,500
    c. $26,000
    d. $25,750

Questions 7 through 10 refer to the following information.

On October 1, 1998, D.A. Bulls Inc. borrowed $10,000 from the bank. As part of the deal, Bulls signed a note agreeing to pay the bank $10,900 on June 30, 1999.

7. What is the annual interest rate on this note?
    a. 9 percent
    b. 12 percent
    c. 10 percent
    d. 110 percent

8. Which of the following is *true* regarding the journal entry required on the day Bulls signed the note?
    a. Discount on Notes Payable should be debited for $500.
    b. Discount on Notes Payable should be credited for $900.
    c. Notes Payable should be credited for $10,900.
    d. Notes Payable should be debited for $10,000.

9. Which of the following is *true* regarding Bulls' balance sheet on December 31, 1998?
    a. Discount on Notes Payable is $600.
    b. Carrying value of Notes Payable is $10,000.
    c. Discount on Notes Payable is $300.
    d. Carrying value of Notes Payable is $10,600.

10. Which of the following is *true* regarding Bulls' income statement for 1998?
    a. Interest Payable is $300.
    b. Interest Expense is $300.
    c. Interest Payable is $900.
    d. Interest Expense is $900.

11. On January 1, 1999, Buckeye Inc. signed a five-year, 10 percent, $50,000 note. As part of the agreement, Buckeye promised to make annual interest payments on January 1 of each year. Which of the following is correct regarding the effect of the note on Buckeye's financial statements on December 31, 1999?
    a. Buckeye should report $55,000 of long-term debt.
    b. Interest expense will be $0.
    c. Buckeye should report a current liability of Notes Payable of $50,000.
    d. Buckeye should report current liabilities of $5,000.

12. Arnie's Pro Shop has a 100% satisfaction guaranteed policy for all golf clubs sold. If a customer isn't completely satisfied, he can return the clubs for a full refund. Arnie's currently has a credit balance in Contingent Warranty Liability of $1,000. What is the effect on Arnie's Warranty Expense when a customer returns a golf club?
    a. Decrease
    b. Increase
    c. No effect
    d. We need more information.

Questions 13 and 14 refer to the following information.

Wolverine Inc. sells football helmets. Each helmet costs Wolverine $10, sells for $25, and includes a money-back guarantee. Sales history indicates that 2 percent of the helmets sold are returned. During 1998, Wolverine had $100,000 of net sales.

13. What is Guarantee Expense for the year?
     a. $800
     b. $2,000
     c. $80
     d. $50,000

14. Assume that Guarantee Expense for 1998 was $1,000. Wolverine had a $1,200 credit balance in Contingent Guarantee Liability on January 1, 1998. During 1998, customers returned 90 helmets. What is the balance in Contingent Guarantee Liability at the end of 1998?
     a. $50 debit balance
     b. $200 credit balance
     c. $2,200 credit balance
     d. $1,300 credit balance

Questions 15 and 16 refer to the following information.

Nittany Company sells stopwatches. Each watch costs Nittany $10, sells for $25, and is guaranteed for life. If a watch ever fails, Nittany will replace it at no cost to the customer. Sales history indicates that 2 percent of the stopwatches sold are returned. During 1998, Nittany sold 100,000 stopwatches.

15. What is Warranty Expense for the year?
     a. $100,000
     b. $2,000
     c. $50,000
     d. $20,000

16. Assume that Warranty Expense for 1998 was $10,000. Nittany had a $12,000 credit balance in Contingent Warranty Liability on January 1, 1998. During 1998, customers returned 1,500 stopwatches. What is the balance in Contingent Warranty Liability at the beginning of 1999?
     a. $18,000 credit balance
     b. $22,000 credit balance
     c. $3,000 debit balance
     d. $7,000 credit balance

17. Under which of the following conditions should a loss contingency be accrued?
     a. When it is estimable
     b. When it is highly probable
     c. When it is either estimable or highly probable
     d. When it is both estimable and highly probable

18. Which of the following plans requires no actuarial assumptions?
    a. A post-retirement health care plan
    b. A post-retirement life insurance plan
    c. A defined-benefit pension plan
    d. A defined-contribution pension plan

Questions 19 and 20 refer to the following information.

Campus Bus Services began operations on January 1, 1999. Campus Bus Service sells monthly passes good for thirty days of unlimited travel. During 1999, Campus sold monthly passes for a total of $63,000. On December 31, 1999, Campus estimates that unexpired passes are outstanding with a value of $1,850.

19. What is the Unearned Revenue and Monthly Pass Revenue for 1999?

	Unearned Revenue	Monthly Pass Revenue
a.	$0	$63,000
b.	$1,850	$63,000
c.	$1,850	$61,150
d.	$63,000	$63,000

20. If instead, Campus had a beginning balance in Unearned Revenue of $5,000, what would be the Monthly Pass Revenue for 1999?
    a. $61,150
    b. $63,000
    c. $66,150
    d. $68,000

21. Hawkeye Stereo and Electronics recognizes most expenses when the cash payments are made. Hawkeye began doing business in June 1998. Hawkeye made the following payments during December 1998:

    12/1/98   Prepaid insurance premium of $600 for a policy covering the six months ending May 31, 1999. Recorded entire amount as insurance expense.
    12/1/98   Paid $500 interest on an outstanding note payable. Under the terms of the note, Hawkeye makes an interest payment on the first of each month for the prior month's expense.
    12/10/98 Paid $400 in rent for the month ended November 30.
    12/16/98 Paid employee wages of $5,000. Employees are paid on the first and sixteenth of each month for the half-month just ended. The next payday is January 1, 1999.

    On December 31, 1998, Hawkeye reported total current assets of $30,000 and total current liabilities of $20,000. Hawkeye's income statement showed a net income (cash basis) of $12,000 for the partial year ended December 31, 1998.

a.   What is Hawkeye's current ratio, before any accrual adjustments?

b.   Prepare all required adjusting journal entries to convert from Hawkeye's cash basis to the accrual basis of accounting for the above listed expenses.

c.   What is Hawkeye's net income on the accrual basis?

d.   What is Hawkeye's current ratio on the accrual basis?

22. The following relates to Phillips Inc.:

Income before taxes	$100,000
Income tax expense	35,000
Reported net income	$ 65,000
Decrease in deferred tax liability balance	$ 5,000

    a.   Compute estimated taxes payable for the year.

    b.   Compute the estimated effective tax rate.

    c.   Compute estimated taxable income.

23. Bates Motel Construction instituted a defined-benefit pension plan for its employees on December 31, 1997. Bates makes annual contributions in the amount of $25,000 to the Last National Bank, which manages the pension plan. The first deposit was made on December 31, 1997. The bank invests the funds for the plan and earns a 10 percent annual return. The annual return is deposited directly to the fund; it does not go to Bates. On December 31, 1999, prior to making the 1999 contribution, Bates estimates that promised future retirement payments under the plan would require a total fund of $100,000.

   a. Prepare all journal entries that have been made by Bates related to the pension plan.

   b. What amount of pension liability should appear on Bates' December 31, 1999, balance sheet?

   c. What would be Bates' December 31, 1999, journal entry if the pension were a defined-contribution plan, rather than the defined-benefit plan?

    d.   What would be Bates' December 31, 1999, pension liability if the pension were a defined-contribution plan, rather than the defined-benefit plan?

24.   Wolverine Company operates a local sporting goods retail store. On a typical Michigan spring day, after a heavy snowfall, a customer, Robert Night, slipped and fell on the icy sidewalk as he was leaving the store. Mr. Night contends that everyone should realize that snow and ice are common in this area in late April, and Wolverine should have cleared and salted the sidewalks. Night sued Wolverine for $2,000,000 in damages for injuries sustained in the accident. The suit had not been settled on December 31, 1998.

John Bo, Wolverine's attorney, believes that Night has a valid claim for at least part of the damages. Bo estimates that the final settlement will be somewhere between $500,000 and $1,200,000. Bo's best guess is that the suit will result in a loss of $800,000.

Night and Wolverine finally agree to settle out of court for $850,000 on April 15, 1999.

    a.   Assume that Wolverine agrees that a contingent liability exists on December 31, 1998. What journal entry is required to record this contingency?

    b.   What journal entry is required to record the final settlement on April 15, 1999?

25. Panther Corporation has $40,000 of net income before inclusion of depreciation expense. The only depreciable asset Panther owns is a new delivery truck. The truck was purchased on January 1, 1999, for $30,000. Panther plans on using the truck for five years, at which point it will be worthless. Panther depreciates the truck using the straight-line method for financial reporting purposes. For tax purposes, the IRS will allow depreciation of $12,000, $8,000, $5,000, $3,000, and $2,000 for years one through five, respectively. There are no other differences between financial reporting and tax return income. Panther's federal income tax rate is 30 percent.

Prepare Panther's journal entry to record its 1999 tax liability. Show all supporting calculations.

CHAPTER 10-SOLUTIONS

1.	a	6.	c	11.	d	16.	d
2.	b	7.	b	12.	c	17.	d
3.	d	8.	c	13.	b	18.	d
4.	c	9.	a	14.	d	19.	c
5.	a	10.	b	15.	d	20.	c

21. a. Current ratio = Current assets / Current liabilities
$30,000 ÷ $20,000 = 1.50

b. Prepaid Insurance (+A)   500
        Insurance Expense (-E,+SE)   500
    Adjust for the prepaid portion of insurance expense.
    Hawkeye would have recorded the entire $600
    as Insurance Expense under the cash basis.

    Interest Expense (E,-SE)   500
        Accrued Interest Payable (+L)   500
    Record accrued expense for December. Hawkeye
    made an entry on December 1, but that
    represented the November expense.

    Rent Expense (E,-SE)   400
        Accrued Rent Payable (+L)   400
    Record accrued expense for December. Hawkeye
    made an entry on December 10, but that
    represented the November expense.

    Wage Expense (E,-SE)   5,000
        Accrued Wages Payable (+L)   5,000
    Record accrued expense for the last half
    of December. Hawkeye made an entry on
    December 16, but that represented the
    expense for the first half of the month.

c. Net income as reported (cash basis) $12,000
    Plus: Reduction in insurance expense   500
    Less: Accrued expenses   (5,900)
    Net income on accrual basis $ 6,600

d. Current ratio = Current assets / Current liabilities
    $30,500 ÷ $25,900 = 1.18

22. a. Estimated taxes payable for the year are:

Income Tax Expense	35,000	
Deferred Tax Liability	5,000	
Income Tax Payable		40,000

b. Estimated effective tax rate is:

Income tax expense / Reported income before tax =
$35,000 ÷ $100,000 = 0.35

c. Estimated taxable income is:
Taxable income x Effective tax rate = Income tax payable
Taxable income = Income tax payable / Effective tax rate
Taxable income = $40,000 ÷ 0.35 = $114,286

23. 1997

Pension Expense (E,-SE)	25,000	
Pension Liability (+L)		25,000

Recognized $25,000 pension liability.

Pension Liability (-L)	25,000	
Cash (-A)		25,000

Paid $25,000 to pension fund.

1998

Pension Expense (E,-SE)	25,000	
Pension Liability (+L)		25,000

Recognized $25,000 pension liability.

Pension Liability (-L)	25,000	
Cash (-A)		25,000

Paid $25,000 to pension fund.

12/31/99

Pension Expense (E,-SE)	42,500	
Pension Liability (+L)		42,500

*Recognized $42,500 additional pension
liability based on revised estimates
from the actuary. The total fund
balance should be $100,000. The current
balance is only $57,500 [$25,000 (1997
contribution) + $25,000 (1998 contribution)
+ $2,500 (10% interest earned in 1998)
+ $5,000 (10% interest earned in 1999)].*

b. The total Pension Liability should be $100,000, based on the estimate.

23. c. Pension Expense (E,-SE)   25,000
            Cash (-A)   25,000
        Paid defined contribution of $25,000
        to pension fund.

    d. Bates' pension liability is zero under a defined-contribution plan. Bates records no liability unless a required contribution has not been made. The actuarially determined liability does not apply to defined-contribution plans.

24. a. Contingent Loss (Lo,-SE)   800,000
            Contingent Liability (+L)   800,000
        Accrued contingent liability due
        to Night lawsuit.

    b. Contingent Liability (-L)   800,000
        Contingent Loss (Lo,-SE)   50,000
            Cash (-A)   850,000
        Settled accrued contingent liability
        due to Night lawsuit.

25. Panther's taxable income (per the tax return) is $28,000. This is calculated by subtracting the tax depreciation expense of $12,000 from the $40,000 operating income. Panther's Income Tax Payable (the current liability) is $8,400. This is calculated by multiplying the $28,000 taxable income by the tax rate of 30 percent.

    Panther's tax benefit is due to the difference in depreciation expense between the tax return and the income statement.

Tax depreciation	$12,000
Straight-line depreciation	(6,000)
Excess depreciation	$ 6,000
x Tax rate	x 30%
Tax benefit	$ 1,800

    Panther's journal entry for 1999 is:

    Income Tax Expense (E,-SE)   10,200
        Income Tax Payable (+L)   8,400
        Deferred Tax Liability (+L)   1,800

    Note that Income Tax Payable and Deferred Tax Liability are calculated directly. Income Tax Expense is "plugged" for an amount needed to balance the journal entry.

CHAPTER 11

Long-Term Liabilities: Notes, Bonds, and Leases

REVIEW OF KEY CONCEPTS

This chapter extends the discussion of liabilities from Chapter 10 to include long-term liabilities. There are three primary types of long-term liabilities: notes payable, bonds payable, and lease liabilities. The discussion here will focus on accounting for bonds payable, which represent an important source of capital financing for many companies.

Before continuing with this chapter, you should review several important items, if you have not already done so. First, be certain that you understand the **time value of money** concepts presented in Appendix B to the text. These concepts are critical to understanding accounting for long-term liabilities. Second, go back and carefully reread the sections titled **EFFECTIVE INTEREST RATE** and **ACCOUNTING FOR LONG-TERM OBLIGATIONS: THE EFFECTIVE INTEREST METHOD** in Chapter 11 of your text. These sections provide an excellent introduction to the concepts being discussed below in accounting for bonds payable.

Before beginning the discussion of bonds payable, recall an important definition from your text:

The effective interest rate is the actual interest rate paid by the issuer of the obligation. It is determined by finding the discount rate that sets the present value of the obligation's cash outflows equal to the fair market value of that which is received in the exchange.

As in Chapter 10, the approach here will be to look at accounting for long-term liabilities (1) when originally recorded, (2) during the holding period, and (3) when discharged.

Understanding How a Bond Works

A bond payable is a long-term debt security issued by a company to private investors. Under the terms of a standard bond contract (called an indenture), the investors lend money to the company. The company agrees to repay the *principal amount* (the face value or the amount borrowed) at a future *maturity date*. Typically, bonds are issued for long time periods, often 10 or 20 years.

In addition to the principal repayment, the issuer (borrower) agrees to make periodic cash interest payments to the investors. Most bonds issued by corporations pay interest on a semiannual basis. The amount of the interest payments is determined by the terms of the indenture. Bonds pay interest based on the face value of the bond and the stated (or coupon) interest rate. For example, assume Nittany Corporation issues a $10,000, eight percent bond which pays interest semiannually on January 1 and July 1. On each interest payment date, Nittany will write investors a check for $400,based on the stated terms ($10,000 x 0.08 x 1/2 year). The cash payments for interest are based on the stated rate and the face value; the payments are not affected by changes in the fair market price of the bonds or the effective interest rate.

Accounting for Issuance of Bonds Payable

The issuer initially records the liability for bonds payable based on the face value of the bond issue. The issuer also records the receipt of cash from the bond issue, which is known as the **proceeds** of the bond issue.

Bonds are always sold at *fair market value*. The fair market value of a bond is determined by the riskiness of the company's business operations, the time period until maturity, and the general market rate of interest. The market rate of interest for a bond of a given risk level and term to maturity is known as the **effective interest rate**. The effective interest rate can change over time due to changing economic conditions. For example, a company may diversify into several different lines of business, decreasing its overall operating risk. The decrease in risk will lead to a decrease in the effective interest rate. However, the stated rate on a bond is fixed by the indenture and will not respond to changing economic conditions. Bond prices will adjust for differences between the stated rate and the effective rate, so that the bond always sells for its fair market value.

Bond prices adjust to fair market value as follows. If the stated interest rate is equal to the effective interest rate, the bond will sell for its face value. If the stated interest rate is less than the effective interest rate, the bond will sell for less than its face value. The bond is then said to sell at a **discount**. If the stated interest rate is greater than the effective interest rate, the bond will sell for more than its face value. The bond is then said to sell at a **premium**.

Investors seek to earn a fair rate of return on investments. Rate of return is calculated by dividing the interest received by the cost of the investment. Consider the case of a bond selling at a discount. Since the cash payments for interest are fixed by the indenture, the investors can earn the fair market rate of return (the effective interest rate) by reducing the price they are willing to pay for the bond. The numerator of the rate of return is fixed by the bond indenture. The rate of return can only be changed by adjusting the denominator (the bond price).

Example. Illini Corporation decides to raise needed funds for a major plant expansion by issuing $800,000 in ten-year, 8 percent bonds. The bonds will be issued on January 1, 1999. The bonds will pay interest semiannually on June 30 and December 31.

Bonds Issued at Face Value

Assume that the effective interest rate is 8 percent on January 1, 1999. The bonds have a stated rate equal to the effective rate, and should sell for the face value of $800,000. You can verify that this is the fair market value of the bonds.

First, identify the future cash flows associated with the bond. There will be an $800,000 outflow at the end of 20 periods (ten years, with semiannual interest payments) for repayment of the face value. There will be semiannual payments of $32,000 each (an annuity) representing the cash payments for interest. This is calculated by multiplying the stated interest rate (8 percent or 4 percent per semiannual payment period) times the principal amount of the bond ($800,000).

Next, calculate the present value of these future cash flows using the effective interest rate of 8 percent (4 percent per semiannual payment period) for the 20 periods until maturity.

The table factor for the present value of a dollar for 20 periods, discounted at 4 percent, is 0.4564. Multiplying by the principal amount gives the present value of the $800,000 principal repayment as $365,120.

The table factor for the present value of an ordinary annuity for 20 periods, discounted at 4 percent, is 13.5903. Multiplying by the interest payment amount gives the present value of the $32,000 annuity as $434,890.

Adding the present values together gives the total present value of the remaining cash flows as $800,010. This amount is equal to the face value of $800,000. (There is a $10 difference due to rounding). The present value of the future cash flows is the fair market value of the bond. Illini would make the following journal entry to record the issue of the bond.

Cash (+A)	800,000	
Bonds Payable (+L)		800,000

Bonds Issued at More Than Face Value

Assume that the effective interest rate is 6 percent on January 1, 1999. The bonds have a stated rate greater than the effective rate, and should sell for a premium over the face value of $800,000. With this information, you can determine the price of the bonds.

First, identify the future cash flows associated with the bond. There will be an $800,000 outflow at the end of 20 periods (ten years, with semiannual interest payments) for repayment of the face value. There will be semiannual payments of $32,000 each (an annuity) representing the cash payments for interest. This is calculated by multiplying the stated interest rate (8 percent or 4 percent per semiannual payment period) times the principal amount of the bond ($800,000).

Next, calculate the present value of these future cash flows using the effective interest rate of 6 percent (3 percent per semiannual payment period) for the 20 periods until maturity.

The table factor for the present value of a dollar for 20 periods, discounted at 3 percent, is 0.5537. Multiplying by the principal amount gives the present value of the $800,000 principal repayment as $442,960. The table factor for the present value of an ordinary annuity for 20 periods, discounted at 3 percent is 14.8775. Multiplying by the interest payment amount gives the present value of the $32,000 annuity as $476,080.

Adding the present values together gives the total present value of the remaining cash flows as $919,040. This amount is the fair market value of the bond. The bond will sell for $919,040. This price indicates a premium of $119,040 over the face value of the bond. Investors will pay more than face value, because the bond offers stated interest higher than the effective rate at the issue date. Illini would make the following journal entry to record the issue of the bond at a premium.

Cash (+A)	919,040	
Premium on Bonds Payable (+L)		119,040
Bonds Payable (+L)		800,000

Bonds Issued at Less Than Face Value

Assume that the effective interest rate is 10 percent on January 1, 1999. The bonds have a stated rate less than the effective rate, and should sell for a discount. You can determine the price of the bonds, as was done in the above cases. Adding the present values together gives the total present value of the remaining cash flows as $700,310. This amount is the fair market value of the bond. The bond will sell for $700,310. This price indicates a discount of $99,690 from the face value of the bond. Investors will pay less than face value, because the bond offers stated interest lower than the effective rate at the issue date. Illini would make the following journal entry to record the issue of the bond at a discount.

Cash (+A)	700,310	
Discount on Bonds Payable (-L)	99,690	
Bonds Payable (+L)		800,000

Accounting for Bonds at Maturity

Under terms of the bond indenture, the issuer will repay the **face value** at the **maturity date**. Note that this is independent of the original issue price of the bond. In all three of the above cases, Illini would repay the $800,000 face value of the bond when it matures on December 31, 2002. The redemption of the bond is recorded with the following journal entry.

Bonds Payable (-L)	800,000	
Cash (-A)		800,000

Accounting for Bonds During the Holding Period

Bonds Issued at Face Value

Illini makes semiannual interest payments beginning June 30, 1999, continuing until the final payment on December 31, 2002. The amount of interest paid is based on the stated rate and the face value. Interest expense is calculated using the effective interest method. Under the effective interest method, the expense is calculated by multiplying the bond liability amount by the effective interest rate. In this example, interest expense is $32,000 ($800,000 x 0.08 x 1/2 year). Illini would make the following semiannual journal entries to record interest payments on June 30 and December 31 each year.

Interest Expense (E,-SE)	32,000	
Cash (-A)		32,000
Recognized interest expense		
($800,000 x 0.08 x 1/2 year).		

The balance sheet value of the bond liability will always be equal to the balance in the bonds payable account when the bond is originally issued at face value. In this case, Illini will report a bonds payable balance of $800,000 on its balance sheet every year until maturity. Note that since the bond liability does not change over the life of the bond, the interest expense calculated under the effective interest method will be the same each period.

Bonds Issued at a Premium

Illini still makes semiannual interest payments. The amount of the cash interest payment is still based on the stated rate and the face value and the cash payments are still $32,000 each. In the case of the bond issued at a premium, Illini would make the following journal entry to record the June 30, 1999, interest payment.

Interest Expense (E,-SE)	27,571	
Premium on Bonds Payable (-L)	4,429	
Cash (-A)		32,000

[(Bonds payable + Premium on bonds) x 0.06 x 1/2 year]
[(800,000 + 119,040) x 0.06 x 1/2 = 27,571]

By now, you have noted that the interest expense is not equal to the interest payment amount. Interest expense is calculated using the effective interest method. Under the effective interest method, the expense is calculated by multiplying the bond liability amount by the effective interest rate. The total bond liability is $919,040, which includes the bond payable of $800,000 plus the premium on bonds of $119,040. In this example, the interest expense for the six months ended June 30, 1999, is $27,571 ($919,040 x 0.06 x 1/2 year). The amortization of the premium is a plug figure to balance the journal entry for the difference between the interest expense amount and the cash interest payment amount.

The balance sheet value of the bond liability is no longer equal to the balance in the bonds payable account when the bond is originally issued at a premium. Rather, the total bond liability will be equal to the balance in bonds payable plus the balance in the premium on bonds account. The above entry to record the interest payment reduces Premium on Bonds Payable. The interest expense must be recalculated at each interest payment date using the effective interest method. The entry to record the December 31, 1999, payment is as follows.

Interest Expense (E,-SE)	27,438	
Premium on Bonds Payable (-L)	4,562	
Cash (-A)		32,000

[(Bonds payable + Premium on bonds) x 0.06 x 1/2 year]
[(800,000 + (119,040 - 4,429)) x 0.06 x 1/2]

The bond liability at a balance sheet date is equal to the bonds payable balance plus the unamortized balance in Premium on Bonds Payable. The balance sheet values for the bond liability in 1999 are as follows:

	6/30/99	12/31/99
Bonds Payable	$800,000	$800,000
Plus: Premium on Bonds *	114,611	110,049
Balance sheet value	$914,611	$910,049

* The original premium was $119,040. The remaining balance after the two amortization entries ($4,429 and $4,562) is $110,049.

Bonds Issued at a Discount

Illini still makes semiannual interest payments. The amount of the cash interest payment is still based on the stated rate and the face value and the cash payments are still $32,000 each. In the case of the bond issued at a discount, Illini would make the following journal entry to record the June 30, 1999, interest payment.

Interest Expense (E,-SE)	35,016	
Discount on Bonds Payable (+L)		3,016
Cash (-A)		32,000

[(Bonds payable - Discount on bonds) x 0.10 x 1/2 year]
[(800,000 - 99,690) x 0.10 x 1/2 = 35,016]

As for a bond sold at a premium, interest expense is not equal to the interest payment amount. Interest expense is calculated using the effective interest method. Under this method, expense is calculated by multiplying the bond liability amount by the effective interest rate. The total bond liability is $700,310, which includes the bond payable of $800,000 less the discount on bonds of $99,690. In this example, interest expense for the six months ended June 30, 1999, is $35,016. Amortization of the discount is a plug figure to balance the journal entry for the difference between the interest expense and cash interest payment amounts.

The balance sheet value of the bond liability is no longer equal to the balance in the bonds payable account when the bond is originally issued at a discount. Rather, the total bond liability will be equal to the balance in bonds payable less Discount on BondsPayable. The entry to record the interest payment reduces Discount on Bonds Payable. Interest expense must be recalculated at each payment date, using the effective interest method. The entry to record the December 31, 1999, payment is as follows.

Interest Expense (E,-SE)	35,166	
Discount on Bonds Payable (+L)		3,166
Cash (-A)		32,000

[(Bonds payable - Discount on bonds) x 0.10 x 1/2 year]
[800,000 - (99,690 - 3,016) x 0.10 x 1/2]

The bond liability at a balance sheet date is equal to the bonds payable balance plus the unamortized balance in the discount on bonds account. The balance sheet values for the bond liability in 1999 are as follows:

	6/30/99	12/31/99
Bonds payable	$800,000	$800,000
Less: Discount on bonds *	(96,674)	(93,508)
Balance sheet value	$703,326	$706,492

* The original discount was $99,690. The remaining balance after the two amortization entries ($3,016 and $3,166) is $93,508.

You can verify the balance sheet value for the bond liability by applying the concepts of the effective interest rate method. The calculations below illustrate this verification in the case of the Illini bond issued at a discount for December 31, 1999. Once you have reviewed these calculations, you should make a similar verification of the December 31, 1999, balance sheet value for the case of the bond issued at a premium.

First, identify the remaining future cash flows associated with the bond. There will be an $800,000 outflow at the end of 18 periods (nine years, with semiannual interest payments) for repayment of the face value. Note that 18 periods are used, not 20, since one year (2 periods) has elapsed as of December 31, 1999. There will be 18 semiannual payments of $32,000 each (an annuity) representing the cash payments for interest. This is calculated by multiplying the stated interest rate (8 percent or 4 percent per semiannual payment period) times the principal amount of the bond ($800,000).

Next, calculate the present value of these future cash flows using the effective interest rate of 10 percent (5 percent per semiannual payment period) for the 18 periods until maturity. The table factor for the present value of a dollar for 18 periods, discounted at 5 percent is 0.4155. Multiplying by the principal amount gives the present value of the $800,000 principal repayment as $332,400.

The table factor for the present value of an ordinary annuity for 18 periods, discounted at 5 percent, is 11.6896. Multiplying by the interest payment amount gives the present value of the $32,000 annuity as $374,067.

Adding the present values together gives the total present value of the remaining cash flows as $706,467. This amount is equal to the balance sheet value of $706,492 calculated above. (There is a $25 difference due to rounding.) The present value of the future cash flows is the fair market value of the bond.

QUESTIONS FOR YOUR REVIEW

1. Which of the following bond types may be retired before maturity, at the option of the bond issuer?
   a. Callable bonds
   b. Serial bonds
   c. Debenture bonds
   d. Coupon bonds

2. Which of the following describes the impact of issuing a bond at a discount?
    a. The issuer records interest expense at a higher rate of interest than is stated on the bond.
    b. The issuer records a loss on issuance.
    c. The interest payment is greater than the interest expense.
    d. The purchaser pays less than fair market value for the bond.

3. Which of the following describes the impact of issuing a bond at a premium?
    a. The issuer pays a higher rate of interest than is stated on the bond.
    b. The issuer records a gain on issuance.
    c. The interest payment is greater than the interest expense.
    d. The purchaser pays more than fair market value for the bond.

4. When a bond is issued at a discount, the balance sheet value of the bond can be calculated by:
    a. adding the unamortized discount on bonds to bonds payable.
    b. adding the amortized discount on bonds between the issue date and the balance sheet date to bonds payable.
    c. deducting the unamortized discount on bonds from bonds payable.
    d. deducting the amortized discount on bonds between the issue date and the balance sheet date from bonds payable.

5. When a bond is issued at a premium, the balance sheet value of the bond can be calculated by:
    a. adding the unamortized premium on bonds payable to bonds payable.
    b. adding the amortized premium on bonds payable between the issue date and the balance sheet date to bonds payable.
    c. deducting the unamortized premium on bonds payable from bonds payable.
    d. deducting the amortized premium on bonds payable between the issue date and the balance sheet date from bonds payable.

6. Which of the following describes the behavior of interest expense and the amortization of discount on bonds under the effective interest method?
    a. The balance sheet value of the bond increases as the discount on bonds is amortized.
    b. Cash payments for interest are greater than interest expense.
    c. Annual interest expense decreases as the discount on bonds is amortized.
    d. Cash payments for interest increase as the discount on bonds is amortized.

7. Which of the following interest rates, when used to discount the future interest and principal cash payments, results in a present value that is equal to the amount of cash received by the bond issuer?
    a. The stated rate
    b. The coupon rate
    c. The discount rate
    d. The effective interest rate

8. Which of the following explains the impact of amortizing a discount on bonds?
   a. Decreases the cash interest payments
   b. Increases the cash interest payments
   c. Decreases interest expense
   d. Increases interest expense

9. Which of the following statements regarding the recording of a capital lease is true?
   a. It is recorded as an asset by the lessor.
   b. It is recorded as an asset by the lessee.
   c. It is recorded as a liability by the lessee.
   d. All the above are true statements.

10. Which of the following could be recorded as an operating lease?
    a. The lease transfers ownership to the lessee.
    b. The lease contains an option allowing the lessee to purchase the property at its fair market value.
    c. The lease term is 75 percent or more of the useful life of the property.
    d. The present value of the lease payments equals or exceeds 90 percent of the fair market value of the property.

11. Under which of the following circumstances should a company finance additional assets with long-term debt rather than common stock?
    a. The company has a very high debt-to-equity ratio.
    b. The company has a very high current ratio.
    c. The company has a very low interest coverage ratio.
    d. The company expects the return on the assets purchased to be higher than the interest expense on the debt.

12. Northwestern Corporation borrowed $1,000,000, signing a three-year note payable. The note has a 10 percent interest rate, compounded annually, and requires payment of principal plus interest at maturity. What is the *total interest* payment on the note?
    a. $248,700
    b. $300,000
    c. $331,000
    d. $1,331,000

Questions 13 through 16 refer to the following information.

On January 1, 1999, Spartan Sporting Goods Inc. issued $1,000,000 of 5 percent, five-year bonds. The bonds pay interest on January 1 and July 1 of each year. Spartan uses the effective interest method to account for bonds.

13. If Spartan issued the bonds when the effective interest rate was 8 percent, how much cash did Spartan receive?
    a. $439,190
    b. $878,370
    c. $880,240
    d. $1,000,000

14. If the effective interest rate was 8 percent on the issue date, how much interest expense should Spartan record for 1999?
    a. $50,000
    b. $80,000
    c. $70,670
    d. $70,270

15. If the effective interest rate was 8 percent on the date of issue, what is Spartan's balance sheet value on December 31, 1999?
    a. $1,000,000
    b. $899,040
    c. $979,330
    d. $929,330

16. Which of the following is *true*?
    a. Spartan issued the bond at face value.
    b. Spartan issued the bond at a premium.
    c. Spartan issued the bond at a discount.
    d. Spartan's issue price cannot be determined without additional information.

17. Gopher Corporation signed a seven-year lease on equipment, with a fair market value of $150,000. The effective interest rate is 6 percent. Gopher makes annual lease payments. What is the amount of the required annual payment?
    a. $21,428
    b. $26,870
    c. $99,765
    d. $17,870

Questions 18 through 20 refer to the following information. Buckeye Brewing Inc. issues a ten-year $100,000 bond on January 1, 1999. The bond has a stated interest rate of 10 percent and pays interest semiannually starting June 30, 1999. Buckeye bonds uses the effective interest method.

18. If the bond was issued on January 1, when the effective interest rate was 8 percent, how much cash did Buckeye receive?
    a. $113,592
    b. $116,310
    c. $67,952
    d. $100,000

19. If the bond was issued on January 1, when the effective interest rate was 8 percent, what amount of Interest Expense should Buckeye record on June 30, 1999?
    a. $10,000
    b. $5,000
    c. $4,544
    d. $4,500

20. If the bond was issued on January 1, when the effective interest rate was 8 percent, what is the balance sheet value of the bond on June 30, 1999?
    a. $86,864
    b. $100,000
    c. $113,592
    d. $113,136

21. On January 1, 1999, Nittany Enterprises borrowed $42,865 from Joepa National Bank. Nittany gave Joepa a note for $50,000, due December 31, 2000.

    a. Compute the present value of the note's future cash flows at the following discount rates:
       (1) 6 percent

       (2) 8 percent

       (3) 10 percent

    b. What is the effective interest rate? Explain your answer.

22. On January 1, 1999, Wildcat Company issued $50,000 of ten-year bonds, with a stated interest rate of 12 percent, payable semiannually on June 30 and December 31 of each year. The effective interest rate was 12 percent on January 1, 1999.

    a. Prepare all entries associated with these bonds during 1999.

    b. Compute the balance sheet value of the bond liability on December 31, 1999. Explain your answer.

    c. Compute the present value of the bond's remaining cash flows on December 31, 1999, using the effective interest rate at the issue date.

23. On January 1, 1999, Badger Corporation issued $50,000 of ten-year bonds, with a stated interest rate of 12 percent, payable semiannually on June 30 and December 31 each year. The effective interest rate was 10 percent on January 1, 1999.

   a. Prepare all entries associated with these bonds during 1999.

   b. Compute the balance sheet value of the bond liability on December 31, 1999. Explain your answer.

   c. Compute the present value of the bond's remaining cash flows on December 31, 1999, using the effective interest rate at the issue date.

24. On January 1, 1999, Boilermaker Inc. issued $50,000 of ten-year bonds, with a stated interest rate of 10 percent, payable semiannually on June 30 and December 31 each year. The effective interest rate was 12 percent on January 1, 1999.

   a. Prepare all entries associated with these bonds during 1999.

   b. Compute the balance sheet value of the bond liability on December 31, 1999. Explain your answer.

   c. Compute the present value of the bond's remaining cash flows on December 31, 1999, using the effective interest rate at the issue date.

25. Hawkeye Paving Company leases heavy trucks for its road construction business. On January 1, 1999, Hawkeye leased ten trucks for four years at $20,000 per truck, per year. Payments are to be made on December 31 of each year. At the end of the lease, Hawkeye has the option to buy the trucks for a nominal price. The effective interest rate is 6 percent per year.

    a.   Compute the annual rental expense if the lease is treated as an operating lease. Prepare the required journal entries associated with an operating lease for 1999.

    b.   Prepare all required journal entries for 1999 if the lease is treated as a capital lease. Assume that the trucks are depreciated over a five-year useful life, using the straight-line method, and have no expected salvage value. Compute the total rental expense (interest expense plus depreciation expense) for 1999 if the lease is treated as a capital lease.

    c.   Prepare all required journal entries for 2000 if the lease is treated as a capital lease. Compute the total rental expense for 2000.

CHAPTER 11-SOLUTIONS

1.	a	6.	a	11.	d	16.	c
2.	a	7.	d	12.	c	17.	b
3.	c	8.	d	13.	b	18.	a
4.	c	9.	d	14.	c	19.	c
5.	a	10.	b	15.	b	20.	d

21. a. (1) The only cash flow is the repayment of $50,000 at the end of two years. The present value of $50,000, due in two years, discounted at 6 percent is **$44,500**. The table factor is **0.8900**.

  (2) The present value of $50,000, due in two years, discounted at 8 percent is **$42,865**. The table factor is **0.8573**.

  (3) The present value of $50,000, due in two years, discounted at 10 percent is **$41,320**. The table factor is **0.8264**.

  b. The effective interest rate is the rate that, when used to discount the future cash payment, results in a present value equal to the cash received by the borrower. The effective rate is thus *8 percent*.

22. a. 1/1/99   Cash (+A)   50,000
                 Bonds Payable (+L)   50,000
                 Issued bonds.

    6/30/99   Interest Expense (E,-SE)   3,000
                 Cash (-A)   3,000
                 Paid stated interest ($50,000 x 12% x 1/2 year).

    12/31/99 Interest Expense (E,-SE)   3,000
                 Cash (-A)   3,000
                 Paid stated interest.

  b. The bond is issued for its face value of $50,000 since the stated interest rate equals the effective interest rate of 12 percent. The balance sheet value on December 31, 1999, (and at all other dates) will be equal to the face value of $50,000.

c. Begin by identifying the remaining future cash flows associated with the bond. There will be a $50,000 outflow at the end of 18 periods for repayment of the principal. There will be semiannual payments of $3,000 each (an annuity) representing the cash payments for interest. This is calculated by multiplying the stated interest rate (12 percent or 6 percent per semiannual payment period) times the principal amount of the bond ($50,000). Next, calculate the present value of these future cash flows using the effective interest rate of 12 percent (6 percent per semiannual payment period) for the 18 periods remaining until maturity.

The table factor for the present value of a dollar for 18 periods, discounted at 6 percent, is **0.3503**. Multiplying by the principal amount gives the present value of the $50,000 principal repayment as **$17,515**.

The table factor for the present value of an ordinary annuity for 18 periods, discounted at 6 percent, is **10.8276**. Multiplying by the interest payment amount gives the present value of the $3,000 annuity as **$32,483**. (There is a $2 difference due to rounding).

Adding the present values together gives the total present value of the remaining cash flows as **$49,998**. (There is a $2 difference due to rounding). This amount is equal to the balance sheet value on December 31, 1999.

23. a. 1/1/99   Cash (+A)   56,232
                   Premium on Bonds Payable (+L)   6,232
                   Bonds Payable (+L)   50,000
                   Issued bonds.

    6/30/99   Interest Expense (E,-SE)   2,812
                   Premium on Bonds Payable (-L)   188
                      Cash (-A)   3,000
                   Paid stated interest and amortized premium.

    12/31/99 Interest Expense (E,-SE)   2,802
                   Premium on Bonds Payable (-L)   198
                      Cash (-A)   3,000
                   Paid stated interest and amortized premium.

b. Bonds payable $50,000
    Plus: Premium on bonds *   5,846
    Balance sheet value $55,846

* The original premium was $6,232. The remaining balance after the two amortization entries ($188 and $198) is **$5,846**.

c. Begin by identifying the remaining future cash flows associated with the bond. There will be a $50,000 outflow at the end of 18 periods for repayment of the principal. There will be semiannual payments of $3,000 each (an annuity) representing the cash payments for interest. This is calculated by multiplying the stated interest rate (12 percent or 6 percent per semiannual payment period) times the principal amount of the bond ($50,000). Next, calculate the present value of these future cash flows using the effective interest rate of 10 percent (5 percent per semiannual payment period) for the 18 periods remaining until maturity.

The table factor for the present value of a dollar for 18 periods, discounted at 5 percent, is **0.4155**. Multiplying by the principal amount gives the present value of the $50,000 principal repayment as **$20,775**.

The table factor for the present value of an ordinary annuity for 18 periods, discounted at 5 percent, is **11.6896**. Multiplying by the interest payment amount gives the present value of the $3,000 annuity as **$35,069**.

Adding the present values together gives the total present value of the remaining cash flows as **$55,844**. This amount is equal to (there is a $2 difference due to rounding) the balance sheet value on December 31, 1999.

24. a. 1/1/99   Cash (+A)   44,265

24. a. 1/1/99	Cash (+A)	44,265	
	Discount on Bonds Payable (-L)	5,735	
	Bonds Payable (+L)		50,000
	Issued bonds.		
6/30/99	Interest Expense (E,-SE)	2,656	
	Discount on Bonds Payable (+L)		156
	Cash (-A)		2,500
	Paid stated interest and amortized discount.		
12/31/99	Interest Expense (E,-SE)	2,665	
	Discount on Bonds Payable (+L)		165
	Cash (-A)		2,500
	Paid stated interest and amortized discount.		

b.   Bonds payable $50,000
      Less: Discount on bonds *   (5,414)
      Balance sheet value $44,586

* The original discount was $5,735. The remaining balance after the two amortization entries ($156 and $165) is **$5,414**.

c. Begin by identifying the remaining future cash flows associated with the bond. There will be a $50,000 outflow at the end of 18 periods for repayment of the principal. There will be semiannual payments of $2,500 each (an annuity) representing the cash payments for interest. This is calculated by multiplying the stated interest rate (10 percent or 5 percent per semiannual payment period) times the principal amount of the bond ($50,000). Next, calculate the present value of these future cash flows using the effective interest rate of 12 percent (6 percent per semiannual payment period) for the 18 periods remaining until maturity.

The table factor for the present value of a dollar for 18 periods, discounted at 6 percent, is **0.3503**. Multiplying by the principal amount gives the present value of the $50,000 principal repayment as **$17,515**.

The table factor for the present value of an ordinary annuity for 18 periods, discounted at 6 percent, is **10.8276**. Multiplying by the interest payment amount gives the present value of the $2,500 annuity as **$27,069**.

Adding the present values together gives the total present value of the remaining cash flows as **$44,584**. This amount is equal to (there is a $2 difference due to rounding) the balance sheet value on December 31, 1999.

25. a. The rental expense under an operating lease is simply $200,000 ($20,000 x 10).

12/31/99 Rental Expense (E,-SE)	200,000	
Cash (-A)		200,000
Recorded truck rental cost under operating lease.		

No other journal entries are required.

b.
1/1/99 Equipment (+A)	693,020	
Lease Liability (+L)		693,020
Recognized capital lease.		

Annual payments are $200,000. The present value of an ordinary annuity of $200,000 per year for four years, discounted at 6 percent, is **$693,020**. The table factor is **3.4651**.

12/31/99 Depreciation Expense (E,-SE)	138,604	
Accumulated Depreciation (-A)		138,604
Recognized depreciation ($693,020 ÷ 5 years).		

12/31/99 Interest Expense (E,-SE)	41,581	
Lease Liability (-L) (plug)	158,419	
Cash (-A) (payments)		200,000
Made first annual lease payment.		

b. Interest expense is calculated by multiplying the lease liability by the effective interest rate ($693,020 x 0.06). The total rental cost for 1999 is $180,185 ($138,604 + $41,581).

c. 12/31/00 Depreciation Expense (E,-SE)   138,604
                     Accumulated Depreciation (-A)   138,604
               Recognized depreciation ($693,020 ÷ 5 years).

               Interest Expense (E,-SE)   32,076
               Lease Liability (-L) (plug)   167,924
                     Cash (-A) (payments)   200,000
               Made second annual lease payment.

Interest expense is calculated by multiplying the remaining lease liability by the effective interest rate ($534,601 x 0.06). The total rental cost for 2000 is $170,680 ($138,604 + $32,076).

CHAPTER 12

Stockholders' Equity

REVIEW OF KEY CONCEPTS

This chapter initially reviews the similarities and differences among the three major organizational structures of for-profit businesses. The corporation is the focus for the remainder of the review. The major concepts discussed are the structure of corporations, the characteristics of ownership shares, and the rationale behind and accounting for transactions involving the corporation's equity stakeholders. Accounting for the issue and repurchase of preferred and common stock is discussed, including the concept of par value. The review concludes with a discussion of accounting for dividend declaration and payment.

Organizational Structure

The *sole proprietorship, partnership, and corporation* are the three principal organizational forms of for-profit businesses in the United States. When businesses are formed as sole proprietorships or partnerships, owners invest their personal assets in the business. While the business may be known to the public under a different name from its owners, all contracts entered into under the business's name are the personal responsibility of the owners. For example, if for some reason the business's assets are insufficient to satisfy business obligations, the sole proprietor or partner is personally responsible for the shortfall.

Other evidence that businesses established as proprietorships or partnerships are an extension of the owner is that income or losses of such businesses are not taxed under the business's name. Instead, the proprietor and partners report their share of the business's income on their individual tax returns, their share of business income is taxed as personal income.

In contrast, a **corporation** is a separate legal entity, a status granted to it by the state in which it is incorporated. This status results in significant differences in the legal responsibility of the corporation's owners (the stockholders) compared to sole proprietorships and partnerships.

Stockholders enjoy a **limited liability**. Usually, the most stockholders' can lose is their original investment and any corporate earnings reinvested in the business. If the assets of the corporation are insufficient to satisfy the corporation's debts, the stockholders are not liable for the shortfall. Creditors do not have recourse against the stockholders. Obviously, the limited liability feature of corporations makes this organizational form very attractive to investors.

Since the ownership shares of corporations are usually traded in markets, the potential investor pool is large relative to the other organizational forms. Corporations typically raise large amounts of money from stockholders.

221

The corporate form of business organization is not without its disadvantages. The costs of applying for corporate status and issuing shares are prohibitive for most small businesses. Usually, businesses begin as sole proprietorships and partnerships and, after reaching a certain size, apply for corporate status. Another disadvantage of the corporate form is *double taxation*. Corporate income is taxed by the government under corporate tax law. The corporation must file annual tax returns and pay taxes on reported corporate income. In addition, cash or property dividend distributions to stockholders are taxable to the owners at an individual level. Potentially, every dollar earned by the corporation can be taxed twice.

Accounting for the Issuance of Stock

Corporations may issue two primary classes of ownership shares, common and preferred stock. Common stockholders are the residual equity stakeholders in the corporation. Ownership of a common share normally includes a right to vote on major corporate issues. While dividends are not guaranteed, common stockholders can fully share in profits earned by the company. Common shareholders are exposed to the most risk compared to any company creditor or other stakeholder because they are the last parties to be paid if the company files for bankruptcy.

Preferred stockholders have rights that common stockholders do not have. Unlike common stock, preferred stock dividends are calculated using a predetermined formula. In addition, preferred stock dividends are required to be declared before common stock cash and property dividends can be declared. If preferred stock is **cumulative**, any preferred stock dividend not previously paid must be paid before common stockholders can receive dividends. The text discusses in detail the different characteristics that preferred stock can possess.

Both preferred and common stock are recorded initially at the price received from the investor purchasing the stock. As mentioned above, corporate status is granted by state governments. At the time the corporation is chartered by the state, the number of shares of preferred and common stock it can sell is specified or **authorized**. **Issued shares** are shares previously sold by the corporation. **Treasury shares** are shares which have been repurchased and retained by the corporation. **Outstanding shares** are shares actually held by investors outside of the business. The total of treasury shares and outstanding shares equals the number of shares issued. Dividends are declared, and earnings per share is calculated using the number of shares outstanding. For example, Hayes Company is authorized to issue 1,000,000 shares of common stock. It has issued and received payment for 600,000 and bought back 25,000 shares. Its shares outstanding would be 575,000, which would be the shares on which it would pay dividends.

Some states require that corporations set **par** or **stated values** when the stock is authorized. The par or stated value sets a minimum per-share amount for which stockholders are personally liable. If the stock initially sells for less than the par or stated value, then the stockholders are personally, contingently liable for the difference between the original market price and the par value. For example, if the par value of the stock is $100 per share and it sells for $90, then the shareholders are contingently liable for $10 per share. If the corporation's assets are insufficient to satisfy its debts, the creditors can require that stockholders pay up to $10 per share to satisfy the debt. While the par or stated value concept was instituted by states to protect creditors, most stock issues are sold at above par or stated value, because today par and stated values are initially set at very low amounts. Par value is used occasionally in the preferred stock dividend formula. For example, 8 percent, $50 par preferred stock pays dividends of $4 per share, per year.

Accounting for Preferred and Common Stock with Par or Stated Value

When stock has a par or stated value, the preferred stock and common stock accounts are used to record transactions based on the number of shares issued and the par value. Any difference between the par value and the issue is recorded in a separate account, Additional Paid-In Capital.

Example. Lopez Construction sells 1,000 shares of its $100 par value, preferred stock for $120 cash per share. Lopez would make the following journal entry.

Cash (+A)	120,000	
Preferred Stock, $100 par (+SE)		100,000
Additional Paid-In Capital-P/S (+SE)		20,000

The par account is increased by $100 x 1,000 shares, the difference between the total amount received and the total par value is recorded in Additional Paid-In Capital.

Example. Marks Corporation sells 2,000 shares of its $5 par value, common stock for $25 per share. Marks would make the following entry.

Cash (+A)	50,000	
Common Stock, $5 par (+SE)		10,000
Additional Paid-In Capital-C/S (+SE)		40,000

If a corporation's stock is no par value stock, then the entire amount received at issue is recorded in Preferred Stock or Common Stock. When there is no par or stated value, there is no additional paid-in capital account.

Example. Jones Corporation sells 2,000 shares of its no par, Common Stock for $25 per share. Jones would make the following entry.

Cash (+A)	50,000	
Common Stock, no par (+SE)		50,000

Treasury Stock

As mentioned in the text, corporations may elect to repurchase previously issued stock. The principal reasons to repurchase shares include fending off take-over attempts and acquiring shares for employee stock option plans. The *cost method* is the most widely used method to account for treasury stock. The following transactions illustrate accounting for treasury stock under the cost method.

Assume that Marks repurchases 200 shares of its $5 par value, common stock for $30 per share on June 1. All transactions are recorded at cost in the treasury stock account.

Treasury Stock (-SE)	6,000	
Cash (-A)		6,000

Purchased treasury shares at cost of $30 each.

On July 15, Marks sells 150 of the repurchased treasury shares for $35 each. The excess of the reissue price over the cost of the treasury shares is recorded in a separate additional paid-in capital account.

Cash (+A)	5,250	
Treasury Stock (+SE)		4,500
Additional Paid-In Capital-T/S (+SE)		750

Some shares may be reissued at a price less than cost. Assume Marks sells the remaining 50 treasury shares on July 20, for $27 per share.

Cash (+A)	1,350	
Additional Paid-In Capital-T/S (-SE)	150	
Treasury Stock (+SE)		1,500

Note that the difference between the cost and reissue price is still entered in Additional Paid-In Capital. However, there is a limit to the amount of debits to be recorded in the additional paid-in capital account. Assume instead that Marks sold the 50 remaining shares for $14 per share. The transaction is recorded with the following entry.

Cash (+A)	700	
Additional Paid-In Capital-T/S (-SE)	750	
Retained Earnings (-SE)	50	
Treasury Stock (+SE)		1,500

As the above example illustrates, if the credit balance in Additional Paid-In Capital-Treasury Stock is insufficient to absorb the entire difference between the sale price and the repurchase price, the shortfall reduces retained earnings.

Dividends Declaration and Payment

Cash and Property Dividends

Payments to stockholders (either preferred or common) are known as dividends. Normally, dividends are paid in cash, but a corporation may distribute other assets to stockholders. These other asset distributions are called property dividends. If the corporation distributes shares of its own stock, the dividend is called a stock dividend.

The date that the board of directors votes to pay a cash, property, or stock dividend is the **dividend declaration date**. In the case of cash and property dividends, a liability exists at the declaration date because the corporation is now legally obligated to remit assets to the stockholders. The **date of record** is the date that establishes which stockholders will receive the dividend. Stocks are actively traded on stock exchanges. The individual holding stock on the date of record receives the dividend when it is paid. When the payment is made, the liability is settled.

In the case of stock dividends, the corporation is obligated to issue additional shares of its stock to current stockholders. The formula used to determine the number of shares each stockholder receives is a percentage of shares already owned. Since the corporation is not obligated to remit assets to the shareholders, a liability does not exist.

Example. On June 30, 1999, J. Crafter Inc.'s board of directors declares a $0.50 per share cash dividend on the 100,000 shares of common stock outstanding. The date of record is July 3, 1999. The dividend is scheduled to be paid on July 15, 1999. Crafter would make the following journal entries.

June 30	Cash Dividends Declared (-SE)	50,000	
	Dividends Payable (+L)		50,000
	Declared a cash dividend.		
July 3	*No entry is recorded on the date of record.*		
July 15	Dividends Payable (-L)	50,000	
	Cash (-A)		50,000
	Paid cash dividend previously declared.		
Dec. 31	Retained Earnings (-SE)	50,000	
	Cash Dividends Declared (+SE)		50,000
	To close Cash Dividends Declared (a temporary		
	account) into Retained Earnings.		

Example. On September 30, 1999, L. Davies, Inc.'s board of directors declares a 10 percent stock dividend on the 200,000 shares of its $5 par value, common stock. On September 30, 1999, the stock sold for $50 per share. The stock dividend is scheduled to be distributed on October 15, 1999. The stock dividend is recorded based on the market price of the stock at the declaration date.

Stock Dividends Declared (-SE)	1,000,000	
Common Stock Dividend Distributable (+SE)		100,000
Additional Paid-In Capital-C/S (+SE)		900,000
Declared 10% stock dividend.		
Common Stock Dividend Distributable (-SE)	1,000,000	
Common Stock (+SE)		1,000,000
Distributed stock dividend previously declared.		

Retained earnings (-SE)   1,000,000
   Stock Dividends Declared (+SE)   1,000,000
To close Stock Dividends Declared (a temporary account) into Retained Earnings.

QUESTIONS FOR YOUR REVIEW

1. Palmer Inc. is considering declaring a 10 percent stock dividend. Currently, 100,000 shares of $5 par value, common stock are authorized, 60,000 shares are issued, and 5,000 shares are held in treasury. The total number of shares outstanding after a 10 percent stock dividend is:
    a. 110,000
    b. 66,000
    c. 60,500
    d. 38,500

2. Alcott is considering a two-for-one stock split of its $100 par value, common stock. Currently, 500,000 shares are authorized, 150,000 shares are outstanding, and 10,000 shares are held in treasury. The total number of shares outstanding after a two-for-one split is:
    a. 1,000,000
    b. 680,000
    c. 300,000
    d. 280,000

3. Par value is:
    a. the stock's minimum market price.
    b. the stock's initial book value.
    c. the stock's required total yearly dividend.
    d. sometimes used in the preferred stock dividend formula.

4. McGregor repurchases 1,000 shares of its $5 par value, common stock on the market for $25 per share. If McGregor subsequently resells the stock for $35 per share, the $10,000 received above the amount paid to repurchase the stock is recorded as:
    a. a gain disclosed on the income statement.
    b. a credit to Retained Earnings.
    c. Other Income disclosed on the income statement.
    d. Additional Paid-In Capital-Treasury Stock.

5. In 1996, immediately upon obtaining corporate status, Lynx issued 50,000 shares of 8 percent, $200 par value, cumulative preferred stock. Through the end of 1998 (three years), no dividends of any type have been declared or paid. In 1999, Lynx's board is considering declaring preferred and common dividends. How much is Lynx obligated to pay the preferred stockholders before paying the common stockholders?
    a. $400,000
    b. $800,000
    c. $1,200,000
    d. $3,200,000

The following information refers to questions 6 through 9.

The stockholders' equity section of Caponi Inc.'s December 31, 1999, balance sheet appears as follows:

Preferred stock, 15% nonparticipating, noncumulative, $150 par value, 100,000 shares authorized, issued and outstanding	$ 15,000,000
Additional paid-in capital-preferred stock	10,000,000
Common stock, $10 par value, 2,000,000 shares authorized and issued, 100,000 shares held in treasury	20,000,000
Additional paid-in capital-common stock	30,000,000
Total contributed capital	$ 75,000,000
Retained earnings	50,000,000
Total stockholders' equity before treasury stock	$125,000,000
Less: Treasury stock at cost, 100,000 shares	6,000,000
Total stockholders' equity	$119,000,000

6. How much is Caponi required to pay its preferred stockholders before any common dividends can be paid?
   a. $1,500,000
   b. $2,250,000
   c. It cannot be determined without information regarding dividends in arrears.
   d. Since it is nonparticipating, preferred stockholders must be paid the same amount as common stockholders.

7. If Caponi's board of directors intends to pay $6,250,000 in total dividends, what is the maximum that common stockholders will receive?
   a. $3,125,000
   b. $4,000,000
   c. $6,250,000
   d. It cannot be determined without additional information.

8. The common stock was initially sold for:
   a. $10.00 per share
   b. $23.16 per share
   c. $25.00 per share
   d. $26.32 per share

9. Caponi's book value per share of common stock is:
   a. $47.00
   b. $49.47
   c. $59.50
   d. $62.63

10. Appropriated retained earnings is:
    a. the amount of cash set aside by the board of directors for designated projects.
    b. the amount of reinvested earnings available for dividends during a particular year.
    c. the amount of reinvested earnings not available for dividend declaration at year-end.
    d. the amount that the Internal Revenue Service is entitled to under the Appropriation Act of 1974.

The following information relates to questions 11 and 12.

On January 1, 1999, Nicklaus Inc.'s Treasury Stock was $3,000,000, representing its purchase of 100,000 shares of common stock in December, 1998. At December 31, 1999, the treasury stock account balance was $1,000,000 and Additional Paid-In Capital-Treasury Stock was $1,333,334. Only one treasury stock transaction occurred during 1999.

11. How many shares of treasury stock were sold during 1999?
    a. 33,333
    b. 66,667
    c. 100,000
    d. It is not determinable without par value per share.

12. At what price were the treasury shares sold?
    a. $20
    b. $30
    c. $50
    d. $65

13. Which of the following is not an advantage of the corporate form of organization?
    a. Unlimited life
    b. Limited liability for stockholders
    c. Ease of formation
    d. Ease of transfer of ownership

The following information relates to questions 14 through 17. Each question is independent.

On January 1, 1999, Campbell Corporation has 500,000 shares of $10 par value, common stock issued and outstanding. The stock initially sold for $40 per share. Campbell's Retained Earnings is $100,000,000 on that date. Campbell has no preferred stock outstanding. Campbell's total liabilities are $60,000,000.

14. Campbell declares and distributes a 10 percent stock dividend on January 1 when the market price is $60 per share. What is Campbell's debt to equity ratio after this event (rounded to the nearest thousandth)?
    a. 0.488
    b. 0.500
    c. 0.513
    d. 0.538

15. Campbell declares and pays a $6-per-share cash dividend on January 1. What is Campbell's debt to equity ratio after this event (rounded to the nearest thousandth)?
    a. 0.488
    b. 0.500
    c. 0.513
    d. 0.538

16. On January 1, Campbell sells 50,000 shares of 10 percent, $25 par value, preferred stock for $100 per share. What is Campbell's debt to equity ratio after this event (rounded to the nearest thousandth)?
    a. 0.480
    b. 0.500
    c. 0.520
    d. 0.542

17. On January 1, Campbell signs a 30-year, $5,000,000 note payable which pays interest of 10 percent annually. What is Campbell's debt to equity ratio after this event (rounded to the nearest thousandth)?
    a. 0.480
    b. 0.500
    c. 0.520
    d. 0.542

18. An advantage of issuing debt over preferred stock is:
    a. potential dilution of common stockholders' interests is avoided.
    b. the debt to equity ratio is improved when debt is issued instead of preferred stock.
    c. interest is tax deductible, while dividends are not.
    d. interest payments can be delayed while preferred dividends must be declared.

19. From the investor's perspective, an advantage of issuing cash dividends over stock dividends is:
    a. an asset (cash) is distributed to the stockholders while a stock dividend is not a distribution of corporate assets.
    b. cash dividends are not taxable to the stockholder while stock dividends are taxable.
    c. the total economic resources of the company are unaffected by cash dividends.
    d. the book value per share is unaffected by cash dividends.

20. An advantage of the partnership form of organization over the corporate form is:
    a. partners' liability is unlimited.
    b. partners can withdraw assets from the business more freely than can stockholders.
    c. partnership interests are easily transferred compared to stock investments.
    d. corporations are subject to less regulation than partnerships.

21. Venturi incorporated on January 1, 1999, and was authorized to issue 200,000 shares of $10 par value, common stock and 50,000 shares of $50 par value, 8 percent, noncumulative preferred stock. The following stock-related transactions occurred during 1999:

    1. On April 1, Venturi sold 150,000 shares of common stock for $25 per share.
    2. On July 1, Venturi sold 30,000 shares of preferred stock for $80 per share.
    3. On August 1, Venturi repurchased 10,000 shares of preferred stock for $70 per share.
    4. On October 30, Venturi sold 6,000 of the preferred shares repurchased on August 1 for $75 per share.
    5. On December 1, Venturi sold 3,000 shares of the preferred shares repurchased on August 1 for $65 per share.
    6. Net income for 1999 is $40,000.

    a. Prepare the journal entries for each of the transactions.

    b. Prepare the stockholders' equity section of the balance sheet at December 31, 1999.

22. The board of directors of O'Grady Inc. is considering paying a $3-per-share cash dividend. O'Grady is authorized to issue 100,000 shares of common stock. 80,000 shares have been issued to date and 10,000 reacquired. All the reacquired shares are held in treasury. O'Grady has no preferred stock outstanding.

   a. Compute the total cash dividend that O'Grady will pay.

   b. Prepare the required journal entries at:

   (1) the declaration date

   (2) the date of record

   (3) the payment date

23. Johnson Inc. has 100,000 shares of $30 par value, 8 percent, cumulative preferred stock issued and outstanding. Johnson also has 500,000 shares of $5 par value, common stock issued, and 25,000 shares repurchased for $20 per share held in treasury. Johnson has not paid dividends in 1997 or 1998. Johnson has $1,000,000 available for dividends in 1999.

    a. Determine how much Johnson will pay its common and preferred stockholders, respectively, in 1999.

    b. Determine how these amounts will change if the preferred stock is noncumulative rather than cumulative.

24. The Mochrie Company's September 30, 1999, balances in its no par value common stock, retained earnings, and treasury stock accounts are $100,000, $500,000 and $25,000, respectively. Mochrie has 20,000 shares issued and 2,000 shares held in treasury. The market price of common stock on September 30 is $30 per share. Mochrie's board of directors is considering the following options:

    Option 1: A five percent stock dividend
    Option 2: A fifteen percent stock dividend
    Option 3: A 2-for-1 stock split

    a. Compute the number of shares that Mochrie would issue under each option.

24. b. Prepare the journal entries for each of the options.

     c. How does total stockholders' equity change under each option?

     d. How does the amount available for future cash dividends change under each option?

25. The Parent Company has the following stockholders' equity balance at the end of 1999 and 1998, respectively:

	1999	1998
Preferred stock ($50 par value)	$ 62,500	$ 43,750
Common stock (no par)	100,000	80,000
Additional paid-in capital:		
Preferred stock	16,250	8,750
Treasury stock	3,000	-
Less: Treasury stock	10,000	25,000

a. Provide the journal entry to record the issuance of preferred stock during 1999.

b. Provide the journal entry to record the issuance of common stock during 1999.

c. Provide the journal entry to record the sale of treasury stock during 1999.

CHAPTER 12-SOLUTIONS

1.	c	6.	b	11.	b	16.	a
2.	d	7.	b	12.	c	17.	d
3.	d	8.	c	13.	c	18.	c
4.	d	9.	b	14.	c	19.	a
5.	d	10.	c	15.	c	20.	b

21. 4/1   Cash (+A)   3,750,000
        Common Stock (+SE)   1,500,000
        Additional Paid-In Capital-C/S (+SE)   2,250,000

      7/1   Cash (+A)   2,400,000
        Preferred Stock (+SE)   1,500,000
        Additional Paid-In Capital-P/S (+SE)   900,000

      8/1   Treasury Stock (-SE)   700,000
        Cash (-A)   700,000

     10/30 Cash (+A)   450,000
        Treasury Stock (+SE)   420,000
        Additional Paid-In Capital-T/S (+SE)   30,000

     12/1   Cash (+A)   195,000
        Additional Paid-In Capital-T/S (-SE)   15,000
        Treasury Stock (+SE)   210,000

     12/31 Income Summary (-SE)   40,000
        Retained Earnings (+SE)   40,000

21.

Venturi Inc.
Partial Balance Sheet
Stockholders' Equity Section
December 31, 1999

Preferred stock (8%, $50 par value, 50,000 shares authorized, 30,000 shares issued, 1,000 shares held in treasury)	$1,500,000
Additional paid-in capital-preferred stock	900,000
Common stock ($10 par value, 200,000 shares authorized, 150,000 shares issued and outstanding)	1,500,000
Additional paid-in capital-common stock	2,250,000
Additional paid-in capital-treasury stock	15,000
Total contributed capital	$6,165,000
Retained earnings	40,000
Total stockholders' equity before treasury stock	$6,205,000
Less: Treasury stock, 1,000 shares of preferred stock held in treasury	70,000
Total stockholders' equity	$6,135,000

22. a. $3 per share x 70,000 (shares outstanding, 80,000 - 10,000)
         = $210,000

    b. 1. Cash Dividends (-SE)   210,000
              Cash Dividend Payable (+L)   210,000

       2. No entry

       3. Cash Dividend Payable (-L)   210,000
              Cash (-A)   210,000

23. a. Since the preferred stock is cumulative, all the previously undeclared preferred dividends must be paid before the common stockholders can receive their dividends.

    Annual preferred dividends = 100,000 shares x $30 par value x 0.08 = $240,000 per year

    Total to be declared: $240,000 x 3 = $720,000

    Common stockholders will receive $280,000 ($1,000,000 - $720,000)

    b. Annual preferred dividend = $240,000

    Common stockholders will receive $760,000 ($1,000,000 - $240,000)

24. a.   Option 1: 0.05 x 18,000 (shares outstanding) = 900
Option 2: 0.15 x 18,000 (shares outstanding) = 2,700
Option 3: 2 x 18,000 old shares = 36,000 totally outstanding after the split. Thus, 18,000 new shares must be issued.

b. 1.   Stock Dividends (-SE)   27,000
              Common Stock (+SE)   27,000

2.   Stock Dividends (-SE)   81,000
              Common Stock (+SE)   81,000

3.   No entry.

The stock dividend is valued using the common stock price at the date of declaration, $30 per share.

c.   Total stockholders' equity is unchanged in all three scenarios.

d.   Less is available for dividends in the stock dividend scenarios since the dividends represent a permanent capitalization of earnings.

25. a.   Cash (+A)   26,250
              Preferred Stock (+SE)   18,750
              Additional Paid-In Capital-P/S (+SE)   7,500

b.   Cash (+A)   20,000
              Common Stock (+SE)   20,000

c.   Cash (+A)   18,000
              Treasury Stock (+SE)   15,000
              Additional Paid-In Capital-T/S (+SE)   3,000

CHAPTER 13

The Complete Income Statement

REVIEW OF KEY CONCEPTS

Transactions included in the income statement are discussed in detail in this chapter. The format used to organize these transactions within the body of the income statement is also presented. After completing this chapter, you will be able to distinguish between financing, investing, and operating transactions and describe the circumstances under which they are included in the income statement.

While Chapters 6 through 12 have examined accounting for various balance sheet accounts, many of the transactions analyzed also affected income statement accounts. The transactions in which a business engages can be sorted into five categories:

1. Revenues and expenses
2. Purchases, sales, and exchanges of assets
3. Issues and payments of debt
4. Exchanges of liabilities and stockholders' equity
5. Exchanges with stockholders

Revenues and Expenses. Revenues are inflows of net assets (assets minus liabilities) from providing goods or services to customers. Expenses are outflows of net assets from providing those goods or services. Revenues and expenses represent the transactions directly involved in the ongoing operations of the business. They form the core of the transactions included in the income statement.

Purchases, Sales, and Exchanges of Assets. Assets are the economic resources in which capital contributed by creditors and stockholders is invested. The purpose of these investments in economic resources is to establish a wealth-generating structure. These resources are used up or converted into other resources that are eventually used up in order to earn revenues.

Occasionally, long-lived assets and investments in bonds or stocks are sold. These sales are not directly part of the ongoing transactions of the business. Instead, the company's management may decide to rebalance its portfolio of investments into one that is expected to result in larger increases in wealth in the future. Companies may sell plant and equipment that is not consistent with the company's evolving strategy. Gains or losses on the sale of assets are included in the income statement since these transactions relate to the operating strategy of the company.

Issues and Payments of Debt. One reason a company incurs debt instead of issuing additional shares of stock is that the expected return on the project the money is invested in exceeds the after-tax cost of the debt. Stockholders' wealth is increased by this difference. To measure the change in wealth because of operations, the cost of debt (i.e., interest expense) is included on the income statement. Usually, interest expense is reported as a separate line item after all the operating expenses.

Debt may be retired early by the company. For example, if the market price of bonds is less than the maturity value, companies may elect to repurchase bonds payable in the bond market. The retirement price is likely to differ from the book value of the bond (principal plus premium on bonds payable or, less discount on bonds payable). This difference is included in the income statement as a gain or loss.

Exchanges of Liabilities and Stockholders' Equity. These exchanges involve replacing a liability with another liability (debt refinancing) and conversion of convertible bonds and preferred stock into common stock. Usually, these transactions are not reported in the income statement because they are removed from the ongoing operating activities of the business. These transactions affect the capital structure of the business which is the relative proportion of assets claimed by creditors and stockholders.

Exchanges with Stockholders. These exchanges involve selling stock, distributing dividends, and treasury stock transactions. According to GAAP, these transactions are not reported in the income statement. Even though net assets can change because of these transactions, they are considered activities so far removed from the normal ongoing operating activities of the business that they are excluded from income.

For example, if treasury stock is resold at a different price than the corporation initially paid to repurchase it, the difference is not reported as a gain or loss on the income statement. If the resale price is higher than cost, Additional Paid-In Capital-Treasury Stock is increased by the difference. Stockholders' equity increases, but the increase is not disclosed on the income statement.

Revenues and expenses are called operating transactions because they involve the actual conduct of operating activities. Categories two through five (above) are capital transactions because they involve acquiring resources to conduct business and investing those resources in productive assets to allow the company to conduct operations.

A Complete Income Statement: Disclosure and Presentation

The accounts listed in the income statement are organized in a manner that reflects the categories of transactions described above. The sale of goods or services is the activity that the business was formed to conduct. Investors base investment decisions on the expectation that the business's primary operations will result in the growth of wealth invested in the business. Accordingly, **operating revenue and expense transactions** are listed in a separate section of the income statement. These transactions are the normal, recurring operating transactions of the business. Investors analyze changes in these revenue and expense categories to determine how the business is performing its primary activity.

As mentioned above, certain capital transactions are also included in the income statement; these are listed after operating income items. Most of these transactions are included in the *Other revenues and expenses* section. Common examples of these transactions are interest expense, interest and dividend revenue from investments, and gains and losses on disposal of assets. After the net of other revenues and expenses is deducted from operating income, income tax expense is presented.

While most nonoperating transactions are included in the other revenues and expenses section, GAAP requires the disclosure of three types of events in a special section of the income statement. These events are *disposal of a business segment, extraordinary items,* and *changes in accounting principle.* These events are reported after operating items and other revenues and expenses. If these special items exist, the income tax effect for these items is presented separately from the income tax expense related to the income determined from operating items and other revenues and expenses. **Intra-period tax allocation** is the process of separating the tax effect of the special items from the tax related to income from operations and other revenues and expenses. The accounting and disclosure of each of these items is briefly described below.

Disposal of a Business Segment

GAAP defines a **business segment** as a separate line of business, product line, or class of customers involving an operation independent from other company operations. The disposal of a segment represents a major shift in the strategy of the business, which warrants this additional disclosure.

Since the segment is discontinued, operating income of the segment is backed out of the operating income from continuing operations to enable the investor or creditor to develop expectations regarding the company in the future. The operating income of the discontinued segment is computed from the beginning of the fiscal year to the disposal date.

Usually, a company will attempt to sell the segment to another company. Occasionally, the segment's assets may be sold separately. In any event, the book value of the segment is likely to differ from the selling price received for the segment or its assets. This results in a gain or loss on the disposal. Both the operating results of the segment and the gain or loss on disposal are presented in the discontinued operations section, net of their specific tax effect.

Example. Beaux Inc., a cosmetics manufacturer, decides to discontinue sales to beauty salons and focus on department stores only. This constitutes discontinuing a major line of customer. During the year, Beaux Inc.'s net income before tax is $300,000, which includes the loss on salon operating activities for the year, $25,000, and the gain on sale of the assets of the beauty salon division, $60,000. The assets' book value was $200,000. Beaux is subject to a 30 percent income tax rate.

Net income before tax on continuing operations for the year is $265,000 ($300,000 + Loss on salon operating activities, $25,000 - Gain on sale of the assets, $60,000). The income tax on continuing operations income is $79,500 ($265,000 x 0.30). Income from continuing operations is $185,500 ($265,000 - $79,500).

The information regarding the discontinued segment is presented after income from continuing operations on the income statement. The loss on salon operating activities after tax is $17,500 [$25,000 - (0.30 x $25,000)]; the after tax gain on the sale of salon assets is $42,000 [$60,000 - (0.30 x $60,000)]. The partial income statement for Beaux follows:

Beaux Inc.
Partial Income Statement
For the Year Ended December 31, 2000

Income from continuing operations before tax	$265,000
Income tax	79,500
Income from continuing operations	$185,500
Discontinued operations:	
Operating loss on salon division	$(17,500)
(net of $7,500 tax benefit)	
Gain on disposal of salon division assets	42,000
(net of $18,000 tax expense)	
Income from discontinued operations	$ 24,500
Net income	$210,000

Extraordinary Items

GAAP defines **extraordinary items** as material events which are *both unusual* and *infrequent* in nature. These events must differ from the business's normal operating and capital transactions. They must be nonrecurring as well, since investors' predictions of future performance are likely to exclude such events. If they are recurring, investors should factor them into predictions. For example, damage resulting from a tornado in Kansas is clearly not a usual operating or capital transaction. However, tornados occur in certain regions, including Kansas, on a regular basis. The investor may wish to factor the cost of the damage into future performance projections, since this is an additional risk due to operating in Kansas. This loss would be disclosed in the other revenue and expense section with accompanying footnotes describing the damage.

In addition to applying the unusual and infrequent criteria to transactions, certain events are required to be disclosed as extraordinary by specific GAAP pronouncements. For example, the gain or loss from early retirement of long-term debt and the gain or loss from pension plan terminations must be disclosed as extraordinary items.

Extraordinary items are disclosed in the same manner as discontinued operations. For example, assume that Beaux Inc. retired $100,000 face amount of bonds payable, with a book value of $100,000, for $98,000. The gain on retirement is $2,000 before tax. The tax expense associated with the gain is $600, and the gain is reported as an extraordinary item (net of tax) for $1,400 in the income statement. Revising Beaux's income statement:

Beaux Inc.
Partial Income Statement
For the Year Ended December 31, 2000

Income from continuing operations before tax	$265,000
Income tax	79,500
Income from continuing operations	$185,500
Discontinued operations:	
Operating loss on salon division	$ (17,500)
(net of $7,500 tax benefit)	
Gain on disposal of salon division assets	42,000
(net of $18,000 tax expense)	
Income from discontinued operations	$ 24,500
Extraordinary item:	
Gain from the early extinguishment of bonds payable	
(net of tax expense, $600)	$ 1,400
Net income	$211,400

Changes in Accounting Principle

Because of operating environment changes, companies occasionally decide that their current methods of calculating particular revenue or expense accounts and the related balance sheet accounts are no longer effective. If the company can convince its auditors that a new method better reflects the economic condition of the company, a change in accounting principle is enacted.

The financial statements are in a sense converted to the new method. For example, assume Beaux Inc. decides to change its depreciation method from an accelerated method to straight-line for its ongoing operating assets. The balance sheet account affected by this change is Accumulated Depreciation. Assume that at the beginning of the year the accumulated depreciation balance was $75,000, reflecting the use of the accelerated method. If straight-line had always been used, the accumulated depreciation's balance would have been $60,000. 2000 income already reflects straight-line. To convert Accumulated Depreciation to the straight-line basis, $15,000 is backed out of the account. Clearly, if straight-line had been used all along, reported income would have been higher by $15,000 before tax and $10,500 after tax since depreciation expense would have been lower in past years. After-tax income is closed each year into retained earnings. Thus, in some way, retained earnings must also reflect the change.

For most accounting principle changes, the cumulative effect of the change (in this example, $15,000 before tax and $10,500 after tax) is disclosed in a special section as the very last item before net income on the income statement. Since net income is closed into retained earnings after the financial statements are prepared, Retained Earnings will reflect the change to straight-line on the balance sheet and the general ledger.

Beaux made the following entry to record the cumulative effect of the accounting principle change:

Accumulated Depreciation (+A)	15,000	
Cumulative Gain from Accounting Change (Ga,+SE)		10,500
Income Tax Liability (+L)		4,500

Beaux's revised income statement is:

Beaux Inc.
Partial Income Statement
For the Year Ended December 31, 2000

Income from continuing operations before tax	$265,000
Income tax	79,500
Income from continuing operations	$185,500
Discontinued operations:	
Operating loss on salon division	$(17,500)
(net of $7,500 tax benefit)	
Gain on disposal of salon division assets	42,000
(net of $18,000 tax expense)	
Income from discontinued operations	$ 24,500
Extraordinary item:	
Gain from the early extinguishment of bonds payable	
(net of tax expense, $600)	$ 1,400
Cumulative gain from accounting change:	
Accelerated depreciation to straight-line	
(net of tax, $4,500)	$ 10,500
Net income	$221,900

Comprehensive Income

The FASB issued a new standard in 1997, which will require companies to disclose **Comprehensive Income**. This is a broader concept than net income, and includes all changes in equity arising from transactions with nonowners. The most significant differences from net income are likely to arise from unrealized market value gains and losses on available-for-sale securities and foreign currency translation adjustments. (Foreign currency translation adjustments are beyond the scope of this introductory course. They arise from investments in foreign subsidiary companies and changes in relative currency values over time.) Comprehensive income may be disclosed in a separate statement of comprehensive income, as an adjustment on the income statement, or as a part of **the statement of stockholders' equity.**

Assume Beaux Inc. has a foreign currency translation gain of $10,000 and unrealized losses on available-for-sale securities of $4,000 during 2000. Both are items subject to a 30 percent effective tax rate. If Beaux chooses to prepare a separate statement, it would appear as follows:

Beaux Inc.
Comprehensive Income Statement
For the Year Ended December 31, 2000

Net income (from the income statement)	$221,900
Other comprehensive income:	
Foreign currency translation adjustment	10,000
Tax effect	(3,000)
Unrealized losses on available-for-sale securities	(4,000)
Tax effect	1,200
Comprehensive income	$226,100

The comprehensive income amount also requires earnings per share disclosure effects.

QUESTIONS FOR YOUR REVIEW

1. The capital maintenance approach to measuring income involves:
   a. determining the change in total assets during the year and backing out additional stockholder contributions and dividends.
   b. determining the change in net assets during the year and backing out additional stockholder contributions and dividends.
   c. determining the change in productive capital (inventory and plant and equipment) during the year and backing out additional stockholder contributions and dividends.
   d. determining the change in the total market value of stock (shares outstanding times market price) during the year and backing out additional stockholder contributions and dividends.

2. An example of a transaction which is not reported on the income statement is:
   a. the sale of equipment at a price above its book value.
   b. the sale of treasury stock at a price below its cost.
   c. the sale of inventory at a price above its book value.
   d. the change in accounting for inventory from the FIFO cost flow assumption to average cost flow assumption.

3. An example of a capital transaction is the:
   a. issuance of common stock.
   b. sale of inventory at a price above its cost.
   c. payment for utilities expense.
   d. recognition of depreciation expense on machinery.

4. An example of an operating transaction is the:
   a. declaration of a stock dividend.
   b. purchase of machinery.
   c. purchase of inventory on account.
   d. recognition of depreciation expense on machinery.

5. Net assets are:
   a. total assets less related contra accounts, such as Accumulated Depreciation.
   b. current assets net of current liabilities.
   c. the total assets contributed by stockholders during a period less dividends distributed during the period.
   d. total assets less total liabilities.

6. Michael Inc.'s beginning and ending total stockholders' equity are $600,000 and $750,000, respectively. During the year, stock dividends of $60,000 and cash dividends of $100,000 were distributed. Michael purchased 3,000 shares of its own stock for $40,000 which are still held as Treasury Stock at year-end. Michael's net income for the year is:
   a. $250,000
   b. $290,000
   c. $310,000
   d. $350,000

7. An example of an operating transaction is the:
   a. collection of an account receivable.
   b. recognition of prepaid rent used during the period.
   c. purchase of inventory for cash.
   d. purchase of equipment using a long-term note payable.

8. The category of transactions whose results are never reported on the income statement is:
   a. operating transactions.
   b. issues and payments of debt.
   c. purchases, sales, and exchanges of assets.
   d. exchanges with stockholders.

9. The category of transactions whose results form the core of the transactions reported on the income statement is:
   a. operating transactions.
   b. issues and payments of debt.
   c. purchases, sales, and exchanges of assets.
   d. exchanges with stockholders.

10. A transaction reported under *Other revenues and expenses* in the income statement is:
    a. the sale of inventory at below its cost.
    b. the sale of equipment at above its book value.
    c. the recognition of depreciation expense on machinery.
    d. the recognition of supplies used during the period.

11. Chambers Inc.'s total income before tax is $200,000. Included in this amount is a $50,000 loss from the disposal of a business segment. Chambers is subject to a 30 percent tax rate. What is Chambers' income tax expense for the year?
    a. $45,000
    b. $60,000
    c. $75,000
    d. $0, since a loss has been incurred.

12. Refer to question 11. What is Chambers' income after tax from continuing operations?
    a. $105,000
    b. $140,000
    c. $175,000
    d. $0, since a loss has been incurred.

13. Refer to question 11. What amount is reported as discontinued operations for Chambers?
    a. $50,000 loss
    b. $35,000 loss
    c. $50,000 gain
    d. $0, since this is a financing and investing, not an operating transaction.

14. The correction of an error detected in prior years' reported income is:
    a. ignored, since investors' decisions are primarily based upon current year's income.
    b. reported in current year's income as an extraordinary item.
    c. recorded directly in retained earnings, bypassing the current year's income statement.
    d. reported in current year's income as other revenue and expense.

15. Which of the following is likely to be reported as an extraordinary item in the income statement?
    a. Switch from accelerated depreciation method to straight-line
    b. Loss from a hurricane in Tampa, Florida
    c. Loss from an earthquake in Los Angeles
    d. Loss from a blizzard in Hawaii

16. Amber Inc. switches its inventory method from FIFO to LIFO at the beginning of 2000. 2000 inventory and cost of goods sold are accounted for using LIFO. Beginning inventory is $40,000 under FIFO and $35,000 under LIFO. Amber has always been subject to a 30 percent tax rate. Where, and at what amount, is the change reported in the 2000 income statement?
    a. Inventory is an operating item, the $5,000 extra expense is included in cost of goods sold.
    b. Since prior years' income would have been $3,500 ($5,000 - (0.3 x $5,000)] lower, retained earnings is reduced by $3,500. The item is not presented in the income statement.
    c. The cumulative effect of the accounting change, a $5,000 deduction, is reported in its own special section just before net income.
    d. The cumulative effect of the accounting change, net of tax, a $3,500 deduction, is reported in its own special section just before net income.

17. Comprehensive income is to be reported:
    a. in a separate statement of comprehensive income.
    b. as a component of the statement of stockholders' equity.
    c. as an additional component of the income statement.
    d. All the above are acceptable alternative disclosures.

18. The denominator in computing diluted earnings per share is:
    a. the average number of preferred and common shares outstanding during the year.
    b. the average number of common shares outstanding adjusted for shares held in treasury.
    c. the average number of common shares outstanding plus the number of additional shares outstanding if options and securities which are convertible into common shares were exercised.
    d. the authorized number of common shares, since this is the maximum number of shares that could be issued.

19. The transactions approach for presenting income is preferred over the capital maintenance approach because:
    a. income is more accurately measured under the transactions approach.
    b. the transactions approach is less costly to apply than the capital maintenance approach.
    c. the transactions approach allows the investor to more fully examine the reasons behind a company's performance during the year than does the capital maintenance approach.
    d. for most companies, the accounting system can produce only the transactions approach income statement.

20. The group of transactions disclosed in the income statement which are expected to be the most persistent in the future is:
    a. operating revenues and expenses.
    b. other revenues and expenses.
    c. disposal of segments.
    d. extraordinary items.

21. The Lewis and Clarke Company's December 31, 1999, balance sheet is presented below.

Assets	$100,000	Liabilities	$ 60,000
		Stockholders' equity	40,000
		Total liabilities and	
Total assets	$100,000	stockholders' equity	$100,000

During 2000, the following transactions occurred:

1. Land was purchased for $20,000 by issuing a long-term note payable.
2. Common stock was issued for $50,000 cash.
3. Dividends of $15,000 were declared and paid.
4. Services were performed for $45,000. $20,000 cash was received, the remainder was on account.
5. Cash expenses of $45,000 were incurred.

Classify each transaction as operating or financing and investing and prepare an income statement.

22. Kalember Inc. decides to sell its mainframe computer division, retaining its personal computer division. On June 1, 2000, the division is sold for $500,000 cash. The following mainframe division financial information at June 1, 2000, was pulled from the books (all numbers are before tax):

Sales (January 1 through June 1, 2000)	$ 700,000
Operating expenses	730,000
Operating loss	$ (30,000)
Assets	$ 3,000,000
Liabilities	$ 2,800,000

At December 31, 2000, Kalember's personal computer division reports income before tax of $500,000. Kalember's corporate tax rate is 30 percent.

a. Prepare the journal entry (entries) to record the sale of the mainframe division.

b. Prepare Kalember's income statement beginning with income from continuing operations before tax.

23. The following is from Mica's adjusted trial balance at December 31, 2000.

	Debit	Credit
Retained Earnings, January 1, 2000		1,000,000
Sales Revenue		400,000
Gain from Sale of Equipment		3,000
Cost of Goods Sold	190,000	
Salaries Expense	30,000	
Depreciation Expense	50,000	
Interest Expense	25,000	
Interest Revenue		10,000
Loss from Early Extinguishment of Debt	45,000	
Income Tax Expense	35,400	
Dividends	75,000	

Mica's corporate tax rate is 30 percent. The loss from the early extinguishment is already recorded net of its tax effect.

a. Determine the income tax liability for Mica for the year.

b. Prepare a multi-step income statement for Mica.

c. Prepare the statement of retained earnings for Mica.

24. Inkspot Inc.'s manager's bonus is 5 percent of pre-bonus income from continuing operations after tax. During 2000, Inkspot sold a plant in Europe, but continues to produce the product in its remaining plants and sell it worldwide. The plant lost $100,000 from operations in 2000 before it was sold. The plant was sold at a loss of $300,000. Both losses are before tax. Inkspot's other operations earned $2,000,000 before tax. Inkspot is subject to a 30 percent tax rate.

   a.   Compute the manager's bonus if the sale is not considered a disposal of a segment.

   b.   Compute the manager's bonus if the sale is considered a disposal of a segment.

   c.   Assuming the manager is primarily concerned about his or her take-home pay, which classification would he or she prefer? Why?

   d.   What do you believe the appropriate classification of the disposal should be? Why?

25. Cafe Au Latte, a producer of fine teas and coffees, decides to switch its depreciation method from straight-line to an accelerated method. Its auditors concur with the change. On January 1, 2000, accumulated depreciation is $50,000. If the company had used an accelerated method all along, accumulated depreciation would have been $80,000. Depreciation expense is recorded using the accelerated method during 2000. The company is subject to a 30 percent tax rate.

   a.   Prepare the journal entry (entries) to record the change in depreciation method.

   b.   Prepare the income statement section which discloses the change, if income before the cumulative effect of the accounting change is $200,000 (net of tax).

CHAPTER 13-SOLUTIONS

1.	b	6.	b	11.	c	16.	d
2.	b	7.	b	12.	c	17.	d
3.	a	8.	d	13.	b	18.	c
4.	d	9.	a	14.	c	19.	c
5.	d	10.	b	15.	d	20.	a

21. Classification of transactions:

1. Financing and investing, purchase of an asset
2. Financing and investing, exchange with stockholders
3. Financing and investing, exchange with stockholders
4. Operating
5. Operating

The Lewis and Clarke Company
Income Statement
For the Year Ended December 31, 2000

Service revenue	$45,000	
Expenses	(45,000)	
Net income	$ 0	

22. a.

Cash (+A)	500,000	
Liabilities (-L)	2,800,000	
Assets (-A)		3,000,000
Gain on Disposal of the		
Mainframe Division (Ga,+SE)		300,000
Gain on Disposal of the		
Mainframe Division (-Ga,-SE)	90,000	
Income Tax Payable(+L)		90,000

b.

Kalember Inc.
Income Statement
For the Year Ended December 31, 2000

Income from continuing operations before tax	$500,000
Income tax expense	(150,000)
Income from continuing operations	$350,000
Discontinued operations:	
Operating loss from mainframe division	
(net of $9,000 tax benefit)	$ (21,000)
Gain on sale of mainframe division	
(net of $90,000 tax expense)	210,000
Income from discontinued operations	$189,000
Net income	$539,000

23. a. Mica's total income tax expense:

Income before tax and extraordinary loss:
$400,000 + 3,000 - 190,000 - 30,000 - 50,000 - 25,000 + 10,000
    = $118,000 x 0.30 = $ 35,400
Tax benefit from the extraordinary loss:
    $45,000 = Pretax Loss - Pretax Loss x 0.30
    $45,000 = Pretax Loss (1 - 0.30)
    $64,286 = Pretax Loss

Tax benefit = .30 x 64,286 = $19,286

Total income tax liability = $35,400 - $19,286 = $16,114

b.

Mica Inc.
Income Statement
For the Year Ended December 31, 2000

Sales		$400,000
Less: Cost of goods sold		190,000
Gross profit		$210,000
Less operating expenses:		
Salaries	$30,000	
Depreciation	50,000	80,000
Operating income		$130,000
Other revenues and expenses:		
Gain on equipment sale	$ 3,000	
Interest revenue	10,000	
Interest expense	(25,000)	(12,000)
Income before tax and extraordinary loss		$118,000
Income tax expense		35,400
Income before extraordinary loss		$ 82,600
Extraordinary loss from early extinguishment of debt		
(net of $19,286 tax benefit)		(45,000)
Net income		$ 37,600

c.

Mica Inc.
Statement of Retained Earnings
For the Year Ended December 31, 2000

Retained earnings, January 1, 2000	$1,000,000
Add: 2000 net income	37,600
Less: Dividends declared	(75,000)
Retained earnings, December 31, 2000	$ 962,600

24. a. His bonus based upon income from continuing operations after tax including the loss on the plant asset is:

Income from continuing plants - Loss from discontinued plant operations - Loss on discontinued plant sale.
$2,000,000 - $100,000 - $300,000 = $1,600,000

$1,600,000 - $480,000 (tax at 30%) = $1,120,000

The bonus is: $1,120,000 x 0.05 = $56,000

24. b. If the sale is considered a segment disposal, the basis for the bonus is:
$2,000,000 - $600,000 (tax at 30%) = $1,400,000

The bonus is: $ 1,400,000 x 0.05 = $70,000

c. Clearly, the manager would prefer the discontinued segment designation because his/her bonus is higher under that accounting treatment.

d. Discontinued segment designation is inappropriate because the company's remaining plants absorb the discontinued plant's production and the entire world continues to be served. The plant's operating loss should not be separated from the continuing plants. The loss on the plant disposal should be reported in the *Other revenue and expense* section of the income statement.

25. a. Accumulated depreciation is higher under accelerated than under straight-line. The change increases accumulated depreciation. The cumulative effect, $21,000 after tax, is a reduction of income.

Cumulative effect of an accounting principle change:

Straight-Line to Accelerated Depreciation (-SE)	21,000	
Income Tax Receivable (+A)	9,000	
Accumulated Depreciation (-A)		30,000

b.

Cafe Au Latte
Partial Income Statement
For the Year Ended December 31, 2000

Income before the cumulative effect of accounting principle change	$200,000
Cumulative effect of an accounting principle change: Straight-line depreciation method to accelerated depreciation (net of $9,000 tax benefit)	(21,000)
Net income	$179,000

CHAPTER 14

The Statement of Cash Flows

REVIEW OF KEY CONCEPTS

This chapter focuses upon the preparation and use of the *statement of cash flows*. The review of key concepts focuses primarily upon the preparation of the statement. The text's discussion on interpretation of the statement is excellent. Questions emphasizing the preparation of the statement are included at the end of this study guide chapter for your review.

A business's ability to generate adequate amounts of cash from operating activities is critical to its long-run success. Eventually, most assets used to produce the services or products sold by the business are paid for with cash. Some assets are purchased directly with cash, others are purchased with short-term or long-term notes, which are subsequently retired with cash. Investors usually receive a portion of the earnings of the business in dividends. The statement of cash flows provides information about transactions that resulted in the change in the cash balance over a period of time.

Preparation of the Statement of Cash Flows

Activities that provide or use cash are included in one of three categories in the statement: *operating activities, investing activities,* and *financing activities*. Transactions directly related to the sale of products or services are categorized as operating activities. Investing activities involve the purchase and sale of the company's noncurrent assets. Financing activities involve cash receipts from, and payments to, the providers of capital, creditors and stockholders. The income statement and balance sheet of Lopez Inc., presented below, are used to illustrate the preparation of a statement of cash flows.

Lopez Inc.
Income Statement
For the Year Ended June 30, 1999

Sales	$1,000,000	
Gain from land sale	10,000	
Total revenues and gains		$1,010,000
Cost of goods sold	$ 700,000	
Salaries expense	150,000	
Depreciation expense	50,000	
Utilities expense	20,000	
Total expenses		920,000
Income before taxes		$ 90,000
Income taxes		36,000
Net income		$ 54,000

Lopez Inc.
Balance Sheet
June 30, 1999 and 1998

	1999	1998
Cash	$ 40,000	$ 60,000
Accounts receivable	260,000	250,000
Inventory	160,000	175,000
Land	100,000	125,000
Building	520,000	375,000
Less: Accumulated depreciation	(210,000)	(160,000)
Total assets	$870,000	$825,000
Accounts payable	$ 50,000	$ 57,000
Salaries payable	15,000	10,000
Utilities payable	1,000	0
Income tax payable	2,000	5,000
Total liabilities	$ 68,000	$ 72,000
Common stock, no par value	$400,000	$400,000
Retained earnings	402,000	353,000
Total stockholders' equity	$802,000	$753,000
Total liabilities and stockholders' equity	$870,000	$825,000

Additional information: All sales and merchandise purchases are on account.

Cash Provided (Used) by Operating Activities-the Direct Method

The same types of transactions are included in cash provided by operating activities as are included in net income. The income statement is prepared under the accrual basis of accounting. The revenue realization and matching rules are used to determine when operating transactions are included in income. The timing of the related cash receipt or payment determines when a transaction is included in cash generated from operations. By examining the income statement, the types of transactions to be included in the cash provided (used) by operations section are identified for Lopez.

Income Statement Account	Comparable Cash Transaction Category
Sales	Cash collections from customers (either through cash sales or collections of accounts receivable).
Cost of goods sold	Cash paid for merchandise (either through cash payments or payments of accounts payable).
Salaries expense	Cash paid for salaries (either through cash payments or payments of salaries payable).
Depreciation expense	The purchase of long-lived assets is included in the investing activities section. No comparable cash transaction is included for depreciation expense.
Utilities expense	Cash paid for utilities (either through cash payments or payments of utilities payable).
Gain on land sale	Cash received from the sale of land is included in the investing activities section. No comparable transaction for gains or losses on sales of assets is included here.
Income tax expense	Cash paid for income taxes (either through cash payments or payments of income taxes payable).

The income statement accounts are separated into two categories. The gain on land sale and depreciation expense accounts are excluded from the cash provided (used) by operating activities section because the related cash flows are located elsewhere in the statement of cash flows. In particular, the cash received from the sale of land is included in the *investing activities* section because land is a long-lived asset. While depreciation expense represents the allocation of a long-lived asset's cost over time, the cash paid to acquire the asset was reported in the *investing activities* section when the asset was acquired. Thus, depreciation expense is not included in the computation of cash from operations. Goodwill amortization and losses on long-lived asset sales are other examples of income statement items excluded from cash from operations.

The second category of income statement accounts are items with comparable operating cash flow transactions. The relation between the accrual and cash bases is used to identify the balance sheet accounts, aside from the cash account itself, which involves both the accrual and cash items listed above. From analyzing changes in the current asset and liability accounts, the cash received or paid related to each of these items can be identified as illustrated on the following page, using Lopez Inc.'s information.

Cash provided (used) by operations computed using the direct method is:

Cash collections from customers [a]	$990,000
Cash payments for:	
Merchandise [b]	$692,000
Salaries [c]	145,000
Utilities [d]	19,000
Income taxes [e]	39,000
Total cash payments	$895,000
Cash generated from operations	$ 95,000

The T-account analysis of Lopez's balance sheet accounts follows. Use the superscripted cross-references from above to determine how these numbers were computed (B.B. = beginning balance, E.B. = ending balance).

Accounts Receivable

B.B.	250,000	Cash	
Sales	1,000,000	Collections ?	
E.B.	260,000		

B.B. + Sales - Cash collections = E.B.
250,000 + 1,000,000 - ? = 260,000

? = 990,000 = Cash collections from customers [a]

Inventory

B.B.	175,000		
Pur.	?	CGS 700,000	
E.B.	160,000		

Accounts Payable

Cash		B.B.	57,000
Payments ?		Pur.	?
		E.B.	50,000

B.B. + Purchases - CGS = E.B.
175,000 + ? - 700,000 = 160,000

? = 685,000 = Purchases

B.B. + Pur. - Cash payments = E.B.
57,000 + 685,000 - ? = 50,000

? = 692,000 = Cash payments for merchandise [b]

Salaries Payable		
Cash Payments ?	B.B.	10,000
	Sal. Exp.	150,000
	E.B.	15,000

Utilities Payable		
Cash Payments ?	B.B.	0
	Util. Exp.	20,000
	E.B.	1,000

B.B. + Exp - Cash payments = E.B.
10,000 + 150,000 - ? = 15,000

? = 145,000 = Cash payments for Salaries [c]

B.B. + Exp. - Cash payments = E.B.
0 + 20,000 - ? = 1,000

? = 19,000 = Cash payments for Utilities [d]

Income Tax Payable		
Cash Payments ?	B.B.	5,000
	Inc.Tax Exp.	36,000
	E.B.	2,000

B.B. + Expense - Cash Payments = E.B.
5,000 + 36,000 - ? = 2,000

? = 39,000 = Cash payments for income taxes [e]

Reconciling Net Income to Cash Provided (Used) by Operating Activities-the Indirect Method

An alternative approach to computing cash provided (used) by operating activities is the **indirect method**, which some companies use instead of the direct method. Both methods result in the same figure for cash provided by operating activities. The difference is a procedural one. The reasoning behind the indirect method is presented on the following page.

The direct method T-account analysis can be organized as follows:

Cash received from customers	= Sales + Beginning A/R - Ending A/R = Sales - (Ending A/R - Beginning A/R) = Sales - Change in accounts receivable
Purchases **Cash paid to vendors**	= Cost of goods sold + Change in inventory = Purchases - Change in accounts payable = Cost of goods sold + Change in inventory - Change in accounts payable
Cash paid for salaries	= Salaries expense - Change in salaries payable
Cash paid for utilities	= Utilities expense - Change in utilities payable
Cash paid for income tax	= Income tax expense - Change in income tax payable

You'll notice that each of the formulas above contains an income statement account (such as sales, cost of goods sold and salaries expense) and the change in a balance sheet account from the beginning of the year to the end. The indirect method uses net income (the net of all of the income statement accounts) as a starting point to compute cash from operations. Net income is then adjusted for the changes in account balances and for income statement accounts that have the cash consequence reported elsewhere in the statement of cash flows. An example is a gain or loss on an asset sale, the proceeds of which are reported in the investing activities section, or depreciation expense, where the cash paid to originally acquire the asset is included in the investing activities section in the year of acquisition.

The following formula can be used to compute cash provided by operations under the indirect method for Lopez Inc.:

Cash provided (used) by operations =
Net income + Depreciation expense - Gain on land sale - Change in accounts receivable -
Change in inventory + Change in accounts payable + Change in salaries payable + Change
in utilities payable + Change in income tax payable

Notice that the items that are not related to cash from operations are backed out of net income: depreciation expense and gain on land sale. The other adjustments involve the change in the current asset and current liability accounts. Increases (decreases) in current asset accounts are subtracted (added) and increases (decreases) in current liabilities are added (subtracted) to arrive at cash provided from operations.

This alternative approach can be applied to the Lopez example, as follows.

54,000 (net income) + 50,000 (depreciation expense) - 10,000 (gain) - 10,000 (increase in accounts receivable) + 15,000 (decrease in inventory) - 7,000 (decrease in accounts payable) + 5,000 (increase in salaries payable) + 1,000 (increase in utilities payable) - 3,000 (decrease in income tax payable) = 95,000.

Notice that the direct and indirect methods yield the same amount of cash provided by operating activities. The difference in the two methods is in procedure.

Cash Provided (Used) by Investing Activities

The cash transactions related to the purchase and sale of noncurrent assets are summarized here. Referring to the Lopez balance sheet, the only long-lived asset accounts are Land and Building. The income statement reports a gain on land sale of $10,000. This means that the land was sold for $10,000 more than its cost. Changes in the land account are examined to determine the cost of the land sold. Land decreased by $25,000 (125,000 B.B. - 100,000 E.B.). No other transactions affected the land account during the year. Thus, the land was sold for $35,000 ($25,000 + $10,000).

The building account increased by $145,000 ($520,000 E.B. - $375,000 B.B.). No sales occurred during the year. Thus, a building was acquired for $125,000.

Cash Provided (Used) by Financing Activities

Cash transactions related to receiving capital or making payments to capital sources (long-term creditors and stockholders) are presented in this section. Referring to the Lopez balance sheet, Lopez has no long-term liabilities. Lopez's common stock balance is unchanged. Retained earnings increased by $49,000 and net income is $54,000. Lopez must have paid $5,000 in dividends to explain the $49,000 increase ($54,000 - $5,000).

The statement of cash flows for Lopez is presented using the indirect method to compute cash provided by operating activities.

Lopez Inc.
Statement of Cash Flows
For the Year Ended December 31, 1999

Cash provided (used) by operating activities:

Net income	$ 54,000
+ Depreciation expense	50,000
- Gain on land sale	(10,000)
- Increase in accounts receivable	(10,000)
+ Decrease in inventory	15,000
- Decrease in accounts payable	(7,000)
+ Increase in salaries payable	5,000
+ Increase in utilities payable	1,000
- Decrease in income tax payable	(3,000)
Net cash provided by operating activities	$ 95,000

Cash provided (used) by investing activities:

Proceeds from land sale	$ 35,000
Purchase of building	(145,000)
Net cash used by investing activities	$(110,000)

Cash provided (used) by financing activities:

Cash dividends paid to stockholders	$ (5,000)
Net cash used by financing activities	$ (5,000)

Net change in the cash balance	$ (20,000)
Beginning cash balance	60,000
Ending cash balance	$ 40,000

QUESTIONS FOR YOUR REVIEW

The following information relates to questions 1 through 3.

All of Mochrie Inc.'s sales and merchandise purchases are on account. Mochrie Inc.'s records reveal:

	1999	1998
Prepaid rent	$ 12,000	$ 14,000
Wages payable	0	7,000
Rent expense	15,000	13,000
Wages expense	75,000	72,000
Accounts receivable	150,000	170,000
Sales	800,000	750,000

1. During 1999, cash collected from customers is:
   a. $780,000
   b. $800,000
   c. $820,000
   d. $970,000

2. During 1999, cash paid for rent is:
   a. $13,000
   b. $15,000
   c. $17,000
   d. $27,000

3. During 1999, cash paid for wages is:
   a. $67,000
   b. $75,000
   c. $79,000
   d. $82,000

4. Inkster Corporation's 1999 cost of goods sold is $700,000. Beginning inventory is $50,000 and ending inventory is $40,000. Beginning accounts payable is $70,000 and ending accounts payable is $75,000. Cash paid for merchandise during 1999 is:
   a. $685,000
   b. $690,000
   c. $695,000
   d. $700,000

5. A purchase of land in exchange for a corporation's common stock is disclosed:
   a. in the operating activities section of the statement of cash flows.
   b. in the investing activities section of the statement of cash flows.
   c. in the investing and financing activities sections of the statement of cash flows.
   d. in the footnotes to the financial statements.

6. Net income can be less than cash provided (used) by operating activities if:
   a. land is sold at a gain.
   b. the balance in Accounts Receivable increases.
   c. the balance in Accounts Payable increases.
   d. the balance in Income Taxes Payable decreases.

The following information relates to questions 7 and 8.

Chamberlain, Inc.'s books revealed the following:

	1999	1998
Equipment	$50,000	$40,000
Accumulated depreciation	10,500	10,000
Depreciation expense	5,000	5,000
Loss on equipment sale	2,000	1,000

Additional information: Equipment which originally cost $8,000 was sold during 1999.

7. How much cash was collected on the sale of the equipment in 1999?
    a. $1,500
    b. $2,000
    c. $5,500
    d. $6,000

8. How much equipment was purchased in 1999?
    a. $9,500
    b. $10,000
    c. $18,000
    d. $20,000

9. Which of the following transactions is not a financing activity disclosed on Henry Inc.'s statement of cash flows?
    a. Repurchased 10,000 shares of 10 percent preferred stock at $20 per share.
    b. Declared and paid a $2 per share cash dividend on common stock.
    c. Sold 25,000 shares of Fonda Inc.'s common stock for $30 per share.
    d. Retired $100,000 of bonds payable by paying them off.

10. Which of the following is not an investing activity disclosed on Jones Inc.'s statement of cash flows?
    a. Sold land which originally cost $30,000, for $30,000. $20,000 cash and $10,000 long-term notes receivable were received in exchange.
    b. Purchased Indiana Sports Inc.'s bonds for $70,000 cash.
    c. Purchased Milwaukee Ale Company stock.
    d. Declared and paid a dividend to common stockholders.

The following information relates to questions 11 and 12. Fox Trot Inc.'s books reveal the following:

	1999	1998
Accounts receivable	$200,000	$205,000
Allowance for doubtful accounts	10,000	14,000
Bad debt expense	35,000	40,000
Sales	700,000	650,000

11. The accounts written off during 1999 totaled:
    a. $4,000
    b. $5,000
    c. $35,000
    d. $39,000

12. Cash collected from charge customers totaled:
    a. $666,000
    b. $670,000
    c. $700,000
    d. $705,000

The following information relates to questions 13 through 15. Antioch Inc.'s stockholders' equity section shows the following:

	1999	1998
Common stock, $5 par value	$ 700,000	$ 650,000
Additional paid-in capital	300,000	200,000
Retained earnings	500,000	560,000
Less: Treasury stock	(80,000)	(90,000)
Net stockholders' equity	$1,420,000	$1,320,000

Additional Information:

1. The 1998 treasury stock, which cost $90,000, was sold for $85,000 on January 15, 1999. The ending 1999 treasury stock was purchased for $80,000 on December 12, 1999. 8,000 shares were purchased on that date. No other treasury stock transactions occurred during the year.
2. Additional common stock was issued on December 20, 1999.
3. A 5 percent stock dividend was declared and issued on October 15, 1999, when the stock price was $10 per share.
4. 1999 net income is $40,000.

13. The number of shares issued through the common stock dividend is:
    a. 3,500
    b. 6,500
    c. 10,000
    d. 30,000

14. Total cash received through the common stock sale is:
    a. $60,000
    b. $85,000
    c. $90,000
    d. $150,000

15. Cash dividends declared total:
    a. $35,000
    b. $50,000
    c. $60,000
    d. $100,000

16. Which of the following is added to net income to arrive at cash provided (used) by operating activities?
    a. Gain on land sale
    b. Increase in accounts receivable
    c. Increase in interest payable
    d. Decrease in accounts payable

17. Which of the following decisions might temporarily improve the appearance of reported cash provided (used) by operating activities?
    a. Purchase long-lived asset with a long-term note payable
    b. Delay declaring and paying preferred dividends
    c. Delay paying a long-term note payable
    d. Delay paying accounts payable

The following information relates to questions 18 and 19.

	1999	1998
Sales	$900,000	$750,000
Accounts receivable	150,000	160,000
Allowance for doubtful accounts	15,000	14,000
Bad debt expense	55,000	40,000

All sales are on credit.

18. Accounts receivable written off during 1999 total:
    a. $1,000
    b. $10,000
    c. $54,000
    d. $55,000

19. Collections on accounts receivable total:
    a. $800,000
    b. $856,000
    c. $1,060,000
    d. $1,114,000

20. Net income can be greater than cash provided (used) by operating activities if:
    a. accounts receivable decrease.
    b. premium on bonds payable decreases.
    c. accounts payable increase.
    d. prepaid rent decreases.

21. Peaks Enterprises engaged in the following transactions during 1999:

    1. Sold 20,000 shares of preferred stock ($50 par value) for $75 per share.
    2. Purchased $100,000 of Jefferson Company's 10 percent, 20-year bonds for $92,000. Peaks intends to hold the bonds until maturity.
    3. Paid $48,000 for four years of rent in advance.
    4. Purchased equipment for $500,000; $50,000 cash down payment and the balance financed through a 20-year mortgage.

    a. Prepare the journal entries to record each of the above transactions.

    b. What is the cash effect of each item, and in which section of the statement of cash flows does the item appear? At what amount?

22. Compute the cash outflows associated with interest and rent during 1999, using the following information:

	1999	1998
Interest expense	$ 20,000	$ 15,000
Interest payable	5,000	8,000
Discount on note payable	48,000	50,000
Prepaid rent	60,000	68,000
Rent expense	300,000	312,000

Additional information: No notes were issued during 1999.

23. Apple Inc.'s statement of cash flows calculated under both the direct and indirect methods is presented below. Prepare an income statement from this data.

Direct Method

Customer collections	$ 70,000
Payments to vendors	(40,000)
Payments for operating expenses	(36,000)
Cash provided (used) by operations	$ (6,000)

Indirect Method

Net income	$ 12,000
Noncash charges to noncurrent accounts:	
Depreciation	10,000
Gain on equipment sale	(6,000)
Changes in current accounts other than cash:	
Increase in accounts receivable	(9,000)
Decrease in inventory	5,000
Decrease in accounts payable	(20,000)
Increase in accrued payables	2,000
Cash provided (used) by operations	$ (6,000)

The following information relates to questions 24 and 25.

The following are the balance sheets and income statement of Marks Corporation.

Marks Corporation
Balance Sheets
December 31, 1999 and 1998

	1999	1998
Cash	$ 23,000	$ 16,000
Accounts receivable	300,000	325,000
Inventory	400,000	390,000
Prepaid rent	12,000	16,000
Plant equipment	500,000	450,000
Less: Accumulated depreciation	(225,000)	(200,000)
Total assets	$1,010,000	$997,000
Accounts payable	$ 200,000	$195,000
Bonds payable	300,000	300,000
Premium on bonds payable	20,000	22,000
Common stock - no par	300,000	300,000
Retained earnings	190,000	180,000
Total equity	$1,010,000	$997,000

Marks Corporation
Income Statement
For the Year Ended December 31, 1999

Sales	$600,000
Less expenses and losses:	
Cost of goods sold	(450,000)
Rent expense	(25,000)
Depreciation expense	(50,000)
Interest expense	(40,000)
Other expenses	(5,000)
Loss on plant equipment sale	(5,000)
Net income	$ 25,000

24. Prepare the statement of cash flows for Marks Corporation using the direct method to compute cash provided (used) by operating activities.

25. Prepare the operating activities section of Marks Corporation's statement of cash flows using the indirect method.

CHAPTER 14-SOLUTIONS

1.	c	6.	c	11.	d	16.	c
2.	a	7.	a	12.	a	17.	d
3.	d	8.	c	13.	b	18.	c
4.	a	9.	c	14.	c	19.	b
5.	d	10.	d	15.	a	20.	b

21. a.

Cash (+A)	1,500,000	
Preferred Stock $50 par (+SE)		1,000,000
Additional Paid-In Capital-P/S (+SE)		500,000

Sold preferred stock.

| Investment in Jefferson Co. Bonds (+A) | 92,000 | |
| Cash (-A) | | 92,000 |

Purchased bonds.

| Prepaid Rent (+A) | 48,000 | |
| Cash (-A) | | 48,000 |

Prepaid rent.

Equipment (+A)	500,000	
Cash (-A)		50,000
Mortgage Payable (+L)		450,000

Purchased equipment with cash and debt.

b.   1.   Cash increased by $1,500,000. This item is reported in the financing activities section since capital is being contributed by the preferred stockholders.

2.   Cash is decreased by $92,000. This item is reported in the investing activities section since a noncurrent asset is being purchased with cash.

3.   Cash is decreased by $48,000. This item is reported in the operating activities section since rent is an operating expenditure.

4.   Cash is decreased by $50,000. This item is reported in the investing activities section since a long-lived productive asset is purchased. The mortgage payable portion of the transaction is disclosed in a footnote since it does not involve the receipt or disbursement of cash.

22. **Interest:** From Chapter 11, the entry to record interest expense when a note payable is issued at a discount is:

Interest Expense (E,-SE)	xxx	
Discount on Notes Payable (+L)		xxx
Cash (-A) or Interest Payable (+L)		xxx

The payment of the note's face amount at maturity will include a portion of the interest expense accumulated over the note's duration. The total amount of interest included in the face amount is the original balance in Discount on Notes Payable. This account is amortized as interest accumulates over time.

In this problem, Interest expense ($20,000) - Change in discount on notes payable ($2,000) = Current year's increase in interest payable ($18,000).

The interest payable account decreased from the beginning of the year by $3,000. This means that $3,000 of last year's accrued interest was paid this year.

Total cash paid for interest = $18,000 + $3,000 = $21,000.

Rent: The prepaid rent account is increased by prepayments of rent and decreased as the rented space is used. During the year, the prepaid rent balance decreased by $8,000 (E.B., $60,000 - B.B., $68,000). This means that rent expense exceeded cash payments by $8,000. Total cash rent payments = Rent expense payments ($300,000) - Decrease in prepaid rent ($8,000) = $292,000.

23. To construct the income statement, the revenue and expense balances are determined by using the relation between cash collections and cash payments and current asset and liability account balance changes. These relations are summarized in the review of key concepts.

Cash received from customers	= Sales + Beginning A/R - Ending A/R
	= Sales - (Ending A/R - Beginning A/R)
	= Sales - Change in accounts receivable
	= Sales - ($9,000)
$70,000	**= Sales = $79,000**
Purchases	= Cost of goods sold + Change in inventory
	= Purchases - Change in accounts payable
Cash paid to vendors	= Cost of goods sold + Change in inventory -
	Change in accounts payable
Cash paid to vendors	
	= Cost of goods sold + $5,000 + $20,000
$40,000	**= Cost of goods sold = $25,000**

Cash paid for operating expenses $36,000	= Operating expenses - Change in accrued payables = Operating expenses - ($2,000) = **Operating expenses = $38,000**

These items are combined with the noncurrent items backed out of income in the indirect method, Depreciation Expense and Gain on Equipment, to prepare the income statement.

Sales	$79,000
Gain on equipment sale	6,000
Total revenues	$85,000
Less: Cost of goods sold	25,000
Accrued expenses	38,000
Depreciation expense	10,000
Net income	$12,000

24. Direct method: Using the current account and revenue and expense account relations, cash receipts and disbursements due to operations are determined. Then the noncurrent accounts are examined to determine the investing and financing activities.

Cash received from customers	= Sales + Beginning A/R - Ending A/R = Sales - (Ending A/R - Beginning A/R) = Sales - Change in accounts receivable = $600,000 - ($300,000 - $325,000) = **$625,000**

Purchases
 	
Cash paid to vendors
 	
Cash paid to vendors
	= Cost of goods sold + Change in inventory
	= Purchases - Change in accounts payable
	= Cost of goods sold + Change in inventory
	  - Change in accounts payable
	= $450,000 + ($400,000 - $390,000)
	  - ($200,000 - $195,000)
	= **$455,000**

Cash paid for rent	= Rent expense + Change in prepaid rent = $25,000 + ($12,000 - $16,000) = **$21,000**
Cash paid for accrued expenses	= Accrued expense - Change in accrued payable = $5,000 - ($0 - $0) = **$5,000**

Interest payable. From Chapter 11, the entry to record interest expense for a bond issued at a premium is:

Interest Expense (E,-SE)   xxx
    Discount on Notes Payable (+L)   xxx
    Cash (-A) or Interest Payable (+L)   xxx

In this example, interest payable has a zero balance at the end of 1998 and 1999. Thus, the total of interest expense and the decrease in Premium on Bonds Payable equals the cash paid for interest during 1999.

Interest Expense ($40,000) + Decrease in premium on B/P ($2,000)
= $42,000 Cash paid for interest.

Investing activities. The plant equipment account is the only noncurrent asset on the balance sheet. During the year, the company sold an asset that originally cost $50,000, had accumulated depreciation of $25,000, and realized a $5,000 loss (according to the income statement). The cash received on the sale is $25,000 (asset book value) - $5,000 (loss) = $20,000.

The plant equipment account increased by $50,000 over the year. A purchase of $100,000 must have occurred after the sale is considered. $50,000 = $100,000 (purchase) - $50,000 (sale).

Since no information is provided to the contrary, the purchase is made with cash.

Financing activities. The bond payable is unchanged. Common stock is unchanged. Retained earnings increased by $10,000.
    B.B. + Net income - Dividends = E.B.
    Dividends = Net income - (E.B. - B.B.)
= $25,000 - ($190,000 - $180,000)
= $15,000

Marks Corporation
Statement of Cash Flows
For the Year Ended December 31, 1999

Cash provided (used) by operating activities:

Customer collections	$625,000	
Payments to suppliers	(455,000)	
Payments for other expenses	(5,000)	
Payments for interest	(42,000)	
Payments for rent	(21,000)	
Cash provided by operations		$102,000

Cash provided (used) by investing activities:

Proceeds from equipment sale	$ 20,000	
Equipment purchase	(100,000)	
Cash used by investing activities		(80,000)

Cash provided (used) by financing activities:

Payment of cash dividends	$(15,000)	
Cash used by financing activities		(15,000)
Net increase in cash balance		$ 7,000
Beginning cash balance		16,000
Ending cash balance		$ 23,000

25. Indirect method.

Cash provided (used) by operating activities:

Net income	$ 25,000
Add: Loss on equipment sale	5,000
Depreciation expense	50,000
Decrease in accounts receivable	25,000
Decrease in prepaid rent	4,000
Increase in accounts payable	5,000
Less: Increase in inventory	(10,000)
Decrease in premium on bond payable	(2,000)
Cash provided by operations	$102,000